UNEMPLOYMENT IN EUROPE

Unemployment is the most serious economic and social problem currently confronting the European Union. Although the extent varies from region to region, it is generally most extreme in large cities. Over recent years it has continued to increase, despite a plethora of active labour market policies to combat it.

Unemployment in Europe: Problems and Policies asks why European unemployment is so high and looks at the policies designed to curb it. The volume examines:

- why European unemployment is so high in relation to the past and to other developed economies;
- the special factors at a local level that can affect the level of urban unemployment;
- European Union policy on unemployment and the allocation of funds;
- case studies of five major European cities currently experiencing high levels of unemployment;
- an analysis of proposals for the future.

This work will be a valuable guide for all those interested in the wider aspects of urban unemployment in Europe.

Valerie Symes lectures in economics at Goldsmiths College, London. She specialises in European urban problems and has extensive research and practical experience in this area.

UNEMPLOYMENT IN EUROPE

Problems and policies

Valerie Symes

London and New York

First published 1995
by Routledge
11 New Fetter Lane, London EC4P 4EE

Simultaneously published in the USA and Canada
by Routledge
29 West 35th Street, New York, NY 10001

Typeset in Garamond by Florencetype Ltd, Stoodleigh, Devon

Printed and bound in Great Britain by
Biddles Ltd, Guildford and King's Lynn

British Library Cataloguing in Publication Data
A catalogue record for this book is available from the British Library

Library of Congress Cataloging in Publication Data
Symes, Valerie, 1941–
    Unemployment in Europe : problems and policies / Valerie Symes.
       p. cm.
    Includes bibliographical references and index.
    ISBN 0–415–11824–7. — ISBN 0–415–11825–5 (pbk.)
    1. Unemployment—European Economic Community countries.
2. Unemployment—European Economic Community countries—Case
studies. I. Title.
HD5764.5.A6S95 1994
331.13′794—dc20   94–33819
                                                                               CIP

ISBN 0–415–11824–7
0–415–11825–5 (pbk)

In memory of my parents

CONTENTS

FIGURES

TABLES

ACKNOWLEDGEMENTS

Research on cities in five European countries would not have been possible without the help and advice of academics, local agencies and government officials in the cities studied. I should, therefore, like to express my gratitude to the following individuals and organisations for their time, in helping me to understand local labour market problems, and for their advice on local sources of information.

In Montpellier to: Professor Jacques Rouzier and colleagues of the CNRS, University of Montpellier; Madame Anne Bernard, Conseil Régional of Languedoc Roussilon; Mr. Masceocchi, ANPE; Madame Duval, DDTE: Mr. Calvat, INSEE Montpellier.

In Manchester to: Professor Brian Robson, Dr. Jamie Peck, Department of Geography, University of Manchester; Dr. Barron Isherwood and his staff DOE Regional Office, Manchester; Mr. Colin Fishwick, Chief Executive's Department and Mr. Graham Miller, Education Department, Manchester City Council; Mr. Ken Turner, Trafford Park Development Corporation; Mr. Chris Paris, Central Manchester Development Corporation; Mr. Richard Money, Centre for Local Economic Strategies; Mr. Stephen Hyde, Manchester TEC; the Centre for Employment Research, Manchester Metropolitan University; the Greater Manchester Research and Information Planning Unit.

In Rotterdam to: Dr. N. van Wijk, Rotterdam Werkt; Dr. C. van der Werf, Social Services; Dr. G. de Kleijn, Rotterdam City; Dr. L. van Veen, Planning Department Rotterdam City; Dr. Rene Teule OTB Delft Technical University; Professor Niels Prak, ECB Rotterdam; the Central Bureau of Statistics Rotterdam.

In Barcelona to: Professor J. M. Blanc, Barcelona Autonoma University; Madame F. Molinaire, Madame M. Marta and colleagues, Barcelona Activa; Dr. Mireia Belil, Director International Centre for Urban Studies Barcelona; INEM; Barcelona City Government.

In Frankfurt to: Professor Dr. Reinhard Hujer, Professor Dr. Alfons Schmid and colleagues, Johann Wolfgang Goethe University Frankfurt; Professor Stephan Leibfried, University of Bremen; Dr. E. Spitznagel, AMB

Nuremburg; Herr Bernhard Kolbe LAA Hessen; Frau Strotz, Social Services Frankfurt City; Herr Mayer and colleagues, Frankfurt Verein für Soziale Heimstätten; Frankfurt AMB.

I am grateful to Madame M. Milliat, European Social Fund, and other staff at the European Commission for their prompt and efficient help in providing documentation and answering questions.

I should also like to thank those who helped with translation and analysis of documents from Dutch, Catalan, Spanish and German – Gerry Gibson, Antoni Sanchez, Marcos Baer and Pat Thomas. My special thanks to Raija Savage and also Marion Chapman for their help in the preparation of the manuscript.

Finally I should like to acknowledge the important part played by the Nuffield Foundation and the Sir Herbert Manzoni Trust in helping to fund the research into urban and unemployment policy in Europe.

Valerie Symes
Goldsmiths College
November 1994

INTRODUCTION

Unemployment has become the most serious economic problem of the European Union, and despite a plethora of active labour market policies to combat it, has continued to increase.

In mid 1994 the official unemployment rate of the Union as a whole was 12 per cent of the labour force, and it is predicted that by the end of the year eighteen million people could be out of work. Since 1981 the rate of unemployment has never been less than 8 per cent, and has been around 2 per cent higher than the OECD average, representing all developed industrialised economies. It has, therefore, been a persistent problem and attempts to reduce the number unemployed and create more work appear to have had only limited success.

Within Europe rates vary greatly from relatively low levels in West Germany, to very high levels in Spain and Greece. Regions within countries also experience enormous variations. Over half the population of the EU live in large cities, defined as Functional Urban Regions, of three hundred thousand people or over (Cheshire and Hay, 1989). The economic profiles of cities may be very different. Some are growing in population, others declining. Some have suffered economic structural change and decline. Others have a favourable economic structure and are thriving. It was found that they all, however, experienced unemployment rates higher than in the past, and higher than their national average.

Unemployment is, therefore, seen in some of its most severe forms in large cities. This work will examine the structure and causes of unemployment in five major European cities with very different economic profiles. Montpellier has had and continues to have a high knowledge-based service economy and has one of the fastest rates of job creation in France. Manchester is a classic case of a city, once a prosperous manufacturing economy, that has suffered from industrial decline and loss of employment, and where now the dominant employment sector is the service sector. Rotterdam similarly has suffered from manufacturing decline but also loss of employment through technological change in port activities. Barcelona, prior to the 1970s a thriving industrial and port city, experienced loss of employment and has rapidly adapted to a predominantly service economy. At the time of study it had, for the first time, lower unemployment than the region and country as a result of the Olympic effect. Frankfurt, a city with the highest rate of job growth, most favourable economic structure and highest income per head of large cities, also experienced higher unemployment than West Germany as a whole.

Each city has a set of policies in operation reflecting national policies on unemployment, both active and passive, and to a greater or lesser extent influenced by European Union policy initiatives on unemployment. In addition the cities have local policies to combat unemployment and create employment. Other urban policies also affect the level of unemployment. The case studies examine the relevance and effectiveness of major policies in the context of the city. They attempt to evaluate the impact of the European Union, and its relevance to local situations, the degree of flexibility of national policies to meet local needs, and the effect of local policies and organisational structures at urban level. What is happening to cities is a microcosm of what is happening in Europe and highlights the complexity of causes of unemployment and the difficulties of solving unemployment at a Community, or Union[1] level, when national policies vary in type, and levels of expenditure on the unemployed differ to such a great extent.

Chapter 1 discusses the wider problem of why European unemployment is so high, both in relation to the past and to other developed economies. Chapter 2 deals with special factors at a local level that can affect the level of urban unemployment. Chapter 3 looks at how the European Community has formulated policy on unemployment, and how funds are allocated throughout the Community. Chapters 4 to 8 examine the problems and policies within the five cities. Chapter 9 compares causes of and approaches to unemployment in the cities. The final brief chapter looks at proposals for reducing unemployment in Europe in the future.

The case studies were undertaken using information for the period 1990 and 1991. This enabled information in two cities, Montpellier and Manchester, to be more accurate in reflecting joblessness rather than registered unemployment, as census material was used. While this does not make the city studies strictly comparable, it is difficult to gain comparability of studies in any case, as definitions between cities differ. It was worthwhile, therefore, to have full information in some cases.

Valerie Symes
Goldsmiths College
University of London
July 1994

1

UNEMPLOYMENT IN THE EUROPEAN COMMUNITY

Unemployment in the European Union has risen more or less continuously in the past fifteen years and is 'the single most serious challenge facing Member States today' (CEC 1993). In 1994 registered unemployment stood at over 12 per cent, with sixteen million officially unemployed. The number of people seeking work is even higher as official statistics underestimate joblessness. Unemployment levels vary a great deal between Member States, with very much higher rates in certain regions and countries of the Community. The problems arising from unemployment are not only economic problems of inefficiency arising from wastage of human resources, rising public sector deficits and possible monetary instability arising from this, but also an increase in social tension and social costs in terms of ill health, increasing poverty, family and community breakdown, and arguably increasing crime levels.

This chapter will examine the causes of the rise in unemployment in Europe and look at the relative seriousness of the problem for different groups.

European economies are said to have special features that result in higher levels of unemployment than similar advanced industrialised economies. This is the question that will be addressed first of all, as the implication is that if the factors behind the higher unemployment level can be identified, action can follow to reduce the problem.

Unemployment in the period 1981–91 was higher for the European Community as a whole than in other major economies. Table 1.1 shows the unemployment rates (standardised) for the USA, Japan, the EC and selected countries within the EC which will be the focus of later study.

The USA and Japan had lower unemployment rates than the European Community in both 1981 and 1991. Individual countries within the EC show greater disparities in unemployment rates ranging in 1991 from 4.3 per cent in Germany to 16 per cent in Spain. Apart from Germany all other countries under study had higher rates than the USA and Japan in both years.

Figures for the individual countries demonstrate the wide disparities in the problem of unemployment throughout the Community. The amalgamation of West Germany with East Germany in 1989 has resulted in an

Table 1.1 Standardised unemployment rates as a percentage
of total labour force rates, 1981 and 1991

	1981	*1991*
USA	7.5	6.6
Japan	2.2	2.1
EC	9.9	8.8
France	7.4	9.4
Germany	4.2	4.3
Netherlands	8.5	7.0
UK	9.8	8.9
Spain	13.8	16.0

Source: OECD Quarterly Labour Force Statistics
(1992)

increase in unemployment in Germany more recently, and special problems, which will be illustrated by the case study of Frankfurt. Apart from Germany all countries within the study have showed higher levels of unemployment than both of the other major economies shown in the table.

One would expect that as national income rose employment would also rise as there is normally a strong link between growth and employment. In terms of national income growth the EC as a whole and the individual countries did not perform significantly worse than the USA and Japan for the period 1981–89 (see Table 1.2). The average growth rate in Japan was 4.2 per cent, nearly matched by the Netherlands with 4.1 per cent. The USA's growth rate was surpassed by the Netherlands, Spain and the UK. Growth in employment, however, shows a different picture with employment growing at 2 per cent p.a. in the USA, 1.2 per cent p.a. in Japan, but with the exception of the UK at 1.2 per cent all other countries experienced employment growth of below 1 per cent p.a. This could be explained by changes in the labour force (Table 1.2, column 3). The labour force can reflect demographic changes such as the number of young people coming onto the labour market, or social changes such as more married women wishing to work, but the number of people offering themselves for work can also reflect the demand for labour. As working opportunities rise so do the number of people seeking employment. The reverse is also true that as employment opportunities fall the labour force can fall because people feel it is no longer worthwhile to seek employment. This can be particularly relevant where adequate welfare payments provide a real choice between seeking work and not seeking work. It is difficult, therefore, to interpret changes in the labour force in this context. What the figures show is that employment grew faster than the labour force in the USA and in the UK, at the same rate in France and Spain and at lower rates in the EC as a whole and in Germany, the Netherlands and Spain (Table 1.2).

Table 1.2 Growth of real GDP/GNP, employment change and labour force change, 1981–89 (average % change per annum)

	Real GDP/GNP	*Employment*	*Labour force*
USA	2.9	2.0	1.6
Japan	4.2	1.2	1.2
EC	2.5	0.6	0.7
France	2.2	0.3	0.3
Germany	2.5	0.1	0.6
Netherlands	4.1	0.4	0.6
UK	3.2	1.2	0.8
Spain	3.3	0.9	1.3

Source: OECD Employment Outlook (1992)

With the advent of the recession after 1991 the effects of the recession on employment growth were more marked in Europe than in the USA and Japan (Table 1.3).

Table 1.3 Changes in real GDP/GNP and employment growth, 1981–89 and 1992

	GDP/GNP		*Employment Growth*		*Unemployment*	
	1981–89	*1992*	*1981–89*	*1992*	*1981–89*	*1992*
USA	2.9	2.1	2.0	1.1	7.3	7.1
Japan	4.2	1.8	1.2	1.1	2.6	2.2
EC	2.5	1.5	0.6	−0.3	9.9	9.4
France	2.5	1.6	0.1	−0.3	9.4	9.8
Germany	2.1	2.0	0.4	0.2	6.0	4.7
Netherlands	1.9	3.2	0.4	−0.1	9.0	6.5
UK	3.2	0.4	1.2	−2.1	10.0	9.8
Spain	3.3	2.6	0.9	0.6	18.8	16.1

Source: OECD Employment Outlook (1992)

Although in 1992 unemployment grew in the USA and Japan employment also grew by 1.1 per cent whereas in the EC it fell by an average of 0.3 per cent and the UK was worst hit by a fall in employment of 2.1 per cent. For more than a decade the rate of job creation has been lower and the rate of unemployment higher on average in the EC than in either the USA or Japan despite the fact that growth rates have not been significantly different.

Another feature of unemployment in which the European Community is in stark contrast to the USA is in the proportion of the unemployed who have been without a job for longer than a year, the long-term unemployed (Table 1.4).

Table 1.4 Long-term unemployment. Those out of work for over 12 months as a percentage of total unemployment

	1983	1987	1989	1990
USA	13.3	14.0	7.4	5.7
France	42.2	45.5	43.9	38.3
Germany	39.3	48.2	49.0	46.3
Netherlands	50.5	46.2	49.9	48.4
UK	47.0	45.9	40.8	36.0
Spain	52.4	62.0	61.5	54.0

Sources: Eurostat; INSEE; Labour Force Survey; Ministry of Employment and Social Security, Spain; Bureau of Labour Statistics, USA

In 1983, of the unemployed in the USA only 13.3 per cent had been unemployed for more than a year. This had fallen to 5.7 per cent by 1990. In Europe the proportion of long-term unemployed was over three times that in the USA ranging from 39.3 per cent in Germany to 52.4 per cent in Spain. In Germany and Spain the proportions had increased to 46.3 per cent and 54 per cent by 1990. In the three other countries it had reduced but was seven and nine times the rate of the United States.

Many studies have addressed the questions 'Why has European unemployment been persistently higher than that of the USA and Japan?' and 'Why has the number of long-term unemployment differed so much between the United States and European countries?' The explanations for the former can be categorised into the effect of aggregate demand; the role of wages in turn affected by the unemployment compensation and institutional factors; and structural change. Long-term unemployment is again linked to the unemployment benefit system but also to hysteresis effects and discrimination.

Taking the first of these explanations, the role of aggregate demand, Bean, Layard and Nickell (1986), Blanchard and Summers (1986), Lawrence and Schultz (1987), Drèze and Bean (1990) all identify demand conditions in Europe as being important in creating and maintaining high levels of unemployment, especially in the EC. Tight monetary and fiscal contractions in the 1980s in most EC countries, with the exception of Mitterand's expansionary programme in France in the early 1980s, and the interdependence of European economies with high levels of inter-Europe trade, made any expansionary strategy by individual economies impotent. It is argued that these aggregate demand shocks left a serious legacy in destroying investor confidence, and damaged the ability of the labour markets to function effectively. Underutilised capacity affected the demand for investment. The growth of demand is linked to both government expenditure and world trade. Governments were cutting back on expenditure and reducing public deficits. High interest rate policies to control inflation further reduced investment, and at the margin caused closures through rising business costs. European shares of world trade fell as a result of differences in the growth rates of domestic and foreign prices through the price elasticity of demand for imports and exports.

The sustained growth in unemployment in Europe since 1970 challenged the premise of a 'natural' or Non-Accelerating Inflation Rate of Unemployment (NAIRU) toward which an economy will gravitate. The idea is that an increase in unemployment will lower the rate of inflation since wage costs will lower as a result of unemployment, unemployment will then reduce as the demand for labour increases with falling real wages. It was found, however, that high rates of unemployment had little impact on inflation. In fact unemployment and inflation in EC countries often went up together. It was reported (Blanchard and Summers 1986) that the NAIRU rose from 2.4 per cent in 1967–79 to 9.2 per cent in 1981–83 in the UK; from 1.3 per cent to 6.2 per cent in Germany and from 2.2 per cent to 6.9 per cent in France in the same periods. Flanagan (1987) estimated a NAIRU for both France and Germany 1983–87 of 6.0 per cent and NAIRU increased more in most of Europe than in North America. Policy makers in this situation were unwilling to stimulate demand as it was thought that it would lead to higher inflation not higher output.

Control of inflation was the major preoccupation of macroeconomic policy in Europe in the 1980s in an attempt to generate export led growth through more competitive prices and reduced uncertainty on future prices. As previously mentioned any expansionary policy that would be effective in reducing unemployment would have to be a concerted effort by all major EC economies. Expansionary fiscal policy was also seen as capable of exerting only temporary effects as it would induce balance of trade and public deficits and lead therefore to a reversal of policy (Drèze and Bean 1990).

In high unemployment countries the reduction in wage share of value added was low when unemployment was high. Wage theory would suggest that high unemployment would cause a reduction in wages and that this would be reflected in the wage share. Table 1.5 shows average percentage change per annum in employee compensation in the USA, Japan and the EC.

The share of wages in national income rose after the oil price shocks of 1974 and 1979–80, which suggests that workers were compensated for the supply side shocks at the expense of profit. Between 1982 and 1987 in Britain, even with over three million unemployed, wages rose steadily at 7.5 per cent p.a. Productivity gains in the 1970s and 1990s were incorporated into real wages quite rapidly in Europe with a short-run elasticity of 0.4 to 0.8 per cent and a long-run elasticity closer to 1 per cent (Drèze and Bean 1990). Both compensation per employee and unit labour costs in the period 1978–93 grew faster in the EC as a whole than in the USA and Japan despite higher unemployment levels. It has been suggested that the difference in unemployment persistence between Europe and the United States arises

Table 1.5 Business sector labour costs in the USA, Japan and the European Community

	Average % change per annum			
	Compensation per employee		Unit labour costs	
	1978–88	1989–93	1978–88	1989–93
USA	5.9	3.9	5.4	3.5
Japan	4.2	3.9	1.0	1.5
EC	8.9	6.0	6.6	4.1

Source: OECD Employment Outlook (June 1992)

because of the higher persistence of wage aspiration in Europe (Alogoskoufis and Manning 1988) and real wage rigidity (Bruno and Sachs 1985). There are two main reasons put forward for real wage rigidity: institutional wage push, through the objectives and power of trade union bargaining; and the effects of government funded welfare benefits for the unemployed.

One of the reasons for real wage rigidity and the insensitivity of wages to unemployment levels could be explained by the 'insider–outsider' hypothesis (Flanagan 1987, Lindbeck and Snower 1988). In this hypothesis unions' bargaining objectives are set according to the interests of employed union members (insiders) subject to the constraint of employers demand for labour but with no reference to unemployed members (outsiders). When unemployment increases wage objectives are traded against the job security interests of a decreased number of employed union members. After a price shock real wages will rise as the trade unions consider only the effect of prices on the living standards of their working members and not the effect of higher wages on reducing the number of potential jobs for the unemployed. Price shocks and demand shocks which can both reduce employment will mean that more workers lose 'insider' status, and the remaining 'insiders' set the wage to maintain a new lower level of employment. Unemployment, therefore, persists at a new higher level (Blanchard and Summers 1986).

A study by Kaufman (1988) found, however, relatively little difference in wage behaviour across union and non-union sectors in the UK. It does appear, though, that wage correction, in response to unemployment in Europe has been weak and slow. The growth of real wages induces capital/labour substitution. While capital widening – the introduction of new technology – is efficient, capital deepening – the substitution of capital for labour – when it occurs at times of high unemployment, is not.

It has been argued that real wages decline faster in response to increases in unemployment and adverse external shocks in corporatist than in non-corporatist economies (Bean et al. 1986). Corporatist economies are likely to be more egalitarian with wage rates in different industries and locations closer to each other.[1] Unemployed workers are less likely to hold out for good wage offers, and labour market policies are more frequently reviewed, better targeted and command more support from unions and employer groups than in non-corporatist economies (Jackman et al. 1990). While this may help to explain why real wages rose faster in Spain and the UK than in the Netherlands and Germany, it does not explain why the growth in real wages was higher for the EC as a whole than for the USA.

The role of unemployment compensation and its effect on wages and on the behaviour of the unemployed has been put forward as one of the reasons for higher unemployment levels in Europe. Burtless (1987) identifies four aspects of unemployment benefit that could affect behaviour of jobless workers. These are eligibility conditions; generosity of benefits; duration of benefits; and efforts made by authorities to prevent malingering. This study of benefits and unemployment for the UK, France, West Germany, Sweden and the USA concluded 'that neither differences between countries in unemployment level, nor differences in trend unemployment could be principally explained by differences in jobless pay, although replacement ratios were found to be as high as 83 per cent in France. Bentolina and Blanchard (1990) also found no evidence to suppose that there was a link between unemployment benefit and the level of unemployment in Spain. The evidence does not demonstrate that benefits played no role, but they were clearly not the sole or the main cause of unemployment. Atkinson and Micklewright (1991) in a review of studies on the subject found that most of the focus had been on the effects of replacement ratios (percentage of income replaced by benefit) on the probability of exit from and entry to unemployment and found that the evidence of a relationship here was far from robust. Most studies ignored the effects on the duration of unemployment and also the effects of other means tested assistance available. Atkinson (1986) found a statistically significant relationship between the duration of a spell of unemployment and the duration of benefits. On the whole the duration of benefits is between three and four times longer in Germany, Britain and France than in the United States. This could help to explain why there are more long-term unemployed in Europe.

Turning now to the role of structural change on unemployment, evidence does show fundamental changes in the economic structure of European economies from 1970 onwards (Table 1.6) with losses in agricultural and industrial employment particularly during the 1970s and the growth in service jobs more marked in the 1980s.

Table 1.6 shows significant losses of jobs in the agricultural sector in France, Germany and Spain. This has had an impact on cities, as the young and able migrate to the nearest cities to find work, increasing the pressures on the urban labour market. This will be illustrated later in Montpellier and Barcelona. In the industrial sector from 1973–83 the European countries all lost employment at a rate above the OECD average but the Netherlands and

Table 1.6 Employment by sector – average annual percentage change, 1973–90

	Agriculture		Industry		Services	
	1973–83	1983–90	1973–83	1983–90	1973–83	1983–90
France	−3.3	−3.3	−2.0	−1.3	1.8	1.8
Germany	−4.8	−3.1	−1.7	0.6	1.4	1.8
Netherlands	−1.2	2.3	−2.0	2.4	2.1	3.9
Spain	−4.3	−4.6	−1.9	1.9	1.6	3.4
UK	−1.6	−1.4	−2.8	−0.1	1.0	3.0
OECD average	−1.9	1.6	−0.9	0.6	2.2	2.8

Source: OECD Labour Force Statistics; Quarterly Labour Force Statistics (1992)

Spain and to some extent Germany recouped some of the losses in the later period. The service sector grew in all five countries, from 1973 onwards with the Netherlands, Spain and the UK showing the greatest increases in the later years.

Sectoral employment change can come about through sectoral divergence of growth of demand for a product; through technological change; through the uneven sectoral impacts of fluctuations in aggregate demand; or through the relative inflexibility of wages within a sector of economic activity causing it to become less competitive nationally or internationally.

These structural changes have resulted in a mismatch of skills with large regional and industrial differences in unemployment rates. Agricultural areas and older industrial areas have been hardest hit in terms of employment loss (see Manchester study, Chapter 5).

Structural imbalance exists if total unemployment could be reduced by the movement of a worker from one sector to another, but unemployment will rise when the labourer becomes 'trapped' in traditional sectors or certain locations while the demand for labour expands in new sectors and new areas.

This 'trapping' may be voluntary in the sense that unemployed, previously high-paid industrial workers will not consider taking on low-paid, often part-time service work, that may be available.

During the past two decades there has been a shift in the UV (Beveridge) curve for most European countries. This curve measures the relationship between unemployment and job vacancies. At high levels of vacancies one would expect low unemployment and vice-versa. A rightward shift of the curve has occurred showing higher levels of vacancies at all levels of unemployment. One interpretation of this is that there may have been increasing mismatch at a regional level, where structural change has been most evident, with unemployed workers in one location, possibly because of geographical immobility as well as lack of relevant skills, unable to take up the available work in other areas. If this was the result of the structural change, then the continuance of sectoral shift would result in increasing unemployment and

8

increasing vacancies. According to Jackman and Roper (1987) and Thèlot (1985) this has not been the main cause of the shifting UV curve.

This is not to say that sectoral employment changes have not had an impact on unemployment in Europe. They have been very important in certain localities with particular effect on large cities, and the inner areas of large cities (see Chapter 2), but they have not been identified as the major cause of the growth in the level of unemployment in Europe. There is no evidence that structural imbalances have increased in recent years in the main industrialised economies of Western Europe to account for this phenomena (Jackman and Roper 1987).

Regional and industrial differences in unemployment rates do not by themselves explain unemployment growth. An increasing mismatch is needed to make the case that structural change is behind the increase in general unemployment levels in Europe. An efficient labour market with occupational and locational mobility should ensure that the mismatch in skills is only temporary as workers shift from one form of employment to another. A permanent increase in the pace of structural change would, however, tend to raise the long-term level of frictional unemployment as the pool of those unemployed between jobs becomes larger.

Let us now turn to the other main feature where Europe is significantly different from other similar economies – the much higher proportion of long-term unemployed. One factor which may affect the longer duration of unemployment for the individual worker in Europe has already been mentioned, the duration of benefits for the unemployed. It was found that benefits lasted between two and four times longer in European countries than in the United States and it could be argued that this allowed longer search periods for those seeking re-employment. There is evidence, however, that in all countries the rate at which unemployed people find work is much lower for the long-term than the short-term unemployed.

In the UK the rate is one tenth of the initial value for those unemployed over four years. Jackman (1992) and Budd et al. (1986) found that the probability of being employed if you had been on the unemployment register longer than fifteen months was less than a third of the probability for those unemployed less than three months. This has been explained by three factors. Firstly that prolonged unemployment has a psychological effect on workers' morale, motivation and expectations which results in a lowering of job search and finally withdrawal from the labour market. These effects may be compounded by material deprivation and lack of savings, which is not only demoralising but also makes expenditure on job search difficult. Secondly there are the hysteresis effects on human capital. Workers who are unemployed lose the ability to maintain and update their skills and this atrophy of skills may combine with disaffection from the labour force. In a high unemployment environment it is difficult for unemployed workers to signal their quality by holding jobs and being promoted. The lower intensity of job search results in a reduced likelihood of finding work (Bean et al. 1986). The

9

long-term unemployed are also stigmatised in the eyes of employers who tend to select from the more recently unemployed (Budd et al. 1986). Firms continue to prefer 'insiders' whose performance they know rather than make a mistake by hiring workers whose performance is not already known from prior or recent employment experience. They may also be unwilling to employ middle-aged workers as they prefer a longer-term investment in their labour force. The reasons given may explain why people remain unemployed once they have been unemployed for longer than a year but not why the level is higher and persistent in Europe. This may be explained by the demand shocks experienced in Europe from restrictive fiscal policy and deeper recessions. The reduction in demand reduces the outflow from unemployment, leading to a higher proportion of the unemployed experiencing longer periods without work. If economic conditions remain bad many of those who become unemployed will not find work and thus will become long-term unemployed with the above effects.

The outward movement of the Beveridge curve can happen if a slowdown in the economy is coupled with hysteresis effects such as discouragement amongst workers, erosion and loss of skills leading to perceptions of reduced employability of the long-term unemployed on the part of employers.

Having discussed the causes of European unemployment put forward by academic commentators, the Commission's own interpretation now follows.

THE EUROPEAN COMMISSION'S VIEW OF THE CAUSES OF UNEMPLOYMENT

The White Paper on 'Growth, Competitiveness, Employment' of December 1993, popularly known as the Delors Report analysed the employment problems of the Community over the last two decades as arising from fundamental imbalances in the macroeconomic framework, together with a low job content of economic growth. The report points out that the rate of unemployment in the EU was lower than in the USA for all years from 1960 to 1980, and only diverged from that of Japan after the first oil price shock of 1973. In the period 1974–85 the rate of growth in Europe fell to around 2 per cent per annum, employment stagnated, and actually fell in the private sector, at the same time as there was a sharp increase in the labour force, partly for demographic reasons and an increase in young workers, partly because of the increased participation of women in the labour market. Stronger growth of 3.2 per cent per annum occurred in the period 1986–90 but the increases in jobs arising from the growth was only 1.3 per cent per annum. Post 1991 the very low growth rate resulted in a loss of four million jobs in Europe during the recession.

In the 1980s the United States responded to growth in the labour force with a strong increase in job creation, with low productivity increases and high job content of economic growth. Japan had higher productivity

10

increases with growth, but a much stronger growth rate than Europe. From the employment viewpoint Europe suffered from high productivity increases in moderate growth and, therefore, relatively low job creation compared to both the United States and Japan. The reason behind high productivity/low employment content of growth can be found in the operation of macro-economic policy. The effect of externally generated price shocks in Europe resulted in a fall in investment and macroeconomic policies aimed at expansion, because of a lower growth potential than previously, resulted in overheating and acceleration of inflation. Inflation resulted in higher wages, increase in labour costs and capital/labour substitution, hence higher labour productivity but lower job growth. The response to inflationary pressures was restrictive monetary policy, lowering both investment, economic growth and employment. At the same time, levels of public expenditure, especially in the social field, largely as a result of increasing unemployment, used up resources that could have been used in productive investment. The increases in taxation on labour, to help fund increased public expenditure again resulted in increased labour costs, affecting the demand for labour. The reunification of Germany in 1989 was followed by fiscal expansion in Germany to fund adjustment problems. This, however, imposed additional tightening of monetary policy and deepened the recession in Europe in the early 1990s.

The policy recommendations from this analysis are discussed in the final chapter.

WHO ARE THE UNEMPLOYED IN EUROPE?

In the European Community as a whole women are more likely to be unemployed than men, and the young more likely to be unemployed than prime age workers. There is, however, some variation across countries.

Table 1.7 shows that male unemployment in Europe was lower both in 1983 and 1990. Between these years there was a fall in male unemployment from 8.7 per cent to 6.6 per cent, while female unemployment remained fairly constant at 11.8 per cent and 11.2 per cent. In Germany, Spain, France

Table 1.7 Male and female unemployment rates in the European Community and selected countries, 1983 and 1990 (%)

	Eur 12		Germany		Spain		France		Netherlands		UK	
	M	F	M	F	M	F	M	F	M	F	M	F
1983	8.7	11.8	6.2	8.0	16.4	20.8	6.3	10.8	1.1	14.7	11.8	9.8
1990	6.6	11.2	3.9	7.0	11.9	24.1	6.8	12.0	5.8	11.9	7.4	6.6

Source: Eurostat, 1992[2]

and the Netherlands female unemployment was around double that of male unemployment in 1990, while in the UK it was lower for both periods, although male unemployment fell at a slightly higher rate between the two years. In Spain male unemployment reduced quite rapidly from 16.4 per cent to 11.9 per cent while female unemployment actually increased from 20.8 per cent to 24.1 per cent, and in France where male unemployment remained almost static female unemployment again increased.

Women have increased their participation rates in the labour force in the past two decades in all the countries under study (see Table 1.8). This has occurred most dramatically in the Netherlands where the percentage rose from 29.2 per cent in 1973 to 53.0 per cent in 1990, but there has been a marked increase in all countries. At the same time male participation rates have declined. In the 1980s the increase in the number of jobs available benefited women who took two thirds of the extra jobs created in the Community between 1985 and 1989, and by 1991 four out of every ten jobs were held by women. This tendency may be explained by the growth in the services sector where almost 75 per cent of women are employed (Van Winckel 1991). In the UK most of the two and a half million jobs created in the service sector in the 1980s went to women, which may account for the lower levels of female unemployed in Britain despite high participation rates. The growth in employment opportunities together with changes in society – such as an increase in education and qualifications, smaller families, and attitudes to female employment may have encouraged more women onto the labour market in Europe. Migration of agricultural workers to the towns resulting from sectoral change has increased participation by accompanying spouses, as will be seen in Montpellier and Barcelona, and was found by Hartog and Theeuwes (1985) in Holland. This increase in participation does not, however, explain higher unemployment rates in most countries. Nor does it explain why women are particularly prone to long-term unemployment with 55 per cent of the Community's unemployed women being long-term unemployed (although those figures vary between countries from 23 per cent in the UK to 61.5 per cent in Spain). Women also account for over half the long-term unemployed in the Community.

It is argued that women have far more problems than men if they want to enter or return to the labour market. Some 62 per cent are seeking a first job or returning after a career break compared with 41 per cent of men. Of those under 25 who are unemployed 55 per cent are seeking a first job. Here the hysteresis effects apply with women as 'outsiders'. Employers, as we have seen, are less willing to take on workers with no experience or no recent experience. Women returners suffer discouragement and lack of confidence in their ability, thus reducing search frequency (Blanch 1992). Women are also more likely to occupy part-time and temporary jobs where they are at greater risk of redundancy and have less employment protection (Van Winckel 1991).

12

Table 1.8 Labour force participation rates[3] by sex, 1973 and 1990 (%)

	1973		1990	
	Male	*Female*	*Male*	*Female*
France	85.2	50.1	75.2	56.6
Germany	89.6	50.3	81.2	57.0
Netherlands	85.6	29.2	79.6	53.0
Spain	92.9	33.4	76.0	41.1
UK	93.0	53.2	86.7	64.8

Sources: OECD Labour Force Statistics; Quarterly Labour Force Statistics (1992)

The other main feature of unemployment in the European Community is the high level of youth unemployment (see Table 1.9). For the whole of the EC the youth unemployment rate was just over double the average unemployment rate in 1983 and just less than double the rate in 1990. Although all countries reduced youth unemployment between these years Germany was alone in reducing it below the national average, while in France and Spain it still remained at around double the national average and in the Netherlands and the UK some three percentage points higher. In examining the effectiveness of policies in later chapters some explanations will emerge for the disparities in reduction of unemployment amongst this group. One of the most believable explanations for youth unemployment is that in tight labour market suffering from a downturn in economic activity, those seeking work for the first time will be less likely to find a job than an experienced worker as they have no past record on which to be judged. Private companies will also be less willing to take on trainees and apprentices in difficult economic times. It has also been argued that the existence of a minimum wage or a high reservation wage due to high unemployment benefit level (Minford 1985) may cause unemployment amongst the young, by pricing them out of the labour market, but this does not appear to be borne out by the facts, as benefits for the young are virtually non existent in Spain, although there is a very low rate of minimum wage, while relatively high levels of benefit are available in the Netherlands for this age group.

With a changing economic structure the demand for well educated labour will rise as blue-collar jobs decline and white-collar jobs increase. Fewer young people stay on at school after the age of 16 in Spain (55.9 per cent in 1987/88 compared with around 80 per cent in France, Germany and the Netherlands) but the figure is also low in the UK – only 52.1 per cent (OECD 1990). Educational qualifications alone do not explain the high levels although they may contribute to them. The most persuasive argument is similar to that explaining higher unemployment levels for women, that when unemployment is generally high those with little or no experience of

13

Table 1.9 Unemployment rates of young people (under 25) in the European Community, 1983 and 1990 (%)

	1983		1990	
	Under 25s	Total unemp. rate	Under 25s	Total unemp. rate
Euro 12	22.8	9.9	16.5	8.5
France	21.5	8.2	19.0	9.1
Germany	11.8	6.9	4.5	5.1
Netherlands	22.3	12.4	11.8	8.1
Spain	42.6	17.7	31.9	16.1
UK	20.1	11.0	10.8	7.1

Source: Eurostat (1992)

work, even if qualified, will be less likely to be chosen by employers who will view them as a more risky proposition, which could involve them in more training costs than a recently unemployed worker.

POLICIES TOWARDS THE UNEMPLOYED

This section will deal with general types of policy that have been pursued in Community countries in the past few years together with expenditure levels on these policies by the countries under study. The role of the EC and policies that are directly or indirectly concerned with unemployment will be outlined in the following chapter. Furthermore, detailed analysis of policy will be found in the city case studies in later chapters.

Macroeconomic policies, as mentioned earlier, have not on the whole been used by European national governments as it was thought that policies of expansion would lead to increasing inflation. Policies have been based on the rationale that the causes of high unemployment are from the supply-side of the economy, resulting from mismatch of skills with localised consequences, and from the hysteresis effects of long spells of unemployment on skill erosion, lack of work experience and the dis-couraged worker syndrome. Accordingly the main policies pursued are active labour market policies, and fall into the categories of: labour market training and retraining to overcome mismatch and erosion of skills; job creation schemes to provide work experience and make the unemployed better equipped to enter the mainstream labour market; employment subsidies, used especially to encourage employers to take on the long-term unemployed, compensating for any perceived extra cost of doing so; and employment services to provide information, guidance and financial support to assist and encourage the unemployed in finding jobs. Youth unemployment is specifically targeted by training and apprenticeships

14

programmes, as are the disabled. There are rarely policies at national level specifically aimed at unemployed women, although the European Community and some local areas have special programmes to meet their particular needs.

Overall national expenditure on active labour market policies has risen as a percentage of GDP as unemployment has risen, but the proportion of GDP spent on these programmes has varied between countries (see Table 1.10).

As can be seen from Table 1.10 the total amount spent does not vary directly with the rate of unemployment. Germany, with the lowest unemployment rate, spent 1.02 per cent of GDP on the programmes, while Spain with 15.9 per cent unemployment spent 0.75 per cent of GDP. The UK spent least on active programmes and the Netherlands almost twice as much as the UK although it had only slightly higher unemployment. Countries do not spend the money in the same direction even though the problems are similar. France and the UK spend most of their resources on training and youth measures; Germany spends most on training and the disabled; the Netherlands spends three times as much on the disabled as on training, the next highest area of expenditure; and Spain spent nothing on the disabled but over half its budget on subsidised employment. One cannot say, therefore, that across Europe the policies to reduce unemployment are in accord. National priorities for different groups are very different and may be influenced by social priorities and different social institutions. The quality of similar types of programme may also vary. A rough measure of this can be derived from, for example, the outlay per participant on adult training programmes. In 1989 in the five countries this varied between $1,600 in Spain to $7,200 in Germany (OECD 1990).[4] While levels of expenditure on certain groups in some countries may be lower, the effectiveness of the policies may not be very different.

Evaluating active labour market programmes

Very briefly, as research in this area will be presented later in the text where available, outcomes of policy are most commonly evaluated by looking at the value of subsequent activities undertaken by those who have been affected by a policy. For instance, with a training programme the outcome for individuals in terms of value of work gained can be compared to the outcome for individuals with otherwise similar histories. One of the problems inherent in this technique is that participants in programmes may not be similar if they are a self-selected group, but may be more dynamic and intent on gaining employment. The other main area of criticism is that this type of benefit/cost analysis emphasises the benefits of successful short-term outcomes and this itself may limit the sort of intake to a programme, i.e. the organisers may discriminate against the hard-to-place. A wider problem is that evaluations do not often take account of the side-effects on the rest

Table 1.10 Public spending on active labour market programmes as a percentage of GDP, 1990

			% unemployed		
	France	Germany	Netherlands	Spain	UK
	8.9	4.9	7.5	15.9	6.8
1 Public employment services and administration	0.13	0.22	0.10	0.13	(1990–91) 0.15
2 Labour market training	0.33	0.38	0.22	0.10	0.23
(For unemployed and those at risk)	(0.28)	(0.35)	(0.22)	(0.07)	(0.20)
(For employed)	(0.05)	(0.03)	—	(0.03)	(0.03)
3 Youth measures	0.21	0.04	0.07	0.07	0.19
(Unemployed and disadvantaged)	(0.08)	(0.03)	(0.01)	(0.07)	—
(Support of apprenticeships and general training)	(0.44)	(0.01)	(0.05)	—	(0.18)
4 Subsidised employment	0.07	0.15	0.05	0.45	0.02
(in private sector)	(0.03)	(0.05)	(0.02)	(0.12)	—
(Starting enterprises)	(0.02)	—	—	(0.21)	(0.02)
(Direct job creation)	(0.01)	0.10	(0.03)	(0.12)	—
5 Disabled	0.06	0.23	0.64	—	0.03
(Vocational rehabilitation)	—	(0.13)	—	—	0.01
(Work for disabled)	(0.06)	(0.10)	(0.64)	—	0.02
Total active measures	0.80	1.02	1.07	0.75	0.61

Sources: OECD Employment Outlook, OECD Quarterly Labour Force Statistics (1992)

of the economy and the overall level of unemployment. There may be a 'deadweight' cost if the participant would have gained employment without the benefit of a programme. There may be a 'substitution' effect if the new employee, perhaps with the benefit of an employment subsidy, is taking the work of an existing worker. Or there may be a 'displacement' effect if a worker in another firm is made redundant because of unfair competition from a similar firm receiving subsidy. These side-effects are difficult to estimate and are, therefore, often ignored.

We shall be returning to an examination of national policies in their local setting and their effectiveness and relevance to given unemployment situations in the case studies, but firstly we shall examine the special features that affect urban unemployment in Europe.

2

URBAN UNEMPLOYMENT
IN EUROPE

The reasons put forward for national and Europe-wide unemployment, namely lack of effective demand, structural change and mismatch, the role of wages and benefits, together with hysteresis effects and discrimination for longer-term unemployment, can be identified at local level, but there are also special features between and within cities that affect and enhance these causes. In this chapter these features will be examined as a preliminary to the city studies.

The economic success of cities is often measured by growth in population, growth in employment and per capita income. Some large cities are growing and some declining. Yet Cheshire et al. (1988) found that major urban regions (those with a population greater than 330,000 with at least 200,000 in the urban core) were more prone to unemployment than average in the European Community. In 1977–81 unemployment for major urban areas was 9 per cent higher than the overall EC average and in 1983–84 7 per cent higher. Can the answer to this be found in the fact that large cities are all in stages of decline with falling population and employment? It will emerge in the case studies that Montpellier, a city with one of the highest levels of employment growth in Europe also has an unemployment rate above the national average, and that Frankfurt, with the highest per capita income of large European cities, has an unemployment rate higher than Germany as a whole. These two cities also have economies based on the growth service sectors in Europe – financial services, medical research, media and high technology. It is more understandable that cities like Manchester, which has suffered from loss of manufacturing employment, and Rotterdam, where jobs have been lost through the introduction of new technology port facilities, should experience high levels of structural or technological unemployment. The economic base of the city and its growth or decline may explain disparities in unemployment rates between cities but economic structure does not help to explain why even the most successful large cities have relatively high rates of unemployment.

As the sample of cities chosen was based on their different characteristics of growth and decline, it would be relevant, first of all, to examine the definitions of and reasons for growth and decline in European cities. The stages of urban development leading to the existence of large city regions were identified by Van den Berg et al. (1982) as fourfold. Initially the process of urbanisation came about through rural–urban migration as the workforce moved from agricultural to industrial occupations. This stage is succeeded by the process of suburbanisation with the outward movement of population and later of economic activity. Stage three in the process comes with desuburbanisation, or exurbanisation as it is sometimes known, when the external costs of location within the city rise. At this stage not only the core of the city but also the suburbs decline in population, and there is an absolute decline in population within the urban region. The fourth stage described is a process of reurbanisation when a revitalisation of the central city causes population to rise. This process and the effects on population are shown in Figure 2.1. But while the figure describes rises and falls of population in different areas of the city it tells us nothing about ensuing urban problems including unemployment.

Cheshire and Hay (1989), examining the problems of Functional Urban Regions[1] (FURs), used an index which included population in-migration; the unemployment rate and unemployment index above and below the European average; a travel demand index, and mean GDP per capita for the period 1974–84.[2] Out of 117 cities studied Frankfurt ranked lowest in problem score. Montpellier forty-second, Rotterdam eighty-sixth, Manchester ninety-first and Barcelona ninety-sixth.

If one looks at the relationship between population growth or decline (a simplistic measurement of urban growth implying the success of cities

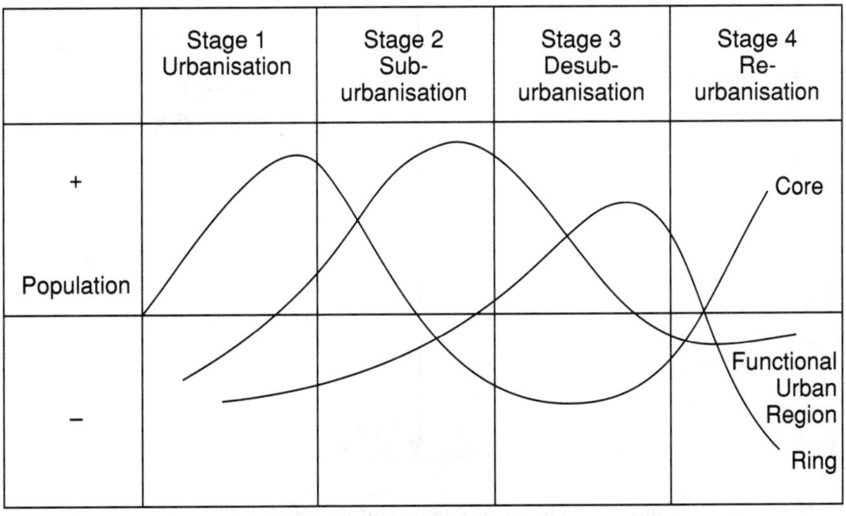

Figure 2.1 Stages of urban growth

that have not reached stage three of the urbanisation process) one finds that Frankfurt, Rotterdam and Manchester have lost population while Montpellier and Barcelona have gained population (Figure 2.2). Population loss does not, therefore, imply a high level of problems, nor gain a low level of problems.

Urban population growth may occur as the result of an increase in the demand for labour, but the increased supply forthcoming may overshoot and result in increased unemployment in the city. This was certainly an explanation put forward for increased unemployment occurring together with increasing employment opportunities in Montpellier and Barcelona, both of which have experienced growth in population, largely from areas of agricultural job loss, and where the rate of new job formation has not been

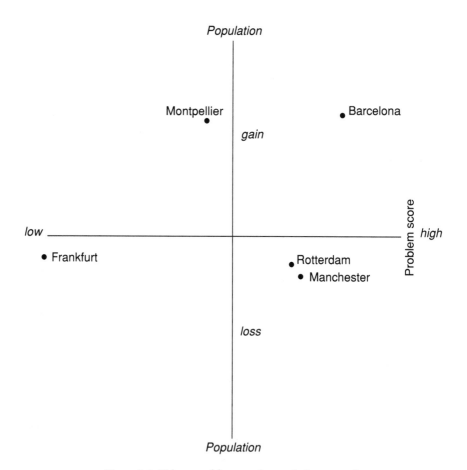

Figure 2.2 Urban problems and population growth
Source: Cheshire and Hay (1989)

able to cope with the increased labour supply. OECD (1990) cites this effect in Barcelona, the wealthiest and most dynamic city in Spain, with an unemployment rate in 1989 of 19 per cent rising to 30 per cent in some districts.

Returning to the question of differential levels of unemployment between the cities, and the growth of unemployment in the 1980s; generally in Europe the priority of price stability as a macroeconomic policy over economic growth accelerated job losses in industries in decline and made restructuring more difficult in a situation of tight demand. This tended to penalise cities with economies concentrating on declining or marginal industries, while those with existing expanding sectors did not suffer from job loss to the same extent, and more often were able to expand employment within the existing economic structure. Pay differentials across Europe also resulted in cities like Barcelona, with relatively lower labour costs, expanding employment, even in manufacturing industry which was in overall decline.

The effects of sectoral change in national economies, often accelerated by a situation of policies of demand restraint, caused some city economies to lose employment at a faster rate, with less replacement in repeated recessions, while others gained employment since their local economy was dominated by growth sectors. These effects were mitigated to some extent if wage levels within the city were lower than the European average. Population growth as such, although the result of a growing local economy, does not necessarily signal a state of lower unemployment; the reverse may be true. Nor does population loss by itself signal urban economic decline and rapidly increasing unemployment.

The different stages of urban growth do, however, have an impact on urban unemployment and it is necessary to look in some detail at the causes of processes of suburbanisation and exurbanisation that have occurred in large cities to see how this comes about. The initial stages of suburbanisation can be seen in the outward movement of households. Traditional economic theory analyses household location in terms of the maximisation of personal welfare. With the growth of population residential areas around the urban core expand but at first the core population remains constant. Households then perceive increasing welfare benefits in outward moves from the urban core in terms of greater space, since land costs are lower in suburban locations; newer housing; and cleaner air and more pleasant surroundings. Suburbanisation will take place if there are adequate transport facilities to provide access to work in the city and accessible public facilities. Transport facilities in terms of availability and cost (both monetary and time costs) are of paramount importance in determining the development of suburbanisation (Van den Berg et al. 1982).

As income per head in the city rises the ability to become owner-occupiers also rises and this encourages further suburbanisation, since the supply of housing for sale in the core is limited. These processes have been seen at

21

work since the 1950s in the more prosperous cities of Northern and Western Europe. They resulted in a decline of population in most inner cores, which also resulted in a change in the social mix of population and increasing social segregation of housing. Lower income households dominated the inner core in those cities where household preference was for suburban benefit and higher income groups could afford to move out. Perception of suburban benefit was by no means the case for all European cities as high income groups sometimes preferred the benefits of city life provided by the availability of cultural and leisure activities and greater social interaction in inner areas.

But the abandonment of cities by the higher income skilled worker resulted in a greater concentration in the inner areas of low-skill, low-income groups in public or often dilapidated private rented housing (Garfield Schwartz 1981). Massive post-war reconstruction of houses in Germany, the Netherlands and the UK resulted in the construction of public housing estates to cater not only for wartime displaced residents but later also for the influx of migrants from Southern Europe and elsewhere into large industrial cities, in the late 1950s and early 1960s to supply the growing demand for unskilled labour in manufacturing industry in France, Germany, the Netherlands and the UK. In France this tended to be on the periphery of cities rather than in central areas (Symes 1992).

Levels of local taxation in city areas rose disproportionately with those of suburban areas as a result of population changes. Social and infrastructure needs in core areas increased at the same time as local population and tax base were falling (Klaasen 1987). Manchester, for example, lost 95,000 people in the period 1971–81. The negative externalities of inner areas, or perception of them by households, continued into the 1980s. Households who could, moved out as a result of the dereliction, crime, poor physical environment and higher taxes, but also because of the availability of new housing on the periphery (Robson 1987).[3]

Employment location patterns also changed in large cities following suburbanisation, which tended to increase outward household moves. In all the cities under study outward shift of employment to the suburbs, and in some cases beyond, has occurred. Explanations for this shift have been either based on microeconomic factors or the consequences, intended or unintended, of local or national policy. Decisions affecting outward moves of industry can be related to cost factors. Land costs are on the whole higher in inner areas than in outer areas. Space constraints inhibiting expansion exist in central areas, and were found to be of major importance by Fothergill et al. (1987) in firms' decisions to locate in suburban or exurban locations. Local pay differentials show a decline in wage rates with distance from the centre of the city (Molho 1991). These factors may have resulted in cost advantages to firms locating outside the city. The availability of an appropriate supply of qualified labour could influence location decision. Jobs may follow qualified people (Ileris 1986). Highly qualified staff moved initially to suburban locations and then outside the large city areas to smaller towns as environment preferences dominated housing moves.[4]

The provision of services and incentives or constraints to location by urban or national governments have also had a significant effect on the location of new employment. The transportation system, especially the building of motorways, can speed the decentralisation of firms and jobs. The existence of an adequate transport system giving access to markets is important. Government planning policy, for example constraints on urban development by the imposition of green zones around a city, can result in either the containment of employment within the city or relocation of expanding firms in exurban localities. Similarly, incentives to dispersal as in New Towns in the UK, or satellite towns in France will affect employment in large cities. Where the whole city is losing employment regional incentives may help to restore the balance. In a recent study of what affects the location of small and medium sized companies in Europe (the largest providers of employment growth) Moore et al. (1991) found that the key factors were the availability of regional development assistance, followed by quality and size of labour supply, the potential for future expansion, and access to customers. Attractive environment as a location factor, unlike for households, was relatively unimportant. All the above reasons for choice of location by firms reinforce the suburbanisation and exurbanisation of employment. Even if they do not result in total job loss in the wider city, suburban areas are likely to benefit from employment growth at the expense of the city core over time. In the UK it was found that inner areas of large conurbations lost most employment, with a slight loss in outer areas while the country as a whole gained employment (see Table 2.1).

The same was true of the Netherlands with more marked losses in the suburban ring in the 1980s (see Table 2.2).

The central city areas of the three main large cities in the Randstadt lost both population and employment over a ten year period, while the suburban ring initially gained employment but subsequently also lost jobs. Large cities in Northern and Western Europe all followed a similar pattern of suburbanisation followed by desuburbanisation of employment. Mediterranean

Table 2.1 Changes in total employment in areas of Great Britain, 1951–81

Area type	1951	1981
Inner areas of six largest conurbations	100	74
Outer areas of six largest conurbations	100	99
Small towns and rural areas	100	118
Great Britain total	100	103

Source: Storey, *Urban Studies* (1990)

Table 2.2 Changes in population and employment: Amsterdam, Rotterdam and the Hague, 1973–83

	Shift in population		Shift in employment	
	Central city	*Suburban ring*	*Central city*	*Suburban ring*
1973–77	−32,000	+18,000	−6,000	+6,000
1977–82	−17,000	+17,000	−4,000	+7,000
1982–83	−17,000	+18,000	−28,000	−4,000
Total				
1973–83	−66,000	+53,000	−38,000	+9,000

Source: Beumer, Harts and Ottens (1983)

cities like Montpellier and Barcelona gained employment and population and are still at the stage of urban expansion. And yet, they too have severe unemployment problems. Employment growth in both these cities is at the suburbanisation stage and this process is being encouraged by local economic generation and planning policy. In the case of Montpellier with the setting up of outer suburban 'poles' and in Barcelona by the Freeport and suburban business parks.[5]

What effect has suburbanisation had on urban unemployment? The loss of employment from the core lowers per capita income and has multiplier effects on local retailers and other services. The outward moves of higher income and higher skill groups causes an imbalance between available employment and local skills in the city core. Employment is taken up largely by higher skill commuters from the suburbs. Central cities have lost unskilled jobs at a faster rate than skilled jobs, so there is a local mismatch between residents and the local demand for labour. This shortfall of local skill can be easily made up by employers advertising in the wider travel-to-work area, so there is no particular incentive for employers to train local inner-city residents for the jobs available.

The residential segregation that has taken place between higher and lower income residents, with the chosen suburbanisation of population in skilled and growth sectors of employment, has resulted in an increase in the social segregation of unskilled and low income residents in certain areas. This is often but need not necessarily be in the inner city. In cities in France such as Nancy, Strasbourg and Montpellier the poor and low-skilled are situated in large peripheral public housing estates.

To what extent does this physical separation of different income and skill groups matter? Manual and unskilled workers gain much of their information on employment opportunities informally via relatives and friends including ex-work mates. In areas of the city where job losses have occurred,

24

and where there is a concentration of large numbers of unemployed, this network of information breaks down and access to work opportunity diminishes. The combination of housing market factors and labour market factors can lead to a concentration of long-term unemployed (Morris 1987). It can also lead to lower participation rates as residents suffer the discouraged worker effect and withdraw from the labour force because of poor prospects (Gordon and Molho 1985). So residential segregation of lower income groups can reinforce unemployment within an area of the city even if the number of jobs available in the city as a whole, and the demand for different types of labour have remained unchanged.

Because traditional methods of gaining employment for the low skilled are either through local informal methods or local employment agencies, information on suitable vacancies elsewhere in the city may not be available to groups marooned in inner cities or outer housing estates (McGregor 1988). If one assumes that information is available, one could argue that if the demand for labour was the same or even increasing within a travel-to-work area then the growth of new jobs at appropriate skill levels could be taken up by the unemployed, who would then commute to the work or alternatively move nearer to the work available in the city. On the latter point the unemployed, or more specifically those unemployed who have only low income earning potential are constrained by the housing market within the city (Gordon 1988). They are able to afford only low-cost housing either within the social housing or private rented sector. In either case their mobility is severely limited; in social housing tenancy because of the inelastic short run supply of vacant tenancies in areas of the city to which they would like to move and the administrative problems of housing allocation; in the private rented sector because a suburban location is likely to be unaffordable and, for instance, in the case of Britain, because private low-rent accommodation forms only a very small percentage of the total housing market in all parts of the city. The great majority of the low-skill urban unemployed are unable to change their residential location in response to employment opportunities.[6] Accepting the high degree of residential immobility of the unemployed within the city there is still the question of whether, if the jobs were available in the city but not in proximity to the place of residence, would the unemployed be able or willing to commute much further than was necessary before relocation of employment took place?

The co-existence of high unemployment and vacancies cannot be explained solely in terms of mismatch. Research on the London labour market by Meadows et al. (1988) came to the conclusion that the unemployed were either uninformed or unwilling to travel far when commuting. Job search and the willingness to commute are very localised for the majority of workers who are either old, unskilled, married women or teenagers. These are the groups in Europe that (as we have seen) are most at risk of both unemployment and long-term unemployment. The main reasons for unwillingness to commute are linked to the availability and cost of transportation in terms of both monetary cost and time cost. In general, the young, women and the unskilled rely on public rather than private transport for commuting. Most urban public transport systems are radial, built at the time when workers needed to be brought to work in the centres of cities. As more work came to be concentrated in the outer city, fixed rapid transit systems did not adapt to link suburban areas to each other, and increasing numbers of workers used cars for commuting purposes. It is still in many cases possible to use existing systems to go out from inner areas to suburbs provided that the new locations of employment are near existing transportation grids. Many are not, and new firms have often located with urban motorway access in mind. Public transport links between suburban locations are normally poor or non-existent thus further reducing the job opportunities of those living in large suburban public housing estates. In cases where public transportation does exist to link the unemployed with available work both fare structures and journey times will affect the ability of the unemployed to take up the opportunity of work.

Where a city operates a flat fare system, as in Barcelona, the monetary cost of commuting distances is irrelevant in deciding what proportion of a wage can be afforded as all locations incur the same cost. Sliding-scale fares will, however, affect the distance a worker is willing to commute. Nabarro (1980) found that commuting costs for inner city residents to get to factories in suburban locations averaged 10–15 per cent of their net wage, and so became an important element in deciding whether to seek work outside the inner city. The third element that will affect whether or not unemployed workers are willing to commute outside their residential area is the time of journey. This is particularly relevant for women with childcare responsibilities who are unwilling to work outside a given area because of the effect of lengthening the working day and making it impossible to fulfil their other obligations. Commuting time, lowering job accessibility, has also been found to have a significant effect on the employment probability of central city youth in the USA, where research results support the view that job decentralisation is a major cause of the increased joblessness among this group (Ihlanfeldt and Sjoquist 1991).

One further point on the location of the unemployed within cities. It has been argued that employers discriminate against applicants who live in certain areas of the city and are unwilling to consider offering employment to residents of specific districts or large 'problem' public housing estates. Evidence on this is anecdotal, but could be a factor in exacerbating already high unemployment rates in these locations.

Ethnic minorities make up a disproportionate number of the unemployed in cities. There is evidence in Britain that they suffer discrimination in the job market. In research in London, Birmingham and Manchester, Brown and Gay (1987) found that white applicants were over a third more likely to receive a positive response from employers than either Asian or Afro-Caribbean applicants. There was, however, no difference between cities or within cities according to whether it was for a manual or non-manual job. McCormick (1985) found that ethnic minority workers travelled between 25 per cent and 35 per cent further than white workers living in the same districts, indicating that discrimination may be the factor behind the longer commuting journey, as ethnic minorities find it necessary to seek work within a larger geographical area before getting a job. There is no particular reason to suppose that racial discrimination in the labour market is more or less in large cities than in other areas. Ethnic minorities are, however, concentrated mainly in inner areas or outer areas of deprivation in the city and will suffer the same effects of job accessibility and mismatch as other groups in these areas, plus discriminatory effects. This could result in ethnic minority unemployed being even more vulnerable to costs of urban transportation. For historical reasons already cited, arising from the high demand for labour in the industrial cities of Europe in the 1950s–1960s, some large cities may have a relatively high proportion of ethnic minorities. The problems of how to reduce urban unemployment may be compounded by the problem of how to eliminate racial discrimination in the labour market in these cities.

There has been no mention, so far, of the role of local government in urban unemployment. The structure and powers of local government are important both in affecting the level of unemployment and in the creation of new employment through economic development. Local government and the labour market is affected passively through the activities of the market, and can react actively according to the responsibilities and power accorded to it. The passive effects will be similar throughout Europe, but the active effects vary according to institutional frameworks and the powers assigned to local tiers of government in different European countries.

Passive effects result from changes in population and business activity, which in turn result in changes in the tax base and/or taxable capacity, and changes in the demand or need for urban services. Cities losing economic activity or experiencing suburbanisation or exurbanisation of activity outside administrative boundaries are losing not only private sector employment but loss in business taxes, which may in turn reduce employment in local public services. Similarly movement of middle and higher income groups out of the city can reduce the ability of local government to raise the same level of revenue from a population with lower average incomes (Klaasen 1987).

The process of urbanisation itself can, therefore, result in loss of employment in the public sector within the city even in situations where the wider urban region may be growing and successful. Fiscal stress in large cities has been evident for many years in the USA where residential and economic suburbanisation came earlier, and has developed to a greater extent than in

Europe. When central government compensates cities for loss of tax revenue, or pays for a large proportion of public urban expenditure, these negative effects of the urbanisation process are mitigated.

Cities, on the other hand, that are growing and that are gaining in economic activity in the central core as well as the wider urban region, can experience growth in local public revenue from an expanding tax base. This can result in an increase in local employment, depending on how the local authorities spend the extra revenue. In the case studies, Manchester and Rotterdam are revenue losers, Montpellier and Barcelona gainers in this urbanisation process.

Active policies of local government can affect unemployment in various ways via policies on physical planning, local economic planning and urban transportation all of which are normally the responsibility of local government in European cities. Land use planning controls the development of different types of activity in areas and neighbourhoods of the city. If these plans are inflexible there can be a resultant loss of potential job-creating activities. Similarly, if external costs of a new development are viewed by planning authorities as being of greater importance in a neighbourhood than new employment, this again will affect local employment and job opportunities. Economic planning at city level can reinforce the market process, for example by releasing suburban land for new activity, providing suburban business parks, and the provision of access and public services appropriate for economic development on greenfield sites. On the whole, local economic planning aims to maximise income and employment for the urban areas as a whole. Cities are in competition with each other for new activity and so are most likely to promote plans that they feel are attractive to private sector investors in terms of location and facilities. In a situation where the majority of the unemployed are locked into the urban core and economic development plans stress outer area expansion the effect on total unemployment levels from new activity may be very small. New employment may be taken up by incomers or extra-urban residents, while, for reasons discussed above, those unemployed in inner areas may be unaffected by economic development. A considerably greater number of jobs has to be generated than the numbers unemployed for it to have an impact on the urban unemployed (Moore and Townroe 1990). If local economic planning is concerned not first with the creation of employment but also with the reduction of unemployment, the location of new employment and the type of new activity encouraged will be important in affecting unemployment levels. Rotterdam, for instance, has a strong policy of reurbanisation, in order to aid the urban unemployed.

Economic planning, although undertaken by all the sample cities, may not have a great impact because resources to promote development may not be available to city governments, either because their revenue does not allow much leeway to devote resources to promoting economic development once the statutory obligations are fulfilled, or because central government funding for this purpose is allocated on a regional rather than an urban level. It may also be the case, as in France, that regional authorities have more powers and resources to carry out economic planning than do city governments. In this case there may be a conflict of interests between the needs of the city and wider issues of economic development in, for example, depressed rural areas within the surrounding region. Regional authorities must balance the interests of small towns and rural communities with those of the urban area when deciding where to subsidise new activity. One of the aims of a regional authority may be to halt migration into the city, since the migration can exacerbate the problems of rural areas and may cause congestion and other increased infrastructure costs in the city. This type of policy may result in too little urban employment creation to lower urban unemployment. The priorities of economic planning and how it is organised and funded within a country can, therefore, affect the level of urban unemployment. The European Community currently awards funds through the European Regional Development Fund for the purpose of regional economic development, normally on infrastructure projects. Some large urban areas can benefit from this if they are within a depressed or underdeveloped region of Europe. Not all large cities with high unemployment and economic problems are so assessed. Rotterdam, for example, is within the relatively wealthy region of Zuid Holland, and so receives no ERDF funding.

Local transportation policy has an important effect on the opportunities for the unemployed to seek employment, as discussed above. Policies that extend and subsidise public transportation, particularly low-cost rapid transit systems, will increase employment opportunities for the urban unemployed by making a wider job search area more viable. The building of outer-urban motorways on the other hand will accelerate processes of economic decentralisation and make access more difficult for low-income workers unable to afford private transportation.

The level of urban unemployment can be raised or lowered not just as a result of employment creation or unemployment policies as such, but also by other policies pursued by city or regional government. Housing, transportation, planning policies and local economic initiatives all have an impact on the level of unemployment and their effects should be considered when examining both the causes of unemployment in cities and the likely outcome of national and EC unemployment policies.

Government structures are also important in their effects on dealing successfully with unemployment. The number of public agencies involved in unemployment policy varies greatly between different countries in Europe. In France there is one, the ANPE, while in Britain and the Netherlands several agencies carry out policies to aid the unemployed. In addition to national agencies operating at local level the city itself may be legally responsible for aiding some categories of the unemployed, as in Frankfurt. Local governments may also fund local voluntary agencies dealing with specific groups of unemployed such as ethnic minorities or the disabled. Policies towards job creation at local level within Europe are not only different but may be more or less responsive and relevant in reducing unemployment levels.

Local employment initiatives (LEIs) have become a popular area of policy in Europe in recent years. The basic argument in favour of LEIs is that national macroeconomic policies still lead to concentration in unemployment in certain geographical areas and amongst certain sectors of the population. The objectives of LEIs can be either job creation or the reduction of unemployment, not necessarily the same thing. The idea is to use public funding to increase private sector activity and bring about economic development in an area. Several strategies can be used including marketing and promotion of the city in general; leverage of private sector investment funds by public sector contributions to a project; provision of consultation services to business; and provision of serviced space for special activities (business parks, technopoles). They can be used to try and increase employment generally within cities with falling levels of activity, or to promote faster growth, or to promote neighbourhood-specific employment for socially disadvantaged areas of the city. There are economic arguments for using these initiatives in social targeting of the poorest areas of the city with the highest unemployment levels, in that, by reducing local high pockets of unemployment external benefits, such as reduction in crime, and housing and environmental improvement may also be generated (Robson 1988). Multiplier effects from an increase in income within the specific area can also lead to further benefit. An additional benefit may be in countering local inertia and the discouraged worker effect, and offsetting downward trends within an area of the city (Keeble and Wever 1986).

LEIs are important in that, if employment is not being generated within the city, national and EC policies for the unemployed, which concentrate on improving the quality of labour supply, will not be successful if no increase in labour demand is forthcoming at a local level. The type of LEI will also matter if urban unemployment level is to be reduced. Initiatives which encourage, for instance, medical research or financial services to locate in the city are going to have little impact in the short term on unemployment, if the vast number of unemployed are of low skill. These sorts of initiative may have only a longer-term effect on unemployment through trickle-down effects on the local economy. One further point on LEIs is that problems can arise according to which tier of government is funding and directing the policy. Where national government subverts the powers of local government and direction of local initiatives are centralised, political conflict can result in less than optimum cooperation at a local level.

The case studies in Chapters 4 to 8 will assess the national active labour market policies for the unemployed operating in the context of five major European cities: Manchester, Montpellier, Rotterdam, Barcelona and

Frankfurt in 1992. The studies will outline the economic structure of the cities and changes that have occurred over the 1980s in population and employment levels. Employment levels will be analysed for different groups and, where information is available, the degree of mismatch in skills existing within the urban area. Locational differences in unemployment levels will also be examined in relation to the location of employment, and both the cost and ease of access of public transportation between areas. In addition to information on national policies on unemployment that are in operation at city level, major policies initiated by local government will, where appropriate, be examined. The studies do not purport to be exhaustive in detailing every initiative for the unemployed at local level, but deal with the major areas of expenditure on active policies.

Eligibility of different groups of the unemployed for unemployment compensation in the city will be detailed together with information comparing the level of benefits to average wages in the city where the information exists. Bearing in mind the importance of economic planning and employment generation policies at local level, the main features of these policies in the cities will be evaluated in relation to their effects on unemployment levels.

Before the case studies though, it would be relevant to look at the role the European Community plays in trying to combat its most serious economic and social problem.

3

THE ROLE OF THE EUROPEAN COMMUNITY IN HELPING THE UNEMPLOYED

'There can be no real united Community in Europe unless there is economic and social cohesion'.[1] Economic cohesion is to be brought about by closing the development gaps between different regions of the European Community, by helping those which are less developed or have suffered from structural change to catch up with the economic level of the most prosperous. Social cohesion is interpreted as achievable by reducing social inequality, particularly in employment and vocational training, between those who have jobs and those who, due to lack of training or special handicaps, have not. Both of these aims are directed at reducing the levels of unemployment and underemployment in Europe.

As has been shown the past decade has brought increasing problems in unemployment to the whole of Europe. The structural changes which have resulted in rural and manufacturing unemployment have been followed, in the recession of the early 1990s, by job losses in the service sector, which have been especially marked in the UK, but have also happened to a greater or lesser extent in other European countries. The challenge of new technologies, particularly information technology, is bringing about changes in working practices and in requirements for higher levels of skills, which will further affect employment of low-skill workers, in both manufacturing and service sectors, in the coming decade. The Single European Market, which came into being in 1993, dismantled trade barriers and allowed freedom of movement of workers and capital, and is expected to result in further shifts in the economic advantages of some areas to the detriment of others, as well as encouraging migratory flows of labour to the Community's more prosperous areas. The opening up of Eastern Europe and the re-unification of Germany has already resulted in a stream of migrant workers from east to west within Germany, and agreements between the EC and Eastern European countries, such as associate membership status, could further increase the number of migrants. The Maastricht Treaty, with its social provisions on minimum wages, workers' protection and health and safety standards, while contributing to the social cohesion of the community, may, by adding to labour costs, result in the unemployment of the low-paid (Addison and Siebert 1992).

So, in addition to the existing problems of unemployment in Europe, the likelihood is that the rate will continue to rise over the coming years. The problem of unemployment is open to both micro- and macroeconomic policy solutions and ideally they should be used together. While improving skills of the labour force to relate to the needs of modern high technology sectors may reduce the level of unemployment by providing jobs for the unemployed in areas of skills shortage, it is not going to provide sixteen million new jobs. The creation of new jobs must rely on expansion of demand. But the European Community, as presently constituted, is not capable itself of acting at a macroeconomic level. This can only be done through policy co-ordination of Member States. High budget deficits within Member States, caused in large part by high unemployment, are keeping long-term interest rates relatively high which militates against expansion of demand. This factor will provide a brake on macroeconomic expansion for the near future, unless there are concerted efforts by national governments to reduce the budget deficits, either by cutting expenditure or raising taxes. The proposed economic and monetary union of 1999 under the Maastricht Treaty would significantly alter the powers of the Community, or more specifically the European Central Bank, to alter macroeconomic circumstances, dependent on its perceived priorities for the European economy. New employment creation can be facilitated by the Community encouraging and subsidising suitable infrastructure for private market development, but it is the private market that is looked to for major new job creation.

The main role of the European Community in relation to the unemployed is, therefore, in financing labour market and other policies to help those areas and those groups amongst the unemployed who are most disadvantaged. It has been noted that a priority of the Community has been to close the gap between the most prosperous and least prosperous regions, and to reduce inequalities in the employment market. Before 1989 responsibility for regional development and employment problems was split between various agencies of the Community. Regional development policy was financed either by the European Regional Development Fund (ERDF), the European Agricultural Guarantee and Guidance Fund (EAGGF) guidance section in rural areas, and the European Coal and Steel Community (ECSC) in declining coal and steel areas. While some policies for the unemployed were dealt with by the ECSC, most employment problems were dealt with by the European Social Fund (ESF) on a cross-Europe basis. Funding was on the basis of individual programmes, and there was little co-ordination between the main agencies.

The ESF is the oldest of the Community's three Structural Funds and was set up by the Treaty of Rome in 1957 to support employment and promote the geographical and professional mobility of workers. This was done in the period 1958–89 by backing vocational training and guidance, and aid for new job creation, for the employed and self-employed, in small firms. During that period around thirty million people received assistance. Major areas of expenditure were on vocational training, particularly in Southern Europe and Ireland; generally with incentives to Member States to keep up training programmes during public spending cuts; and in supporting training for underprivileged groups, especially the disabled, migrant workers, the poor and socially excluded, and young people with low educational attainments. Other schemes included special vocational training for women, and for employment and support for innovation and exchange of information.

REFORM OF THE COMMUNITY STRUCTURAL FUNDS

The Single European Act 1987 led to the reform of structural funds to improve economic and social cohesion by greater co-ordination of all the Community's funding agencies. A new project approach was introduced to replace the decentralised piecemeal programme approach. Funding was doubled in real terms between 1987 and 1993 in response to the increasing problem of unemployment and growing regional disparities which were predicted to worsen after 1992.

The priorities of the Community Structural Funds were:

- *Objective 1*: To promote growth and adjustment of regions that are lagging.
- *Objective 2*: To provide support for regions affected by industrial decline.
- *Objective 3*: To combat long-term unemployment.
- *Objective 4*: To facilitate the occupational integration of young people.
- *Objective 5a*: To adapt agricultural structures and rural development, with a view to
- *Objective 5b*: Reform of the Common Agricultural Policy (CAP).

The current duties of the ESF are, therefore, to back policies for the long-term unemployed and young people, giving particular emphasis to the most vulnerable groups – women, migrants and the disabled – within these groups, and to focus a large part of this assistance on lagging regions and depressed industrial regions. The aid is co-ordinated with aid for regional development, formerly dealt with separately by the ERDF, the ECSC, the EAGGF guidance section, and the European Investment Bank (EIB). The latter gives low interest long-term loans for approved programmes. For example, if one takes a declining industrial region, the EC is interested in converting industries to high technology, in promoting small and medium sized firms, and in improvement of the environment to make it more attractive to potential investors. Within such a programme human resources are considered as part of the general upgrading and change, and training or retraining is important within a plan for economic development. Contributions for an integrated programme would come from the ERDF, the ESF and loan agencies.

Objectives 1, 2 and 5, the regions which receive the majority of the funding, are examined first.

Objective 1: lagging regions

Objective 1 regions are those areas of the Community with a per capita GDP close to, or less than, 75 per cent of the EC average. Included in this definition are the whole of Greece, Portugal, and Ireland; Northern Ireland in the UK; the southern half of Italy and Sardinia; the French overseas departments and Corsica; and a large part of Spain excluding the northern-most regions. The doubling of the financial resources of the Structural Funds is designed to benefit these regions most, and in the period 1989–93 they received 36.2 billion ECU with the ESF providing one third of this sum (CEC 1991). The ERDF finances infrastructure and equipment, and the ESF all types of training and teacher training. Schemes for development of industry, services, tourism, research and technology, energy and the environment have complementary training programmes, in addition to training for the long-term unemployed and the young.

Objective 2: declining industrial areas

Objective 2 regions, under the reform of the Community Structural Funds, are defined as regions or parts of regions, where industry has declined seriously, where unemployment is above the Community average and where industrial employment is higher than average. There are sixty Objective 2

Table 3.1 Assistance from Community Structural Funds for Objective 1 regions, 1989–93

Member State	ERDF	ESF	EAGGF	Total	M.ECU in 1989 prices %
Greece	3,662	1,728	1,277	6,667	18.4
Spain	6,199	2,348	1,232	9,779	27.0
France	406	322	160	888	2.5
Ireland	1,646	1,372	654	3,672	10.1
Italy	4,942	1,700	801	7,443	20.6
Portugal	3,757	2,028	1,173	6,958	19.2
UK (N. Ireland)	348	315	130	793	2.2
Total	20,960	9,813	5,427	36,200	100

Source: CEC, *Social Europe* (1991)

regions or parts of regions in eight EC countries. These regions contain 53.2 million people and many declining major urban centres are included in these areas, including two of the cities under study, Manchester and Barcelona. The ERDF and ESF together fund regeneration of these regions by boosting new activities, rationalising and increasing productivity in existing industries, and generating an environment where new jobs are created. Human resource training other than for the young and long-term unemployed (Objectives 3 and 4) are designed to emphasise conversion of workers to the needs of new activities. The ESF's role between 1989-91 was to give financial aid to and improve the possibilities of creating and developing productive activities. This was done via training and employment measures (ECU112 million); supporting SMEs that use local potential (ECU280 million); supporting various areas of technology by training in innovation and science (ECU80 million); encouraging and developing tourism via training and aid for employment (ECU55 million); and improving the environment and attractiveness of regions (ECU40 million).

Table 3.2 CSF Assistance for Objective 2 regions, 1989–91 (ECU million in 1989 prices)

Member State	ERDF	ESF	Total	% of total CSF assistance
Belgium	145	50	195	5.0
Denmark	22	8	30	0.8
France	514	186	700	17.9
Germany	249	106	355	9.1
Italy	179	86	265	6.8
Luxemburg	15	0	15	0.4
Netherlands	57	38	95	2.4
Spain	576	159	735	18.8
UK	1,159	351	1,510	38.7
Total	2,916	984	3,900	100

Source: CEC, *Social Europe* (1992)

The UK had the lion's share of CSF funds for declining industrial regions, as shown in Table 3.2, with substantial amounts going also to Spain and France. The declining industrial regions received 3.9 billion ECU for the period 1989–91 compared with over 36 billion ECU for Objective 1 regions in the period 1989–93. Cities also received funding under Article 1(2) of the EEC which was to convert 'the regions, frontier regions or parts of regions (including employment areas and urban communities) seriously affected by industrial decline'. This meant that declining industrial cities which were not included in Objective 2 regions could receive similar aid for their problems.

It was a recognition of the fact, for the first time, that cities could experience severe economic and employment problems even though they may be sited in relatively prosperous areas of the Community.

Objective 5: rural areas

Aid for rural development to alleviate low incomes, underemployment and unemployment is available in northern Spain, large areas of France, some parts of central and northern Italy, scattered areas of Germany, northern Holland, the Highlands of Scotland, parts of Wales and parts of the south-west peninsular of England (see Figure 3.1).

Total funding from all agencies of the EC for these areas for the period 1989–93 was 2.6 billion ECU. Of the cities under study Montpellier is within an Objective 5 region, Languedoc-Roussillon, as is Frankfurt, which is in Hesse. The aid given to these regions does not directly affect unemployment in the cities, but may do so indirectly. If regional aid to rural area reduces in-migration of the rural unemployed into the cities, then unemployment in the urban area will not be as high. This is an important factor in the unemployment levels of otherwise prosperous and thriving cities like Montpellier, as will be seen in Chapter 4.

The distribution of CSF indicative funding for the period 1989 to 1993, which includes all priority areas in order of benefit to individual countries is shown in Table 3.3.

As previously mentioned, the European Social Fund provides the finance for employment measures, including development of new employment

Table 3.3 Distribution between Member States of CSF indicative funding, 1989–93

	% of total
Spain	20.2
Italy	15.8
Portugal	13.2
UK	11.3
Greece	11.3
France	10.1
Ireland	8.9
Germany	5.0
Netherlands	1.8
Belgium	1.5
Denmark	0.7
Luxemburg	0.1
Total	100.0

Source: CEC, *Social Europe* (2/91)

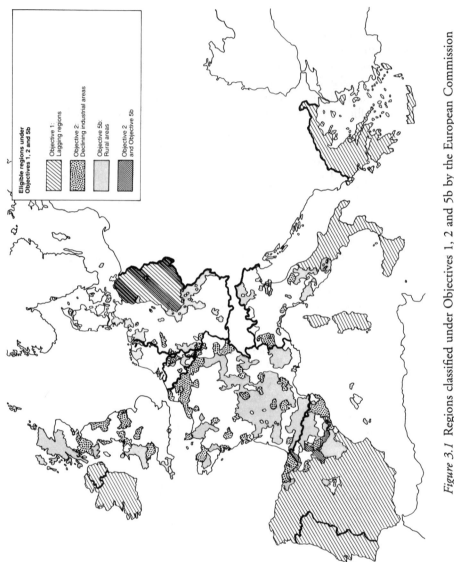

Figure 3.1 Regions classified under Objectives 1, 2 and 5b by the European Commission
Source: Directorate General XVI in CEC, Social Europe (1991)

Eligible regions under
Objectives 1, 2 and 5b

Objective 1:
Lagging regions

Objective 2:
Declining industrial areas

Objective 5b:
Rural areas

Objective 2
and Objective 5b

within the Community Structural Framework. Out of the total funds available from the ESF 63.9 per cent went to Objective 1 regions, 6.4 per cent to Objective 2 regions, 2.8 per cent to Objective 5 regions, and 26.8 per cent to all other areas of the EC, to aid policies under priorities 3 and 4 (the long-term unemployed and the young unemployed). The majority of funding goes, therefore, to lagging regions and poorer countries. The aid for Objective 1 regions may go mainly for development as in Portugal, or mainly in measures to help the long-term unemployed or the young, as in Spain and the UK. In most areas of Europe the main problem is the availability of vacancies in employment, not a mismatch of skills, so funding development together with training makes good sense.

Large cities in Europe, unless they come under Objective 2 criteria, although they all have relatively severe unemployment problems, can only benefit from the general funding available under Objectives 3 and 4. Before looking in more detail at aid available under these priorities a few brief words about the organisation of the ESF. Since 1989 a Committee of the ESF has been in operation, with the aim of helping the Commission to implement the reform of structural funds, with reference to Objectives 3 and 4. The make-up of the Committee is tripartite with two representatives of government, two representatives of workers' unions, and two representatives of employers' organisations from each Member State. It was designed in this way to have a means of ensuring consultation between the various people involved in training and employment throughout the Community.

As has been shown in Chapter 1, the major problems in EC unemployment are the high percentage of those under 25 without a job, nearly double the average rate at 16.5 per cent of the active young population in 1990, and the fact that nearly half those out of work have been unemployed for more than a year. A further problem is the growing number of women who are unemployed, which in many countries exceeds the number of men who are jobless.

The European Social Fund has addressed the first two general problems with Objectives 3 and 4. Within these Objectives the ESF pays particular attention to applications for assistance where the schemes help those with special difficulties: the disabled, migrants, and women in sectors in which they are under-represented. It is up to national governments to devise schemes that would benefit these groups and apply to the Community for funding. Once the programme has been approved the ESF provides 65 per cent of total public spending in Objective 1 regions, and 45 per cent for all other areas. It is very much in the interest of national governments to direct their own expenditure on unemployment policies towards the categories of unemployed benefiting from ESF aid. So while the EC itself cannot directly implement policy in Member States, the high levels of financial incentives provided ensure that national policy is geared in the directions favoured by the Community.

Objective 3: the long-term unemployed

'The extension of the duration of unemployment is the most significant and worrying phenomenon to have affected the labour market of the Community in recent years.' In view of this statement the Community set up specific conditions in 1989 for the support of schemes for the long-term unemployed. In general the aim was to give long-term unemployed workers training opportunities to enable them to move to a higher level of qualifications, appropriate both to their needs and the needs of the labour market. Support was to be given specifically with regard to four criteria. Firstly, the development of operations combining several types of intervention in order that training should be a real factor in promoting occupational and social integration. Secondly, schemes that made the 'most of local employment development potential',[2] thus making actions relevant to local labour markets. Thirdly, the ESF supported financial incentives to recruit the long-term employed. Lastly, concern was shown for the training and occupational integration of women who wished to return to the labour market after a long break.

Objective 4: the young unemployed

High youth unemployment was a feature in Europe throughout the 1980s and was a funding priority of the ESF. Funding rose from 609.5 million ECU in 1980 to more than 2.7 billion in 1989. The main recipients of aid were the UK, Italy, Spain, France and Portugal. After 1989 the ESF spent 75 per cent of its funds to promote employment of those under 25 years of age. This sum includes expenditure in Objective 1 regions as well as elsewhere.

The main aims of policy since 1989 have been to support schemes of four types. Firstly, those designed to help school leavers who do not have qualifications to obtain vocational training to match their own abilities and the needs of the employment market. Secondly, schemes that provide vocational training in a firm or training centre, preferably leading to a recognised qualification. Thirdly, courses involving new technologies that lead to qualifications needed by employers. Lastly, schemes to aid recruitment to newly created, stable jobs and self-employed activity.

Within Objectives 3 and 4, if the basic criteria are fulfilled, preference will be given to programmes that are also aimed at the following:

(a) people encountering special difficulties in the labour market, the disabled, women and migrants;
(b) transnational schemes including exchanges of programmes, teachers and trainers;
(c) training in advanced technology;
(d) innovatory operations in regard to content method or organisation of training;

(e) improved and more effective training structures to ensure more effective vocational training systems.

Women in the labour market and the role of the ESF

As we have seen participation by women in the labour market has increased considerably over the past twenty years, and at the same time female unemployment has risen at a faster rate than average in the European Community. Since 1977, the ESF has recognised the special difficulties of women in the labour market and initially gave priority to training schemes for jobs in which women were under-represented to strike a 'better balance between the sexes in various sectors and throughout the hierarchy particularly in posts of responsibility.'[3] A second priority was to back vocational training schemes in jobs traditionally seen as men's work. Between 1978 and 1983 applications for support for schemes rose from 10.7 million ECU to 118 million ECU. The largest beneficiary was Germany, followed by France and Italy. In 1984 specific budget support for women was withdrawn, but all regulations hindering women's access to all branches of training were abolished. It was hoped that companies would then have a policy of having both sexes properly represented throughout the hierarchy. It was found, however, that in industrialised countries there was a tendency to train women for jobs about to become obsolete, while men were channelled into courses in new technologies. The sexual balance of job training was still to the detriment of women in scientific sectors. It was thought that a balance was needed to ensure that women would not face further exclusion from the job market. By 1989, therefore, the special difficulties faced by women in obtaining training to equip them for long-term jobs and give access to a variety of employment opportunities were recognised.

Migrant workers and the role of the ESF

Articles 48 and 49 of the Treaty of Rome provide for 'freedom of movement for workers', the abolition of any discrimination based on nationality between workers of the Member States as regards employment. Integration of migrant workers was, therefore, recognised as an objective from the inception of the European Community. Ensuring free movement of workers was interpreted as meaning taking proper steps to facilitate the integration of migrants in the host countries. During the late 1950s and the 1960s when manufacturing industry and construction in north-western Europe was suffering from a shortage of labour, vast numbers of migrants went from southern European countries and from ex-colonies to fill the vacancies. The ESF helped originally by backing language and culture classes, not just for the workers, but also for their families. Even if migrants were second or third generation at the time of the Treaty of Rome, integration might still have been a problem because of poor language skills and loss of cultural identity. In many cases this decreased the chances of vocational training for the migrants and their access to the labour market for permanent stable employment. In practice only the least stable, unskilled jobs with no real prospects of promotion were undertaken by most migrants. This is a situation which largely continues to this day as will be shown in the case studies.

Up until 1984 migrants were financed by special budgets. After that time all projects both for young people and the over 25s were open to migrants. In the reform of the ESF in 1984 projects for migrant workers were the only ones to get priority. Political refugees were considered to be in the category of migrant workers. Most of the schemes that applied for funding were run by private, non-profit making associations which often had difficulty in finding the resources needed to qualify for ESF support, since the ESF only provided 50 per cent of the costs. The volume of vocational training and language teaching projects for migrants remained stable from 1984 to 1989 when rules of eligibility changed. The rules were considerably tightened so that workers were only considered migrants if they had arrived in their host country during the previous three years. This excluded all second generation migrants who had previously benefited. So although migrants are a priority for ESF funding, regulations exclude most of those previously falling within this category. Schemes providing training for integration are still supported, and the ESF will also give financial aid to help migrants return to another Member State. Migrant workers from outside the Community cannot receive this aid. This will include North African workers in France and the Netherlands, Turkish workers in Germany, and recent arrivals from the New Commonwealth in the UK, all of whom have special employment problems that are particularly acutely seen in large cities.

Table 3.4 ESF assistance for Objectives 3 and 4 outside Objective 1 regions, 1990–92 by country (ECU million in 1989 prices)

	Objective 3	*Objective 4*	*% of total funds*
Belgium	87.26	79.30	4.21
Denmark	46.00	49.00	2.40
France	399.31	437.81	21.13
Germany	271.73	296.11	13.88
Italy	92.00	466.00	14.17
Luxemburg	1.80	5.20	0.17
Netherlands	123.50	96.80	5.57
Spain	169.35	388.05	13.64
UK	514.00	470.00	24.83
Total	1,704.95	2,288.27	100.00

Source: CEC, *Social Europe* (1991)

42

The total sums to be paid to Member States outside Objective 1 regions for the young and long-term unemployed are shown in Table 3.4.

The largest beneficiaries from the funding are the UK and France who together have nearly half of the available resources. The distribution of these resources between different types of training and different groups is shown in Table 3.5 below.

Basic grounding and updating of knowledge for those without qualifications, who constitute a large proportion of the young unemployed, accounts for nearly 45 per cent of ESF expenditure, compared to training for people who already have some training or job experience and can benefit from a higher level or specialist and technology training – 17 per cent of the total.

As we shall see in the city studies, the groups most liable to unemployment – women, migrants and, in some cases, the disabled receive 5.8 per cent, 3.7 per cent and 9.9 per cent respectively for special programmes to meet their particular needs. This is not to say that this is the total expenditure by the ESF on these groups as many women and migrants will be beneficiaries of general training schemes. Considering, however, that these are priority groups with special difficulties and special needs to help with their integration into the open labour market, it is surprising that

Table 3.5 ESF assistance provided in the CFSs for Objectives 3 and 4 outside Objective 1 regions, 1990–92 – type of training and category of beneficiary (ECU million in 1989 prices)

	Amount	*% of Total funds*
Training		
Basic grounding/updating	1,851,660	44.86
Level two training	322,500	8.05
Technology training	223,645	5.42
Specialised training	165,406	4.00
Training for the LTU	86,217	2.09
Disadvantaged groups		
Women	239,463	5.80
Migrants	154,230	3.73
The disabled	411,018	9.96
Other underprivileged groups	123,369	2.98
Other schemes		
Recruitment subsidies	321,279	7.78
Multi-sectoral	58,165	1.40
Transnational/innovatory schemes	26,204	0.63
Article 1 (2) schemes	134,744	3.28
Total	4,117,900	100.00

Source: CEC, *Social Europe* (1991)

a greater proportion of funding does not go towards support for these groups.

The European Social Fund, in addition to the schemes above, also aids employment creation and special groups of the unemployed via other initiatives. The most important of these initiatives are examined below.

Horizon

Horizon is aimed specifically at helping disabled people, with physical or mental problems, who have difficulties in finding work, and are at risk of greater marginalisation in the labour market because of the increasing use of new technology. Help is also available under this initiative to other people with severe disadvantage, including the ill housed, unqualified, refugees and the multiply socially disadvantaged. The budget for this initiative is 180 million ECU. All projects require co-financing from Member States.

Now

Now addresses the problem of equal opportunities for men and women. Its aims are to develop and promote women's qualifications, and change company culture so that women can set up their own firms and cooperatives. In addition it supports reintegration of women in the regular employment market by guidance and counselling schemes designed to help those who have had a long period at home, or a long period of unemployment. Within Objective 1 regions it promotes child-care schemes and crèches to enable more women to go for training or seek work. The ESF provided 120 million ECU for this initiative.

ILEs – Local Employment Initiatives by women

This scheme supports the creation of Local Employment Initiatives (ILEs) by women. Those benefiting from the grants provided must be committed to providing paid employment for other women. Priority is given in ILEs to creating jobs for the most vulnerable groups – migrant women, disabled women, unemployed women with families to support, and returners to work after a long break.

ECSC/Rechar

The ECSC (European Coal and Steel Community) has been in operation since 1951 to help the re-employment of redundant workers in the coal and steel industries. Between 1976 and 1989 around 600,000 workers benefited from aid by the support of early retirement schemes, tideover allowances, wage support, and resettlement allowances. Rechar is linked to the ECSC and finances measures for retraining redundant miners; giving preparatory training to the less skilled; counselling and assistance to those setting up business; and readaptation aid. In 1990 40 million ECU was provided for this initiative.

ERGO

ERGO was created at the end of 1988 to encourage the pooling and exchange of information, between Member States, on successful programmes to help the long-term unemployed. The initiative also has cooperative links with Austria, Canada, Sweden and the USA. ERGO has also provided a methodology for evaluating national programmes.

LEDA – Local Employment Development Action

LEDA, introduced in 1986, aimed to foster local employment development. It was set up to identify factors underlying successful local development; the best ways to encourage efficient cooperation between local actors and agencies and between them and local, regional, national and Community public bodies; and the best way of ensuring efficient local delivery of national and Community policies. LEDA included twenty-four areas by 1988, all having the characteristics of above average unemployment and structural problems. Barcelona, a case study is one of these areas. Initial findings show that in urban centres of industrial decline, local government and universities play an important part in economic development, as well as development agencies and the private sector. The programme provides no financial aid to local development but disseminates information to local areas on successful employment initiatives, and aims to help those in charge of mainstream Community and national programmes, as well as local agencies, to adapt their policy instruments to local circumstances.

SPEC – Support Programmes for Employment Creation

SPEC was launched in 1990 to provide financial and technical support to innovatory employment creation projects linked to changes in employment. Changes are thought of mainly as those arising from the implementation of the Single European Market. Programmes eligible for subsidy were those which assisted local enterprises or individuals to adapt to either an intensified employment problem or an employment opportunity associated with the single market. Eligible areas were Objective 1, 2 and 5b regions and border areas. EC aid ranged from ECU 5,000 to ECU 20,000 per project. The upper limit was for projects involving training, job creation and industrial restructuring. Co-financing from other sources was at least 30 per cent in Objective 1 areas and 50 per cent elsewhere. SPEC, in addition to financial assistance, aimed to provide technical assistance via special briefing to local authorities and agencies, workshops, technical documentation and guidelines on project design and management.

Transnational schemes

Schemes for employment run cooperatively by two or more EC countries have been an ESF priority since 1985. In the 1989 reforms, subsidy to these schemes was kept if they were concerned with either the long-term unemployed or the young. Very small numbers of applicants have been forthcoming for these schemes. One example has been Euregio, involving cooperation between Germany and the Netherlands to implement cross-border vocational training in the metal and textile industries which needed skilled workers in both countries.

In addition to the above initiatives that directly aid and subsidise employment programmes of different types, the European Community has also set up information systems to help national and local governments dealing with labour market problems. These include ELISE, that collects, processes and distributes information on local development and local employment initiatives; SYSDEM that collects information on studies and reports on employment trends available in Member States; and MISEP which is concerned with a regular exchange of information on employment and the labour market by national governments.

Bearing in mind that the ESF provides substantial funding in order to try and direct national and local government to implement the kinds of policies it considers most appropriate and useful in the context of EC wide unemployment, it is for national governments and national agencies to put forward schemes for subsidy. Schemes that do not come under the various objectives or special measures must be funded totally by national public bodies or voluntary agencies. It is clearly in the interests of national governments and agencies to direct most of the resources available for active policies for the unemployed to programmes that can receive EC subsidy, since some 45 per cent of the costs will be borne by the ESF.

The ESF does not, however, insist that a Member State takes up the amount of indicative funding provided for all different purposes. The decision of whether or not to provide technological training, or have special schemes for some disadvantaged groups is up to the country concerned. The amount of subsidy applied for will also reflect what national governments can themselves afford to pay for employment programmes. There may well be an inverse relationship between the number of unemployed and the ability of national and local governments to fund programmes. Higher levels of unemployment usually mean lowered national incomes, and certainly involve a higher sum paid out in unemployment benefit or social assistance, often thus reducing the amount available for other forms of active aid for the unemployed. It is paradoxical that countries with lower unemployment can afford to fund more expensive and effective programmes to help reintegrate the unemployed, while countries with more serious problems are able to provide less in the way of assistance. Since ESF aid is granted on the basis of matching funds from the recipient country, countries with relatively lower unemployment or higher national income may receive more per head of unemployed than countries with higher unemployment rates and lower national income. Although the ESF gives priority to schemes for the disadvantaged, it is up to national governments to set priorities and implement policies that specifically aid women, the disabled and migrants within the categories of long-term unemployed and youth unemployment.

Table 3.6 shows the amount received by the five countries under study, under Objectives 3 and 4. The contribution of the ESF covers around 45 per cent of most programmes. Table 3.6 shows that France, Germany and Spain aimed to spend more on youth unemployment compared to the long-term unemployed, and that the reverse was true for the UK and the Netherlands.

Within expenditure on programmes for the long-term unemployed, the UK used training subsidies to provide only basic training with nothing on technological training while the Netherlands planned to spend a third of their training budget on technological training, and Germany all of its grant on training leading to qualifications.

The Netherlands spent over a quarter of their budget for the long-term unemployed on recruitment subsidies, compared to around 13 per cent in Spain and the UK, 10 per cent in France and 5 per cent in Germany. The disadvantaged long-term unemployed also accounted for very different amounts of total ESF grants in each country: Germany spent 43 per cent, the Netherlands 35 per cent, France 25 per cent, the UK 23 per cent and Spain only 15 per cent. Within categories of the disadvantaged France and Germany spent most on the disabled, the Netherlands and Spain most on women, and the UK an equal amount on the disabled and women. Considering that women constitute half or over of the long-term unemployed in these countries and have very specific problems in the labour market, it is surprising that the amount spent in every country ranged from a maximum of 23 per cent of the total budget in the Netherlands, to only 5 per cent in France, with the three other countries spending about 10 per cent of programme financing for the long-term unemployed on women's programmes. Programmes for youth unemployment again show differences in the direction of expenditure. France, Spain and the UK use most of their training budget on basic training, while Germany and the Netherlands spend all or most of the budget on technological training. This may well reflect the fact that Germany and the Netherlands have more advanced training for youth within the education system generally, and do not have such a high percentage of unqualified early school leavers as the other countries.

Table 3.6 Total ESF funding on employment measures – Financing Plan,
1990–92 (million ECU)

	France	Germany	Netherlands	Spain	UK
Objective 3 – LTU					
Training	259.1	104.1[1]	36.0	121.8	325.0
Technological	(13.0)	—	(12.4)	(10.0)	—
Basic	(246.1)	—	(23.7)	(111.8)	325.0
Recruitment subsidies	39.1	14.3	35.0	22.2	71.0
Disadvantaged groups	101.2	118.2	42.8	25.4	118.0
Women	(19.2)	(22.3)	(28.5)	(16.0)	(56.0)
Disabled	(66.8)	(57.2)	(8.1)	(8.7)	(56.0)
Migrants	(15.2)	(38.7)	(6.2)	(0.7)	(6.0)
Transnational/Innovatory	—	—	9.7	—	—
Other[2]	—	35.1	—	—	—
Total	399.4	271.7	123.5	169.4	514.0
Objective 4 – Young unemployed					
Training	370.4	33.3[3]	52.6	293.0	405.5
Technological	(74.0)	—	(37.0)	(11.7)	(96.5)[4]
Basic	(296.4)	—	(15.6)	(281.3)	(309.0)
Recruitment subsidies	29.6	—	16.4	74.2	—
Disadvantaged	37.8	231.9	19.5	20.9	64.5
Women	(1.9)	(11.4)	(8.3)	(13.5)	(22.5)
Disabled	(35.6)	(69.6)	(4.3)	(5.6)	(40.5)
Migrants	(0.4)	(31.7)	(7.0)	(1.8)	(1.5)
Other disadvantaged	—	(119.3)	—	—	—
Transnational/Innovatory	—	5.2	8.3	—	—
Other[2]	—	25.8	—	—	—
Total	437.8	296.2	96.8	388.1	470.0
Total 3 and 4	837.2	567.9	220.3	557.5	984.0
Article 1[2]	34.9	5.2	9.7	5.6	41.0
Total ESF	872.1	573.1	230.0	563.1	1025.0

Source: CEC/ESF Community Support Framework 1990–92 for relevant countries (1992)

Notes: (1) specially designed qualification measures; (2) measures relevant to all priorities;
(3) new technologies; (4) higher training.

Recruitment subsidies to encourage employers to take on young unemployed
workers are not used in Germany or the UK, but account for 17 per cent of
grants to the Netherlands and 19 per cent in Spain.

Programmes for disadvantaged youth receive 78 per cent of total financing in Germany, but less than 20 per cent elsewhere. In Germany, France
and the UK this is concentrated on aid to the disabled young, while in the
Netherlands most goes to women and migrants, and in Spain most to
women. Transnational schemes, another EC priority, account for only a tiny
proportion of total expenditure on Objectives 3 and 4 and this only in
Germany and the Netherlands.

Overall the UK received twice as much in ESF financing as Spain, although in 1990 the total number of unemployed in the UK was 1.7 million, whereas in Spain it was 2.4 million. This may well reflect the fact that the UK can afford to co-finance schemes to a greater extent than Spain which has a lower national income per head. This clearly affects levels of expenditure per recipient on employment programmes funded by the ESF. This can be illustrated by Table 3.7 which shows the amount of ESF grant per long-term unemployed worker in the five countries.

Table 3.7 ESF financing per long-term unemployed, 1990

	Number of LTU	Total ESF funding million ECU	Funding per LTU ECU
France	831,300	133.1	160
Germany	673,500	77.9	115
Netherlands	166,980	35.4	212
Spain	1,318,100	61.1	46
UK	607,500	157.0	258

Source: OECD *Labour Force Statistics* (1992); CEC (1992)

The UK and the Netherlands received over four times as much ESF funding for each of the long-term unemployed as Spain, and although all countries had actively supported programmes, the amount of subsidy ranged in 1990 from 46 ECU to 258 ECU per worker. This must clearly be reflected in the quality of the schemes available and appears, in the case of Spain, to indicate that where the need is greatest the amount spent is low, and where numbers are relatively low, as in the Netherlands, programmes are more expensive and sophisticated.

This raises one of the problems of EC grants to aid the unemployed, the question of what national governments are able to afford to co-finance.

While the poorest countries in the Community with lagging economic development do receive a higher proportion of total financing of a scheme from the ESF, they are still required to provide up to half of the costs. In areas outside Objective 1 regions, national financing provides 55 per cent of the finance for a programme. As already pointed out, there is to some extent an inverse relationship between the ability of a country to afford high level programmes and the degree of severity of unemployment. With the economic recession of the 1990s governments are experiencing falling government revenues and rising social security expenditures. It is in this context that those worst hit by unemployment, and those with a lower national income per head can afford least. Some system that involved a sliding scale of grants from the ESF, according to the severity of unemployment rates of the young and those out of work for more than a year, might overcome this problem. It would ensure that the quality of schemes across the Community would be more even, and hence the results from, for example, training, which equipped the unemployed for an increasingly high-skill oriented labour market, would be more positive in job search.

Another point on the direction of ESF funding is the policy change since 1989 towards migrants. Large cities in Europe are the major centres for migrant settlement. In the cities under study a high percentage of migrants, whether first or second generation, are unemployed. The difficulties in finding work are partly to do with low skill levels and partly language problems. Most of these migrants do not come from other EC countries and are not political refugees. They are, however, permanent residents even though they may not be EC nationals. Turkish workers in Germany, North African migrants to France and migrants from ex-colonies in the UK and the Netherlands all face language and cultural differences which may make integration into the workforce more difficult. In some cases fluency in the language of the host country is not high even in second generation migrants. While the ESF sets as a priority help to unemployed internal migrants, these groups are excluded. Social cohesion and the reduction in equalities is a primary aim of the Community. In many large cities social cohesion is threatened when large groups of migrant workers become isolated and ghettoised into an underclass, with up to half of them unemployed, as in Montpellier, and most of the rest in low-skill, low-paid and precarious jobs. The need for special help for these residents is very apparent in most large cities, but is no longer recognised by the EC.

Women in Europe, as already discussed, not only have difficulties in finding work that is appropriate to their skill levels, but also work which is physically possible to undertake given that they may have to care for children or elderly parents. There are also psychological barriers for women returning to work after long spells at home. The ESF recognises the skills problem by subsidising programmes of training to give access for women to all sectors of the work hierarchy. It also recognises problems involved in return to work. The major problem of women in the workforce is, however, concerned with the availability of substitute carers for the children, the disabled and the elderly. Grants directed to workplace crèches and subsidies for help in the home would overcome most women's unemployment problems more effectively than training in non-traditional skills. Even though all general programmes receiving ESF subsidy are open to women, special programmes for women account for only 5.8 per cent of total Objectives 3 and 4 grants. It is small recognition of the problems of this disadvantaged group.

Most large cities in Europe are not within the lagging regions and do not, therefore, receive special development aid from the EC. Declining industrial cities do receive subsidy under Objective 2, but ESF funds for the unemployed are ten times greater in lagging regions than in declining industrial areas. Cities that are not classified as in either Objective 1 or Objective 2 areas share 27 per cent of funding for the unemployed. Over half of the population of the EC lives in large cities and these cities experience above average unemployment compared to other areas of the countries concerned. While those cities in priority areas receive more aid, most cities do not. The work prospects of the majority of Community citizens is tied up with the future of large cities. The case studies will illustrate the particular problems of unemployment in urban economies and may demonstrate the need for further EC policies designed to meet their needs.

4

MONTPELLIER

INTRODUCTION

Montpellier is situated some ten miles from the Mediterranean in one of the poorest regions of France, Languedoc-Roussillon. The city has grown rapidly since the 1960s when it was predominantly a university town with a population of around one hundred thousand, to a core population of 208,000 and a labour market area of 323,000 by 1990.[1] During the 1960s population increased by 10 per cent as it became a major area of settlement for French Algerians (*les pieds noirs*) after Algerian independence. Of the total population of Montpellier in 1990 just over 22 per cent were born outside Metropolitan France.[2] Over a third of the resident population have come from outside the city, including from overseas and the surrounding region, since 1982. Montpellier has, therefore, a high proportion of recent migrants. Following French local government reorganisation in 1967 Montpellier became the regional capital of an area dominated by viticulture, producing mainly low quality wines contributing to the European 'wine lake', and with some nascent tourism. Between 1960 and 1977 the population of the city doubled, as an increasing number of new industries started to locate in the south. IBM set up there in 1962 and was followed by other data processing and electronics firms and by medical technology and medical research industries. From being the least industrialised region of France in 1974, Languedoc-Roussillon attracted the highest proportion of new firms in the early 1980s and most of these were located in and around Montpellier (Aydalot 1986).

The city government was very active in the 1980s coping with the expansion and encouraging it. Public transportation doubled the number of lines and passengers; urban motorways were constructed, and eleven thousand new public housing units were built in the period 1979–86; an extended city centre on largely derelict land, the 'Antigone', was built. The old centre was refurbished and a new opera house and conference centre were opened. The city is now carrying out plans to link Montpellier to the sea with a new marina, Port Marianne, within the central city area. Plans for the 1990s are dominated by the development of Technopoles, of which more later. Montpellier has been described by Donzel (1991) as the pioneer of urban marketing in France combining economic performance, quality of life and extensive culture. While the Languedoc-Roussillon is still marked by economic activities in decline and low income levels, Montpellier itself has one of the most highly qualified workforces in France, showing the greatest value added. Income levels between the regional capital and the rest of the region continue to widen. The success of Montpellier has been put down to the Sun Belt phenomenon, the absence of nineteenth- and twentieth-century industrial development providing an attractive environment for new activities (Aydalot 1986), the suitability of a university town based on medicine, pharmacy and agronomy for the development and relocation of tertiary industries (Berger et al. 1988), as well as aggressive urban marketing. In economic structure Montpellier typifies the new service sector city with over 70 per cent of employment in services (see Table 4.1).

Table 4.1 Montpellier: full-time employees, December 1985

	Number	*%*
Manufacturing industry	11,770	18.2
Construction and public works	6,221	9.6
Services	46,779	72.2
Total	64,770	100

Source: Brunet et al. (1988)

Of the twenty-two regional capitals Montpellier showed the greatest increase in employment in the period 1975–87 with a growth in employment of 23 per cent (INSEE 1990a). Despite the economic vitality and accompanying increased job opportunities, unemployment has also increased from 13.9 per cent in 1982 to 16.6 per cent in 1990.

If we compare unemployment in Montpellier to that of France as a whole, and to the region, the picture is equally puzzling (see Table 4.2).

Table 4.2 Unemployment: France, Languedoc-Roussillon, Montpellier (%)

	1982/83	*1990*
France	8.2	9.1
Languedoc-Roussillon (1988)	NA	13.2
Montpellier	13.9	16.6

Sources: Eurostat Labour Force Survey, 1991; Recensement de la Population INSEE (1990)

Even allowing for the fact that figures may vary slightly according to methods of collection, the basic definition of unemployment in both census and labour force surveys is the same and would not in itself account for disparities. What is shown is that possibly the most successful urban economy in France has, throughout the last decade, had a significantly higher unemployment rate than that of the country as a whole, and similar to that of one of the poorest regions of which it is a part. What follows is an analysis of the unemployed in Montpellier, their characteristics and their location, which may shed light on this apparent paradox.

UNEMPLOYMENT IN MONTPELLIER

The average unemployment rate in 1990 for the active population (those seeking work) in Montpellier was 16.9 per cent. Table 4.3 shows activity rates and unemployment rates by age and sex. In Europe as whole in 1990, and in France, unemployment was seen to be highest for women, both for short-term and long-term unemployment, and for the young under 25 who were twice as likely to be unemployed as the workforce as a whole.

Age and unemployment

Similar to France as a whole, the unemployment in Montpellier is higher for the under 25s and more particularly so for females under 25 – at 32.1 per cent for those under 19 and 29.9 per cent for under 25s, with 21 per cent for males

Table 4.3 Montpellier: activity rate and unemployment rate by age and sex, 1990

Age	Male Activity %	Male Unemp. %	Female Activity %	Female Unemp. %
15–19	12.8	21.0	8.1	32.1
20–24	35.0	24.3	28.7	29.9
25–29	75.3	16.8	72.7	22.6
30–34	88.2	15.0	78.1	20.7
35–39	92.6	12.9	78.6	16.1
40–44	95.1	11.3	79.4	13.3
45–49	94.6	10.5	74.6	11.7
50–54	91.7	11.3	65.0	13.2
55–59	76.4	15.1	50.6	14.7
60–64	27.9	11.6	18.1	12.1
Total % (average)	56.7	14.8	43.2	18.6
Total number	45,057	6,655	41,730	7,769

Source: Recensement de la Population, INSEE (1990)

in age groups 15–19 and 24.3 per cent for the 20–24 age group. Female unemployment is highest in the youngest age group with nearly one third of those seeking work without a job, but female unemployment remains over 20 per cent for all groups up to 35 years of age. The low activity rates for the resident age group 20-24 can be accounted for by the fact that there is a very high student population in this age group in Montpellier. Unemployment rates fall for both men and women up to the age of 50 and then rise during their 50s. Those in their 40s are least likely to be unemployed. The youngest age group is, by definition, those who have not completed higher secondary school nor had experience of work, features that in Europe are given as reasons for the high rates of unemployment in this age group. Because of the low activity rates of the younger age groups the number of unemployed as a percentage of the total is only 20.4 for those aged 15–24, while 66.6 per cent are aged 25–44, and 13 per cent are over 50 years of age.

Male/female unemployment

As seen above in all age groups women are more likely to be unemployed than males. There are greater numbers unemployed, despite lower activity rates for women, with a total of 7,769 women unemployed compared to 6,655 men. Women are also more likely to suffer from long-term unemployment as shown by Figure 4.1.

Duration of unemployment

Of the 14,424 people unemployed in Montpellier in 1990 21.8 per cent had been unemployed for less than three months, 30.7 per cent for between three months and a year, 17.3 per cent between one and two years and 21.7 per cent for over two years.[3] As reported previously employment is generally more difficult to obtain for those unemployed longer than a year and this group constitutes 39 per cent of total unemployment. Women form the greater proportion of those unemployed longer than a year – 57.9 per cent of the total in this group.

Of the total long-term unemployed by age group, the young workers constitute only 13.3 per cent of the total, while prime age workers are 66.4 per cent and older workers 21.3 per cent. This accords roughly with the figures for the percentage unemployed in each group. The propensity to long-term unemployment is in fact slightly less for the young workers and slightly more for older workers over 50 (see Table 4.4).

Of those aged under 25, only 27 per cent had been unemployed for longer than a year. While this does not negate the problem of youth unemployment, which is high as we have seen, it does appear that the problem of long-term unemployment is not very important, or may only be a factor of concern for certain groups of the young.

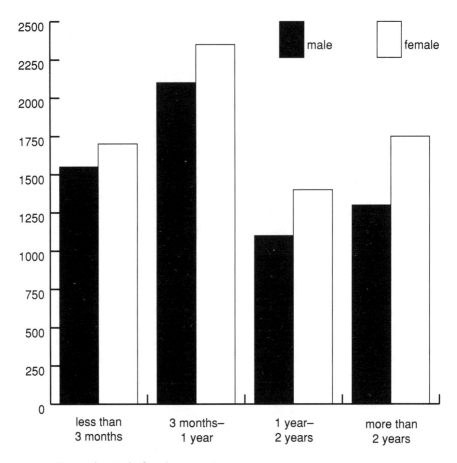

Figure 4.1 Male/female unemployment by duration, Montpellier 1990

Source: Recensement de la Population Montpellier, INSEE (1990)

Note: Figures do not add up to the total unemployed as there is also a category where no precise information on duration is known.

Table 4.4 Montpellier: unemployed and duration of unemployment by age group, 1990

Age group	% of total unemployed	No. of unemployed for less than 1 year	% of total unemployed for over 1 year
15–24	20.4	749	13.3
25–49	66.6	3,751	66.4
50+	13.0	1,150	21.3
Total	100	5,650	100

Source: Recensement de la Population, INSEE (1990)

Country of origin of the unemployed

The French census does not have a breakdown by ethnic origin as such, so racial discrimination in the labour market cannot be fully assessed. Montpellier, however, has a large resident population from North Africa in particular and they would be categorised in the census under non-EC residents. Table 4.5 shows a breakdown of unemployment rates by nationality of workers.

Table 4.5 Montpellier: percentage unemployed by nationality, 1990

Nationality	%
French	15.2
French by naturalisation	20.6
Other EC countries	21.1
Non-EC	36.6
Average unemployment rate	16.9

Source: Recensement de la Population, INSEE (1990)

As shown, the group most likely to suffer unemployment are those coming from outside the EC, with an unemployment rate of 36.6 per cent. The rate is even higher for women originating outside the EC (see Table 4.6).

Table 4.6 Montpellier: percentage unemployed by country of origin and sex, 1990

	French	French by naturalisation	Other EC	Non EC	Average
Male	13.0	17.6	19.0	32.0	14.6
Female	17.3	23.4	24.3	48.6	18.6
Total	15.2	20.6	21.1	36.6	16.9

Source: Recensement de la Population, INSEE (1990)

The highest level of unemployment for any group is found in female non-EC residents, with nearly half (48.6 per cent) of the active population unable to find work.

In summary the least likely groups to suffer unemployment in Montpellier are French, male, prime-age workers, while the young, women and particularly foreign women are more likely to be unemployed. Having said this, the greatest number of the unemployed by far are French born women followed by French born men as they constitute the largest proportion of the population (see Table 4.7).

Table 4.7 Montpellier: numbers unemployed by sex and nationality, 1990

	French	*French by naturalisation*	*Other EC*	*Non EC*
Men	5,137	334	168	1,335
Women	6,846	450	140	781
Total	11,983	784	308	2,116

Source: Recensement de la Population, INSEE (1990)

Table 4.7 illustrates the scale of the problem as a whole in that although certain groups in the population may have a high propensity to unemployment they may form a relatively low proportion of those who are unemployed. This is not to deny the great importance of the problem socially. For non-EC workers skill levels and educational levels are lower, and they tend to be heavily concentrated in certain areas of the city (see Figure 4.2) thus reducing the passing of work opportunities information via neighbours and friends.

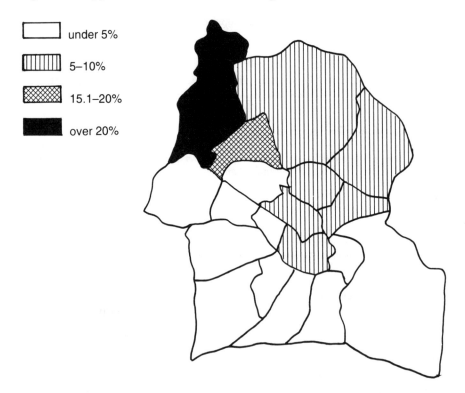

under 5%

5–10%

15.1–20%

over 20%

Figure 4.2 Percentage of non-EC residents by *quartier*, Montpellier, 1990
Source: Recensement de la Population, INSEE (1990)

This is an area of France where the National Front party is strong and as shown later, the only policy in force in 1991 to help this group specifically was repatriation. If we look at the number employed of non-EC residents – 3,668 – and assumed that all the workers wished to be repatriated and assumed further that these jobs would be taken by French citizens, which may not be likely considering many are low-paid anti-social jobs, then unemployment in Montpellier would still be 12.7 per cent – very little improvement.

But if the main concern in reducing unemployment is in order to avoid wastage of human resources then the main problem lies with the reduction of unemployment generally and that of females in particular.

Why is there such a large number of unemployed women in Montpellier? Reasons given[4] are that as the population has increased through in-migration, when men came from the surrounding region and elsewhere in order to take up jobs in expanding industries and the booming construction sector, their wives, who had not previously been formally employed, saw opportunities to work in the city and became active seekers of work. The high cost of living in Montpellier[5] may also act as a push-factor for becoming two-income households. The difficulty in finding employment may be due to lack of suitable employment for given skill levels or discrimination arising from the predominantly male Mediterranean culture.[6] In the Languedoc-Roussillon region the participation of women in the labour market has increased significantly – more than at national level. Between 1975 and 1984 the number of women employed increased by 40,000 at the same time as male employment decreased by 1,200. Fornairon (1987) interprets the greater number of women entering the labour market as the result of the increase in tertiary industries providing suitable employment, and also the increase in the region of active and qualified women from other regions.

Urban factors in unemployment

One of the hypotheses of urban unemployment discussed in Chapter 3 was the physical inaccessibility of jobs, and the cost, including time cost, of travel to work for the unemployed. Also, the likelihood that if in certain areas of the city a large proportion of the population were unemployed, the hysteresis effects would be reinforced.

Areas of the city and their unemployment rates are shown in Figure 4.3. Of the twenty quarters[7] in Montpellier, three have unemployment rates in excess of 20 per cent, two in the north-east and one in the central area. These are also the areas of highest female unemployment, and as shown in Figure 4.2, areas where non-EC residents are concentrated. The first question is whether these areas are easily accessible to employment. The growth areas for employment are to the south and east of the city near the airports and in new industrial estates. More recently technopoles have been promoted by the city government.

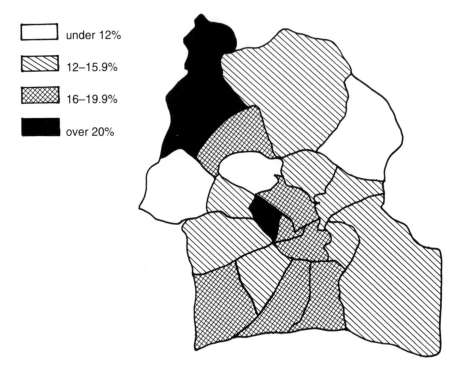

under 12%

12–15.9%

16–19.9%

over 20%

Figure 4.3 Unemployment rate by *quartier*, Montpellier 1990
Source: Recensement de la Population, INSEE 1990

The technopoles are small economic zones specialising in tertiary sector growth activities – medicine and medical research (Parc Euromedecine); agricultural research (Parc Agropolis), media (Pole Antenna), information technology (Pole Informatique) and tourism/leisure (Pole Heliopolis) (see Figure 4.4).

The labour the technopoles require is largely highly skilled and is drawn from all over France and Europe. They are unlikely to provide employment for the majority of the unemployed who do not possess the appropriate skills. So, while two of these poles (Euromedecine and Agropolis) are within or near areas of highest unemployment, their effect on the unemployed in these areas is likely to be minimal. The jobs available where lower levels of skill are required are located in the communes to the south and east. While public transportation is both good and low cost within the city, it is virtually non-existent or infrequent outside the city boundary. Private transportation would be needed for city residents to reach this work, and the areas most affected by unemployment within the city are furthest from the new jobs. The unemployed are unlikely to be able to afford private transportation.

60

The concentration of unemployed away from areas of job growth means they are also less likely to hear informally of jobs available because of their physical distance from the new employment.

While the pattern of concentration for women is similar to that of the total unemployed as shown, non-EC foreign workers suffer high rates of unemployment throughout the city regardless of location. There is, however, a concentration of non-EC population of around 20 per cent in the two north-eastern quarters of the Paillade district which is a huge area of public housing (HLM). Even in areas of the city where there are less than 5 per cent non-EC residents, e.g. Millenarie, Aiquerelles in the south, the unemployment rate of this group is still in excess of 30 per cent. This would lead one to believe that skill levels and discrimination play a greater part in the unemployment chances of this group.

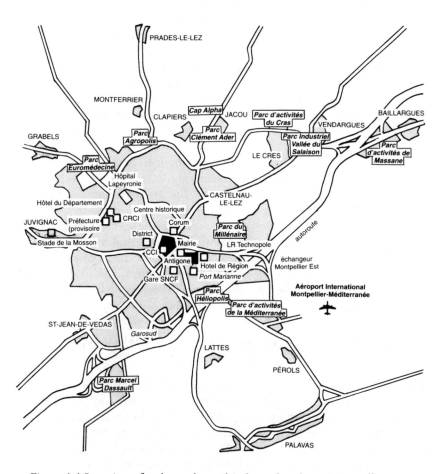

Figure 4.4 Location of technopoles and industrial parks in Montpellier region

Source: Montpellier Languedoc-Roussillon Technopole, 1991 (Synergie 1)

Economic development and its location, while making sense in terms of economic growth for the city, being sited near motorways or the airport for access and in environmentally attractive locations, is not located with access for the unemployed in mind.

So the unemployed in Montpellier suffer from a mismatch of skills. Growth industries draw on appropriate skills from other areas, which in turn can bring partners who wish to be active in the labour market but for whom there is no immediate employment available. The success of Montpellier, measured by its growing population from outside the city, is one of the factors which contributes to the high unemployment rate. Migrants head for areas where there are work opportunities especially in regions where there is little new employment, and where jobs in the basic industry, in the case of Languedoc-Roussillon, viticulture, have declined in numbers, rapidly losing over 200,000 jobs in the period 1950–88.[8] The closure of the mines in Alès had a similar effect in encouraging movement of workers to large towns in search of employment. Unfulfilled demand for jobs in the tertiary sector showed the greatest increase in the region rising by 70 per cent between 1983 and 1990 with 133,000 people in the region seeking work in this sector. As Montpellier is a centre for tertiary growth many of these unemployed workers migrated to the city in hope of employment. Of these job seekers 90 per cent were female and 35 per cent were under 25 years of age.[9]

To put it succinctly, growth of employment and economic success has tended to reap its own problems in the case of Montpellier. Its situation, in a poor region of growing unemployment, has attracted the unemployed in greater numbers and at a faster rate than new jobs can be created. The demand for certain jobs has far outstripped supply, and in many cases the migrants do not fit the skill profile required for new employment opportunities. If unemployment in other areas of the region does not fall significantly the process of population growth by migration is not likely to slow down and Montpellier's unemployment rate will remain high. It is a case of success breeding a specific failure in the economy of the city.

POLICIES TOWARDS THE UNEMPLOYED IN MONTPELLIER

We will now turn to the question of how unemployment is dealt with in the city and examine the main policies that are in operation and the organisations that are charged with operating these policies. In France the responsibility for policy is centralised and active measures to help the unemployed are laid down by central government and operate throughout the country. All finance for the unemployed both for income maintenance and for active measures comes from central government although specific policies such as for the young or women may be aided by the ESF.

Organisational structure

Although policy is centrally directed by the state the implementation is by local public agencies. The two main organisations dealing with unemployment in Montpellier are the local offices of the ANPE (Agence National pour l'Emploi) and a branch of the departmental prefecture the DDTE (Direction Departmentale pour Travail et l'Emploi). They are in close touch with each other and most aspects of policy, as we shall see below, are dealt with by both agencies. The ANPE keeps a register of those seeking employment and of employment vacancies. It also organises training programmes both inside and outside private firms. The DDTE holds information on unemployment throughout the Hèrault department and on labour market areas (the Montpellier labour market area is larger than the city and is similar to a Travel-to-Work-Area in Britain). It organises some schemes or has an input into them, and is normally the public body dealing with the various contracts between employer and potential worker or trainee. The role of regional government, the Conseil Règional pour Languedoc-Roussillon, is mainly concerned with economic development in the region, but it has an observatory which analyses labour market trends in different sectors and geographical areas of the economy. This information is used to help the ANPE and DDTE to formulate long-term training and retraining programmes. The city government of Montpellier does not have any role where the unemployed are concerned. The main economic function of city government is to promote economic growth and development. Although they are influential in creating new employment they are not charged with any responsibility for creating employment specifically designed to reduce unemployment, and their major function is to ensure and handle long-term economic prospects for the city.

Unemployment benefit and income support for the unemployed are provided by ASSEDIC at regional level, the agency which administers the unemployment insurance benefit system, and for other forms of income maintenance the CAF (Caisse d'Allocations Familiale – Family Allowance Fund).

A brief description of 'passive' unemployment policy i.e. income maintenance provision, is provided below, followed by an analysis of active labour market policies for the unemployed or those at risk of unemployment in the city.

The ANPE liaises with ASSEDIC to advise and promote employment of unemployed workers.

Unemployment benefit and income maintenance for the unemployed

Unemployment benefit

Unemployment benefit is paid out to those who have worked for six months in the previous twelve months, or twelve months in the previous two years.

It is paid at the rate of 40 per cent of the last salary + 51.65FF per day (1991) or alternatively 57.4 per cent of the last salary. The level of entitlement to benefit reduces over time and the length of entitlement depends on length of contribution and age, with a minimum of three months and a maximum of 45 months of benefit. Once the benefit is exhausted the unemployed person must rely on social assistance.

The rates for the disabled are greater, at 100 per cent of last salary with a minimum of 4,226FF per month and maximum of 12,676FF per month.

Social assistance

Paid through the CAF, the assistance available differs according to age and family circumstances. The RMI (Revenue Minimum d'Insertion/Minimum Integration Income) is designed to allow everyone the minimum resources to meet their essential needs and to promote the social or vocational integration of the most disadvantaged. Beneficiaries of RMI can also be eligible for sickness insurance and social housing allowance. (The beneficiary of RMI in applying for the allowances undertakes to participate in integration schemes.) The minimum salary in France SMIC (Salarie Minimum Interprofessionnel de Croissance) for the same period was 5,398FF per month. Thus the basic rate of income maintenance for those outside special categories was around 50 per cent of the minimum wage for adults and less than this for the younger age groups. The basic allowance for a single person over 25 years of age is 2,185FF per month (June 1992) rising to 4,807FF for a person with three dependents.

The allowance for the young is 798FF per month for the 16–18 age group and 2,002FF per month for the 18–25 group. For the unemployed disabled, who are seeking work whatever age, the rate is 3,803FF per month. The same rate is also available to other job seekers – single parent mothers, widows, divorcees or separated women and single women looking after an elderly parent.

Many of the training schemes below are based on RMI or RMI plus, but since 1992 the youngest age group are not eligible for RMI if they do not undertake training.

Active labour market policies

The following lists the different policies in operation together with the aims, finances and subsidies, eligibility and benefits. General policies applying to all the unemployed will be followed by policies directed towards special groups – the young, women, the disabled, the LTU, and non-EC nationals. The measures cited apply from January 1991.

Vocational and other training

Vocational rehabilitation course (SRP – Stage de reclassement professionel)

The aim of this policy is to update and extend the skills of the unemployed. The beneficiaries must have some skills and experience, must be over 25 years of age and unemployed less than twelve months. The training is of a similar kind to that available to workers in work having continuous training. An average period of training of 150 hours is given, either by a training establishment or a private firm. The firm receives the same payment as a training establishment. Beneficiaries are paid through ASSEDIC at the rate of 125FF or 127FF per day (AFR/AFRE level – redeployment training allowance). The training is organised or arranged by ANPE.

Training for work (SAE – Stage d'accès a l'emploi)

If the ANPE has jobs available with no registered unemployed to match the skills needed to undertake the work, or if an existing worker could take up another post in his or her firm with further training thus freeing the previous post for an unemployed person, training will be provided at state expense. For the unemployed the cost of around 300 hours training is paid with a maximum of 750 hours for the long-term unemployed. For retraining of an existing worker the hours necessary to allow the worker to take up a new post will be financed. The payment to the unemployed worker is either 125 or 127FF per day (AFR, AFRE). Payment to firms for training is negotiated between the firm and the ANPE. For workers upgrading in the firm the firm is paid 28FF per hour of training to compensate for loss of working time.

Job creation policies

Assistance for creating an enterprise
(ACE – Aide à la création d'entreprises)

The aim is to help the unemployed to start businesses or to rescue failing businesses, within a short time of having registered as unemployed. It is open to those on unemployment benefit or income maintenance, those on training schemes and ex-public sector workers. A company can be created conducting any legal economic activity with the exception of economic interest groups. The ANPE gives guidance, information and help in setting up an application, which is submitted to the DDTE. The decision on grants is made by the prefect within two weeks of receipt of application. The allowance varies between 16,125FF and 43,000FF.

Family employees (Les emplois familiaux)

This is a new scheme introduced in 1992 which encourages job creation through providing tax relief to employers. It is to encourage employment in the home of people who will help look after the disabled, the elderly over 70, and children at home – either young children or older children after school hours. As it is tax relief, the employer, to benefit, must be working and paying tax. The employer must have a proper work contract or letter of hiring with the domestic employee and give paid holidays. Minimum payment is at SMIC rate of 26.50FF per hour with pay increments after two years. Allowances are very generous with 50 per cent of the cost of employment paid by the state through reduction of taxes with a ceiling of 13,500FF per annum. This policy is a double edged tool. Not only does it create domestic jobs, thus providing work for the unemployed, more especially women as they tend to be the main beneficiaries of this kind of work, it also allows the potential employer to work. In Montpellier there is a shortage of highly skilled professional workers, and this measure may well encourage highly skilled women (the main carers), who have family responsibilities, to take up work. Unemployed carers who previously could only undertake part-time work, which is in very short supply, could also now consider full-time jobs because of increased domestic help.

Mobility allowances

Mobility allowances are to encourage employment search particularly for the unemployed who are difficult to place because of low skills and who are finding difficulty in gaining employment. It is also open to those who are in work and likely to become redundant, and for non-EC unemployed workers wanting public help for repatriation.

Financial help is given for these groups with removal expenses for a minimum distance of 15km and a maximum of 1,000km and daily expenses for 2–15 days. For those who wish to undertake training more than 15km from their home, travel expenses are paid, plus a daily allowance for the duration of the training. The scheme is organised by the local ANPE office.

The above measures apply to all adult workers over 25 years of age with no age limit on enterprise creation. There are special measures which apply to the young unemployed, women, the long-term unemployed and the disabled.

Measures for the young unemployed

The measures for young people involve skill training at different levels, job experience, or completing educational qualifications. All these measures are open to the 16–25 age group.

Apprenticeship contract (Contrat d'apprentisage)

This is to allow the young to gain technical professional qualifications on a contract which lasts between one and three years. The training period is a minimum of 400 hours per year, in an apprenticeship centre or with a master worker in a firm. A minimum of 1,500 hours is required for a BAC professional. The young person is paid on a sliding scale 15–75 per cent of SMIC. The contract is arranged by the DDTE and the firm is allowed 100 per cent exemption from social security charges for the apprentice.

Adaptation to employment contract (Contrat d'adaptation)

This provides 200 hours of training within a firm, for a period of between six and twelve months. The contract is between the young person and the firm and is arranged by the DDTE. The worker must be paid at least 80 per cent of the minimum wage payable and not less than SMIC. It is open to young people who have a qualification. The firm receives 50FF per hour of training and 100 per cent reduction of social security payments.

Qualification contract (Contrat de qualification)

This is to allow the young person to gain a recognised vocational qualification. The contract is for between six and twelve months, at least a quarter of which must be spent in a training centre. Pay is in the range of 17–75 per cent of SMIC according to age and length of time in the contract. The firm receives 50FF per hour and 100 per cent reduction of social security payments. The contract between the worker and the firm is arranged by the DDTE.

Employment solidarity contract (Contrat emploi solidarité)

This is to help young people, with a level IV or level V diploma, to become able to accomplish a useful activity, and get used to social working life. Jobs are provided in the public or voluntary sector with a training limited to 400 hours. The contract lasts between three and twelve months and is between the public body and the beneficiary arranged by the DDTE. Pay is at SMIC level. The employer is granted 100 per cent exemption from social security contributions and the state funds 85 per cent of the young person's pay.

Orientation contract (Contrat d'orientation)

This scheme is designed for those aged 16–22, or exceptionally up to 25, who do not have any formal qualifications. It entails a general or vocational training at lower level. It is aimed at those with little or no work experience and is a contract between the young person and a private or public employer with support from the ANPE and DDTE. The contract lasts from three to six months and is non-renewable. Thirty-two hours per month are spent at a training centre. Pay to the young person ranges from 30–65 per cent of SMIC according to age. The employer is granted 100 per cent exemption from social security and receives 50FF per hour of training. In the case of a public body the state funds 15 per cent of the young person's pay.

Youth training credit (Crédit formation – jeunes)

This provides young people who have left school with the opportunity to gain a recognised diploma (CAP or BEP) through a personalised course of training and supervision. Priority is given to young people with a poor educational level. Eight hundred hours of training/tuition are given and the scheme is organised by the ANPE.

Between October 1991 and May 1992 a special policy called 'EXO – Jeunes' was in operation. It was for unqualified young people to facilitate entry into unskilled jobs or jobs where training was available. It involved a reduction of labour costs of 28 per cent for firms, and the subsidy lasted for eighteen months. If payment to the young person was at SMIC level, the subsidy to firms was 31,830FF.

Since 1992 young people aged under 18 who do not belong to one of the approved training or work experience schemes are not entitled to income support.

In Montpellier, according to the 1990 census, the number of people on various training schemes was as shown in Table 4.8. Unfortunately the breakdown does not include all schemes, and does include company trainees who are not subsidised by the state. It shows, however, that of the active age group 16–24 (10,873) 12.7 per cent were in training of some kind. The above figures also show that for the highest level of training, apprenticeships, men filled twice as many places as women, and that more women were on short-term lower level training than men. This may reflect the unwillingness of firms to apprentice women, which in turn results in the lower level of

Table 4.8 Montpellier: those aged 16–24 in training, 1990

	Men	*Women*	*Total*
Contrat d'apprentisage	333	172	505
Contrat d'adaptation/de qualification	165	245	410
Company trainee	88	68	156
Trainees at a training centre	139	172	311
Total	725	657	1,382

Source: Recensement de la Population, INSEE (1990)

qualifications of the female workforce and the higher incidence of female unemployment. Special measures designed to help unemployed women in the workforce are described in the next section.

Measures to aid unemployed women

Aid for 'single' women (Femmes isolèès)

'Single' women are defined as women alone on low income who are bringing up children; women looking after an elderly person; and women seeking work whose partner is long-term unemployed. The aim is to give training or retraining for four to six months to enable these women to work. While training they receive AFR or AFRE (127 or 125FF) or continuation of API (allowance of 3,803FF per month to care for an elderly or disabled parent). The DDTE is responsible for this scheme. The state funds the training with aid from the ESF.

Contract to promote mixed employment in SMEs (Contrat pour la mixitè des emploi dans les PME–PMI)

This policy is to encourage the recruitment, and also promotion of women in occupations in firms where women are very poorly represented, by improving working conditions and training. Companies must employ less than 200 employees. The contract is between the regional prefect, the company and the employee. The state pays for 50 per cent of the teaching costs in training, 50 per cent of other costs (e.g. adaptation of workplace) and 30 per cent of training costs during the training period.

Another policy which does not affect the unemployed woman but might avoid redundancy by improvement of skills is:

Plan for vocational equality (Plan d'egalité professionelle)

The aim of this policy is to train women already employed to take up occupations within a firm traditionally held by men. A contract is made between the company and the state and financial incentives are provided on the same basis as under the policy to promote mixed employment.

Measures for the long-term unemployed

There are three measures in operation in Montpellier to help the long-term unemployed.

Contract for return to employment
(Contrat de retour a l'emploi – CRE)

For those unemployed for at least twelve of the previous eighteen months, recipients of RMI and partners of RMI beneficiaries, and for the disabled, training to help return to work is available for between six and eighteen months. Training is for 200–1,000 hours and can be in a training centre or in a firm with a training body. Pay is at SMIC or the collective wage. The firm gets a 100 per cent reduction of social security contributions for nine months or eighteen months if it takes on a person unemployed for longer than three years, or disabled, or for the whole contract if a person is more than fifty years of age. The firm is also paid 50FF per hour of training or 10,000FF to allow workers to be accompanied by a teacher.

Solidarity employment contract
(Contrat emploi solidarité – CES)

This is aimed to benefit those unemployed for longer than three years, or longer than one year if they are over fifty years of age, or beneficiaries of RMI for longer than a year. It provides public sector work experience paid at SMIC level for between three and twelve months, or up to two years for those in special difficulty. It is arranged by ANPE.

Integration and training schemes
(Actions d'insertion et de formation – AIF)

This scheme favours the long-term unemployed who are particularly hard to place. A personalised training is provided in a training centre, of between 40 and 1,200 hours. Pay is at AFR or AFRE rates (127 or 125FF per day). Training is organised by ANPE but the DDTE has responsibility for the scheme.

The final category of the unemployed for which special policies exist is the disabled.

Measures for the disabled

Contract for return to employment
(Contrat de retour a l'emploi – CRE)

The terms of this contract are as described at the top of this page, but also includes a subsidy of salary, whereby an extra subsidy of 10–20 per cent of a worker's salary is payable by the state where the disabled worker is unable to fulfil the same work as other employees.

Protected employment

Guaranteed pay by the state of 80 per cent of SMIC to the disabled person. The firm is entitled to a 50 per cent tax allowance on the salary of the worker. The scheme is arranged by the DDTE on the advice of COTOREP (Technical Commission for Vocational Guidance and Rehabilitation of Disabled Workers).

Adaptation of workplace (Amènagement des postes de travail)

The firm can claim 80 per cent of expenses for any adaptation needed to make the workplace accessible to disabled workers.

Disabled worker's allowance (Subvention d'installation)

This is a grant of 150,000FF to aid disabled workers to get to work.

Sheltered workshops are organised by COTOREP which pay disabled workers who have a working capacity at least one third of an able-bodied employee but require special working conditions. Participants are paid 90 per cent of SMIC.

All the above measures are aimed at helping those already unemployed. Several measures also exist to avoid the unemployment of those in work. They include various measures to support modernisation and upgrading of the workforce. LIGE (Strategy for Innovation in Employment Management) helps firms to plan increases in employment with the help of consultants; for upgrading qualifications of the existing workforce the state pays for between 20 per cent and 70 per cent of the cost of worker replacement while they are on the course; for low-skill workers whose employment is threatened the firm is paid 50 per cent for the cost of training.

EVALUATION OF EXISTING MEASURES IN MONTPELLIER

There is no information available on any formal evaluation of policies by the ANPE or DDTE. The main problems in Montpellier are high unemployment rates for the young and high rates and numbers for women, especially women under 35 years of age. Also unemployment among female non-EC residents, who are small in number but have a disproportionately high unemployment rate, rising to nearly half of all non-EC women. In this context how well are policies in operation geared to these groups? As far as the young are concerned it has already been noted that only 12.7 per cent of the active population in the youngest age groups were on formal schemes gaining qualifications. It has not been possible to assess how many undertook orientation contracts or youth training credits. It seems justifiable to conclude, however, that a relatively small percentage of these unemployed are engaged in the sort of training scheme where professional recognised qualifications are achieved. As one of the main problems with youth unemployment is lack of formal educational and other qualifications the resolution to this problem is not wholly dealt with. Lack of work experience, another main factor behind unemployment of the young may be better fulfilled by the policies. In the long-term, as Montpellier becomes a local economy increasingly requiring high levels of skills, the prospects of the young unqualified would appear to be bleak as they enter the prime age working group. The prospects are, as noted above, worse for young women than young men, more of whom are on higher level training.

For women generally in the city there are more of them in the prime age work group 25–49 on short-term contracts than men, including the SRP, SAE, CRE, CES and AIF. They appear, therefore, to be represented in these schemes in proportion to their unemployment levels. Just over one third of adults in this group were on schemes at the time of the census. The policy of tax exemptions paying for 50 per cent of the cost of help in the home should allow many more women to have greater flexibility in applying for work that is further from home, or where full-time or unsocial hours are required by the job. The policy will certainly directly provide more employment for women as paid carers. No information is available on the number of participants in the city on special schemes for women, but the two schemes for training women in non-traditional sectors of employment and for promotion should upgrade their skill levels, which are below that of men, and are a greater mismatch with the required skills of the local labour market.

For non-EC residents the only specific policy is payment of expenses for voluntary repatriation. There may be linguistic and cultural difficulties in obtaining employment, in addition to skills mismatch and discrimination. Some of the schemes in general operation do give help with language skills but there is no obligation to provide special measures for this group of the population where unemployment is highest. There is no information on what proportion of places on general schemes are taken up by the non-EC unemployed.

The disabled appear to be well catered for both in terms of type of employment offered, and special facilities and rates of pay above minimum levels.

With regard to the question of whether unemployment in Montpellier is 'voluntary' in the sense of people choosing welfare benefit rather than work, this seems unlikely. Replacement ratios of benefit for the unemployed insured are around 60 per cent of previous wage at the start of unemployment but fall after one year to approximately 30 per cent of average wage level. In 1991 the rate of social assistance (RMI) for the uninsured, or when insurance had run out, was 40 per cent of the minimum wage for a single person over 25; for 18–25s, 37 per cent of minimum wage, and for under 18s, 15 per cent of minimum wage. These subsistence levels would not lead one to conclude that these unemployed had 'chosen' unemployment.

As has already been pointed out the urban policies of local government both in planning the location and type of new enterprises, and in local transport policy do not appear to have been made in relation to the location and needs of the unemployed. While this lack of consideration between planning and social problems is not uncommon, and reinforcing market preferences for new firms to locate outside the city is a feature of recent urban policy in Europe, it does nothing to help the unemployed and could be said to hinder their employment prospects. Urban policy for the central area of Montpellier has resulted in an exodus of poorer residents as gentrification and rehabilitation has taken place.

This may actually have resulted in an increase in unemployment, as low-income central residents who were often casually employed are no longer on the spot to take advantage of opportunities. Those who worked in catering at unsocial hours may also be inhibited by lack of transportation to their new residences. There is no question that the siting of the enormous HLM complex at La Paillade has ghettoised the unemployed in a peripheral sub-urban location, as in many other French cities, and has broken up or reduced informal networks on job information, reinforcing hysteresis effects for the long-term unemployed. No urban employment or national employment policy for the unemployed exists to cope with this localised problem in the city.

While Montpellier is an economically successful city, it has problems because of its location within a poor region, and it may be that unemployment will remain high in the city as long as the wider regional unemployment problem persists.

5

MANCHESTER

INTRODUCTION

The city of Manchester is part of the wider metropolitan area of Greater Manchester and is situated in the North West region of England (see Figure 5.1 on p. 79). The whole region is a classic case of structural change resulting from loss of manufacturing industry and employment from the 1950s onwards, and adaptation of the local economy to growth activities in the service sector. In the nineteenth and early twentieth century Manchester was an industrial power-house and one of the wealthiest cities in Britain, with an economy based on the production of and trade in cotton textiles. Loss of markets to developing countries resulted in major closures in the textile industry in urban areas, leading to failure of dependent industries and vast areas of industrial dereliction within the city. The once dominant textile industry accounted for only 2.4 per cent of employment in the region by 1990. Fall in employment led to losses of population in older industrial areas particularly in the city of Manchester. For the period 1971 to 1991 the city lost 20.8 per cent of its population, a much larger fall than in the metropolitan area as a whole and than the region, while exurban areas within the region, of Cheshire and Lancashire, gained population (see Table 5.1).

Greater Manchester suffered a fall in employment from 1.22 million in 1977 to 1.01 million by 1987. Of the 33,315 redundancies in the area

Table 5.1 Change in population, 1971–91

	000s		% change	
	1971	1981	1991	1971–91
Manchester	554	463	438	−20.8
Greater Manchester	2,750	2,619	2,570	−6.5
North-West Region	6,634	6,459	6,396	−3.6
England and Wales	46,411	49,634	51,099	+10.1

Source: OPCS: Local Base and Small Area Statistics (1991)

74

between 1988 and 1990, 23,152 were in metal goods, engineering and vehicles and other manufacturing sectors. So losses in manufacturing employment have continued into the 1990s. The growth sectors have been in property, financial and professional services and other services. The city of Manchester has had a higher rate of redundancies than other parts of the metropolitan area, with 28 per cent of all redundancies in Greater Manchester in 1989 within the city compared to 10–12 per cent for other urban boroughs.

The structure of employment in Greater Manchester changed during the 1980s with the continuing decline of large scale businesses and an increase in jobs in small businesses (see Table 5.2).

Table 5.2 Size of firms and employment, Greater Manchester, 1977–87

Size of firm by number of employees	1977 Employees	1987 Employees	Change 1977–87
1–100	438,629	500,750	+62,121
101–500	422,000	262,218	−159,782
501 +	363,272	254,399	−108,873
Total	1,223,901	1,017,367	−206,534

Source: GMRIPU (1991a)[1]

Employment in small firms increased from 36 per cent to 49 per cent, while employment in larger firms declined, with the greatest losses in firms employing over five hundred people. Using net VAT registrations as a proxy of the growth rate of small firms in the period 1980–89, it was found that the highest rate of growth was in the extraurban area of Cheshire with a 33 per cent increase, with Greater Manchester at 13.7 per cent increase, but the city lost 11.7 per cent of small businesses (GMRIPU 1991a). Despite enormous losses of manufacturing employment the North West has the second largest service sector in the United Kingdom, with Manchester as its centre. Manchester has the regional offices of several major government departments – the Department of Trade and Industry, the Department of the Environment and the Department of Employment. The financial services sector has also grown and accounts for the employment of 8.5 per cent of male workers and 10.3 per cent of female workers. The city is an exporter of both financial and other professional services. Electronics industries are major employers in the metropolitan area with large companies in defence, aerospace and electrical components. ICL's £21 million development in Manchester provides Europe's largest computer hall.

Information technology has been promoted in the city by the Manchester

Host initiative, whereby small businesses, voluntary organisations, community groups and other public sector organisations are linked via their personal computers with direct access to electronic mail, fax, telex, computer conferences, databases and software libraries. The city has also become a media centre with two major broadcasting companies, and is the cultural capital of the North West with museums, art galleries, theatres and concert halls. Sporting facilities of international standard are under construction despite the failure to attract the Olympic Games to the city.

The construction of urban motorways linked to national motorway systems has provided easy access to other areas of the country, while the international airport serves most areas of the world.

Employment in new service sectors in the local economy compensated for losses in employment in the manufacturing sector.

The structure of employment in the city and metropolitan area is shown in Table 5.3.

Table 5.3 Manchester: employment by sector, 1987

	Greater Manchester %	Manchester City %
Primary and energy	2.0	0.5
Manufacturing	28.7	19.5
Construction, distribution + Transport, hotels and catering	30.2	31.0
Financial and other services	39.1	49.0
Total	100.0	100.0

Source: Employment Census (1987)

While service sector employment has grown in the local economy, and manufacturing declined, manufacturing still accounts for 35 per cent of all male employees, but only 15 per cent of female employees. Greater levels of redundancies have been experienced by males (both skilled and unskilled) in the manufacturing sector, while two thirds of new vacancies are in the services sector. The new jobs in services have been disproportionately taken up by women, and activity rates for women have risen, while those for men have fallen slightly.

Between 1984 and 1990 economic activity rates for women in Greater Manchester rose from 49.4 per cent to 53.2 per cent, and for men fell from 75.9 per cent to 75.5 per cent. (The growth in activity rates for women has increased most for married women, from 52 per cent to 58.6 per cent.) In 1990 women made up 44 per cent of the labour force, estimated to rise to at least 50 per cent by 1995 (GMRIPU 1991b). Because of the loss of jobs in the traditional manufacturing industries, and its consequent effect on unemployment, particularly male unemployment, the inner areas of Manchester city, Salford and Trafford have been designated an Integrated Development Area (IDA) by the European Commission. IDAs were designed to concentrate European funding more effectively on problem areas, similar to priority regions, but usually relating to depressed urban economies.

Table 5.4 shows the relative unemployment rates of the city, the metropolitan area, the region and Great Britain.

Table 5.4 Percentage of unemployment: UK, the North West, Greater Manchester and Manchester, 1984 and 1991

	1984	*1991*
UK	12.9	9.7
North West	17.0	11.1
Greater Manchester	15.0	10.7
Manchester	NA	15.7

Source: GMRIPU (1991b and 1991d)[1]

Greater Manchester had an unemployment rate above the national average, but below the regional average in both 1984 and 1991. The difference in unemployment rates of Greater Manchester and Great Britain narrowed in this period from 2.1 per cent to 1 per cent. The city of Manchester, the inner centre of nearly half a million people, within the urban area of two and a half million, has an unemployment rate well above the national, regional and metropolitan average. This suggests that the more suburban outer areas of Greater Manchester suffered unemployment rates at or below the national average, and that rates in Manchester itself reflect the effects of suburbanisation of economic activity and mismatch of skills caused by residential suburbanisation of the more skilled, and a residual population in the city of unskilled or low skilled.

For this reason the rest of the analysis on unemployment and active labour market policies will concentrate mainly on the city of Manchester itself.

UNEMPLOYMENT IN MANCHESTER

The average unemployment rate in 1991 according to census figures, which are a measure of joblessness, that is, they reflect all those seeking work whether claimants at employment offices or not, is 19.2 per cent, well above the official Department of Employment figure of 15.7 per cent, based on claimants.

Table 5.5 shows the activity and unemployment rates by age and sex in the city.

Table 5.5 Manchester: activity and unemployment rates by age and sex, 1991

Age	Male		Female	
	Activity rate %	*Unemployment %*	*Activity rate %*	*Unemployment %*
16–19	64.1	37.0	51.9	30.8
20–24	79.4	30.5	60.7	19.8
25–34	89.9	22.7	59.7	12.5
35–44	88.5	19.4	65.0	8.8
45–54	81.3	18.2	63.7	9.1
55–64	59.0	21.3	52.8	8.9
Total average %	79.7	23.3	60.4	13.5
Total number	97,331	22,604	70,231	9,491

Source: OPCS, Local Base and Small Area Statistics (1991)

Age and unemployment

As in the UK as a whole and in other cities the unemployment rate is considerably higher for those aged under 25, but, unlike Montpellier, the unemployment rate, calculated on the same basis, is higher for men than for women. For males under 25 the rate is above 30 per cent with 37 per cent in the youngest age group 16–19. For females again the 16–19 age group is the highest for all age groups at 30.8 per cent, but this falls back to 19.8 per cent for those 20–24 years of age. After the age of 25 unemployment falls by several percentage points, but the 25–34 age group is more likely to be unemployed than older age groups. For both males and females the lowest rates of unemployment are for prime age workers of between 35 and 54, with unemployment increasing slightly for males over 55, but remaining fairly constant for women in that age group.

The young (16–24) are most at risk of unemployment and constitute 33.7 per cent of all those unemployed in Manchester, representing 30 per cent of male unemployment and 42 per cent of female unemployment.

Male/female unemployment

In contrast to the situation in the other cities under study, men rather than women experience higher unemployment rates in all age groups, and there are over twice as many men as women unemployed – 22,604 compared to 9,491. This is taking into account the fact that official figures do not adequately reflect female joblessness. Unemployed claimants, on which official figures are based, shows 20.7 per cent male unemployment and 8.4 per cent female unemployment, a much greater disparity than the census figures of joblessness, but even with joblessness taken as the measure disparities still remain at 23.2 per cent for men and 13.5 per cent for women.

Comparing official rates of long-term unemployment for men and women is less reliable as most married women are excluded from contributory or other benefits after one year if their spouse is earning, and so will not appear on the official figures. Numbers affected will, therefore, be underestimated more for females than for males, in the figures where Department of Employment statistics are cited.

The diagram in Figure 5.1 shows that, in Manchester, of those unemployed 32.8 per cent of men and 27.2 per cent of women had been out of work for more than a year and 19.4 per cent of men and 12.4 per cent of women for longer than two years at the end of 1991. Greater Manchester had figures one to two percentage points lower for both groups. By the end of 1993 long-term unemployment had become very much more serious with nearly half of unemployed men and a third of unemployed women out of work in the city for more than one year. Rates for those unemployed for over two years had also increased, although not so much for women as men.

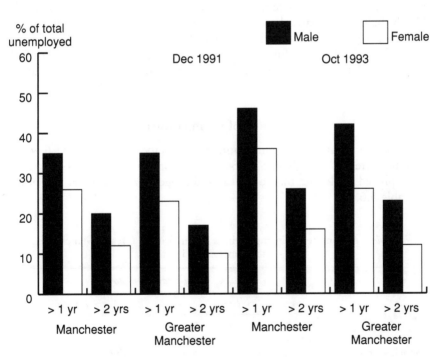

Figure 5.1 Percentage of those unemployed more than one year and more than two years in Manchester and Greater Manchester, 1991 and 1993

Source: GMRIPU (1991c, 1993) based on Department of Employment data

79

To understand why there is a distinct difference in employment and unemployment patterns between Manchester and other cities in the study one must look at general trends in activity rates and employment of women, and at the role of part-time work in Great Britain. The percentage of economically active women in employment rose by almost 20 per cent in the period 1979–90. Over the same period men in employment increased only slightly. In Manchester the proportion of females in the labour force was 42 per cent of employees in 1977 but had risen to 46 per cent by 1987 (Census of Employment 1987). As noted previously women are taking up a disproportionate number of jobs in the service sector of the economy where new jobs were created at a faster rate. Of women in employment in 1989 just over half (52 per cent) were working full-time and 39 per cent part-time.[2] Nearly three quarters of the two and a half million jobs in Britain created in the mid to late 1980s were part-time jobs, and were predominantly filled by women. Some of the reasons for the growth in part-time jobs is that they provide greater flexibility for the employer who does not have to pay the same level of non-wage costs and is not bound by the same redundancy agreements for part-time or temporary workers.[3] Thus women, in particular married women, have taken up part-time service sector work. Nearly half of all married women working found part-time employment, and 25 per cent of non-married women. In 1990 women made up 44 per cent of the total labour force in the UK and if trends continue, by 2001 are expected to form at least half the labour force (Labour Force Survey 1990).

Duration of unemployment

The median duration of unemployment in the city in 1991 was 31.6 weeks and for Greater Manchester 24.6 weeks. Comparative figures for those unemployed for longer than one year and longer than two years are shown in Table 5.6.

Table 5.6 Long-term unemployment Great Britain, Greater Manchester and Manchester, 1991

| | % of total unemployed | | | |
| | > 1 year | | > 2 years | |
	No.	*%*	*No.*	*%*
Manchester	10,890	34.4	5,698	18.0
Greater Manchester	32,712	27.1	16,732	13.9
Great Britain	542,334	24.0	263,055	11.6

Source: GMRIPU (1991c) based on Department of Employment data

The rate for Manchester is higher than that for Greater Manchester, which is in turn higher than the average for Great Britain. This applies to those unemployed for over a year and those unemployed for over two years.

If we look at the breakdown by age groups, again the rates of long-term unemployment are higher for the city than the urban area as a whole as shown in Table 5.7.

Table 5.7 Those unemployed for more than 1 year by age group, Manchester and Greater Manchester, 1991[4]

Age group	Manchester		Greater Manchester	
	No.	*%*	*No.*	*%*
16–19[5]	362	11.9	883	7.6
20–24	244	29.2	5,920	19.9
25–54	7,632	40.3	21,402	30.5
55 +	1,111	58.5	4,557	47.0
All ages	11,549	35.8	32,712	27.1

Source: Department of Employment data accessed via NOMIS by GMRIPU

The average percentage long-term unemployed continued to rise in Manchester with 43.2 per cent of all ages in this category. In October 1993, 17.5 per cent of 16–19 year olds, 35.5 per cent of 20–24 year olds, 49.1 per cent of prime age workers, and 58.7 per cent of those over 55 years old had been without a job for longer than a year.

Rates of long-term unemployment did not vary a great deal in different areas of the city with a low rate of 25.8 per cent and a high rate of 43.9 per cent with most areas having around 30–35 per cent long-term unemployed workers.

Unemployment and ethnic origin

As noted in Chapter 2 ethnic minority groups tend to be concentrated in large cities and to suffer various disadvantages in the labour market, resulting in higher levels of unemployment compared to the dominant group.

This is the case for some but not all ethnic minority groups in Manchester, as shown in Table 5.8.

All non-white unemployed constituted 15.8 per cent of the total unemployed in the city with 15.4 per cent of non-white males, and 16.5 per cent of non-white female workers. The overall rate for non-white ethnic groups was around 50 per cent higher than for white groups, but for males Indian and Chinese workers had lower unemployment rates than white workers. For female workers white unemployment was lowest and women of Pakistani

Table 5.8 Unemployment rate by ethnic group Manchester, 1991

	Male		Female		All	
	No.	%	*No.*	%	*No.*	%
White	19,165	21.9	8,000	12.0	27,165	17.6
Afro/Caribbean	965	35.5	470	19.6	1,435	28.0
Indian	217	18.7	106	15.6	323	17.5
Pakistan	1,050	31.9	336	29.1	1,386	31.2
All non-white	3,503	31.1	1,582	22.8	5,085	27.9
Total	22,668	23.2	9,582	13.5	32,250	19.2

Source: OPCS (1991) Local Base and Small Area Statistics

origin had the highest unemployment rates at 29.1 per cent, but female workers in all ethnic groups had unemployment rates below that of males.

Activity rates for males were higher for all non-white than white workers at over 70 per cent (white 66.9 per cent) while the highest activity rate for women was amongst Afro/Caribbean groups at 58.8 per cent followed by white females at 44 per cent, with an average female activity rate of 44.3 per cent.

If one looks at the figures for youth unemployment, where the highest levels of unemployment occur, by ethnic group, the same picture emerges (see Table 5.9).

Table 5.9 Youth unemployment (16–24 years) by ethnic group Manchester, 1991

	Male		Female		All	
	No.	%	*No.*	%	*No.*	%
White	5,805	31.1	3,281	21.5	9,086	26.8
All non-white ethnic groups	994	43.8	739	36.3	1,733	40.3
Total	6,799	32.5	4,020	23.2	10,819	28.3

Source: OPCS (1991) Local Base and Small Area Statistics

For all non white groups the unemployment rate amongst the young is over 50 per cent higher than for young white workers. There is considerable variation within ethnic groups however. The lowest rates of unemployed youth are amongst the Chinese community with 26.4 per cent males and 18.0 per cent females unemployed while the highest rates are amongst black Africans at 59.7 per cent and 50.9 per cent respectively (although the latter constitute less than 1 per cent of the young unemployed).

As shown, unemployment rates among ethnic minorities, with some exceptions, are higher both for workers as a whole and for young age groups. For black groups the rates are consistently several points higher than for whites in all wards of the city, while for Asians they are higher in twenty-seven of the thirty-three wards in the city. Ten wards in the city had an over-all unemployment rate of over 25 per cent, but black workers had an unemployment rate of over 25 per cent in nineteen wards, and Asian workers in ten wards, with white workers in seven wards (Census 1991). Ethnic minorities tended, therefore, to have significantly higher unemployment rates in all areas of the city, whether the areas had high or low unemployment. Forty-six per cent of the non-white population reside in the eight wards of the city with an unemployment rate over 25 per cent (see Figure 5.2 on p. 85). This will add to the local effect of high unemployment in making it more difficult to hear of work opportunities, and in affecting discouragement and low job search for nearly half the non-white population.

The highest unemployment rate in Manchester was for young non-white workers at 43.8 per cent with lowest rates for females in age groups 35 and over at around 9 per cent. The greatest number of unemployed are, however, white male workers who constituted 59.4 per cent of those who are jobless, with over nineteen thousand unemployed in 1991.

Mismatch of skills

Skill shortages reported in 1991 by the Manchester City Chamber of Commerce related largely to professional and managerial labour. Job vacancies registered at Job Centres[6] show that in Greater Manchester 70.7 per cent of all vacancies in July 1991 were for service sector jobs in clerical, sales, cleaning and personal services, and catering. These jobs are predominantly taken up by women.

If we look at a profile of the unemployed by educational level it shows that those with A levels and degrees in the North-West Region were only 7.7 per cent of those unemployed, while those with no formal educational qualification of any kind formed 49 per cent of the unemployed (see Table 5.10).

There is clearly a mismatch between the large numbers of male workers without qualification and the growing demand for professional, managerial and service workers in the local economy. The mismatch between qualification level and needs of the workforce may explain the higher levels of ethnic minority unemployment. In the North-West generally, white people were more likely to have qualifications than ethnic minorities, with the biggest difference in the over 45 age group (Centre for Employment Research 1990). The level of qualifications of young people from different ethnic origins also varies. According to the Labour Force Survey (1990) the white population is more likely than the population of all other ethnic

Table 5.10 Percentage of unemployed by educational
group – North-West, 1990

Qualification level	% of those unemployed
Degree	4.0
'A' level	3.7
City and Guilds (vocational qualification)	8.0
Apprenticeship	5.6
'O' level (GCSE)	13.1
CSE	8.9
Other	5.7
No qualification	49.0

Source: Centre for Employment Research (1990)

groups combined to have formal qualifications of some kind, with only 23 per cent having no qualifications compared to 28 per cent from other groups. Females from ethnic minority groups, however, have a higher rate of higher education, at A level or above, than either white males or females, but also the highest level with no qualification. These factors may help to explain the higher unemployment rates of certain ethnic minorities in Manchester.

The major problems in Manchester are to generate enough jobs to provide work for those unemployed in what has been an area of great economic change, where a mismatch of skills exists between redundant workers and the needs of a growing service sector economy with a demand particularly for high skill levels in the city itself. Older male workers and the young lacking high levels of qualification are particularly at risk of unemployment and long-term unemployment. In this context examination of policies operating at local level will be examined.

Urban factors in unemployment

In order to assess factors of accessibility of jobs to the unemployed, and the hysteresis effects resulting from concentrations of the unemployed, areas of the city of Manchester where the unemployed are concentrated are shown in Figure 5.2. The analysis is concentrating on the city itself as it has the highest rates of unemployment, youth unemployment and ethnic minority unemployment within its administrative area,[7] but it is nevertheless affected by what is going on in the Metropolitan area.

Of the thirty-three wards[8] in Manchester, thirteen had an unemployment rate in excess of 20 per cent, with four with a rate over 30 per cent. The areas of highest unemployment are situated around the centre of the city of Manchester. The other area of heavy unemployment is in the south of the city,

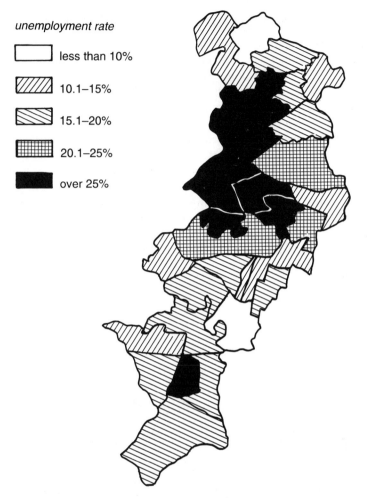

Figure 5.2 Unemployment rates by ward in Manchester, 1991
Source: Census, 1991

Benchill, where the vast inter-war public housing estate of Wythenshawe is situated. This area suffers from lack of access, being served by buses as the only form of public transportation, giving limited access only to certain areas, and is expensive in both money and time costs for long journeys. There is very little local employment in this residential area.

As previously stated the city lost small businesses, a generator of employment, in the period 1980–89, while in other areas of Greater Manchester there was a gain. In the extraurban areas of Cheshire, to the South and West, there was a 33 per cent increase in small businesses. This accords with the observed patterns of an increasing tendency to locate in peripheral areas of the urban area.

Economic development planning in Manchester

Because of the fragmentation of local government powers after the abolition of the metropolitan layer of government in 1985[9] economic planning, previously the responsibility of a Greater Manchester authority, now devolved largely to the boroughs (see Figure 5.3). Outer boroughs took into account the needs of their own area, rather than those of the agglomeration, and so the tendency is for all to wish to generate new economic activity within their area, with little reference to the employment needs of neighbouring areas, although the Association of Greater Manchester Authorities does cooperate on economic development issues. The major stated aim of Manchester City Council's economic strategy was to retain existing jobs and maximise opportunity for new employment by, amongst other policies, providing four sites for high-technology industries, two in central Manchester and two in suburban Manchester near the airport (Manchester City Council 1992). The Department of the Environment, a ministry of central govern-

Figure 5.3 Greater Manchester

86

ment with a regional headquarters in Manchester, has powers to control development and is trying, in Manchester, to stop the spread of economic activity into the Green Belt around the city, partly to protect the environment, but mainly to divert development to the city area.

These relatively new policies to reurbanise the central areas of the urban region are in reaction to the loss of employment and rise in unemployment in the city. Market forces, and to some extent past development policy, had favoured suburban expansion. Since the recession beginning in 1992 there has been little new activity to be reurbanised, and further job losses have occurred.

The position still stands that vacancies, where they occur, are higher in the outer than the inner urban area, and it is relevant, therefore, to examine the availability and cost of public transportation. Most people travelled to work by car in Greater Manchester, with only 17 per cent of men and 31 per cent of women using the bus service (Census 1981). Buses were the only option until the opening of a very limited tram service in 1992, and still dominate public transportation. Bus fares increased after deregulation and loss of subsidy in 1985, and increases have been greater for longer distance journeys over three miles. Daily commuting costs from inner to outer areas can be as much as a fifth of the net wage of low-income workers. So both time and money costs are high, militating against wide area job search for the young and the low-paid. Public transportation is not available to all growth areas in exurban locations outside the metropolitan area and is limited within it, largely to main radial routes to the centre.

Policies towards the unemployed in Manchester

Organisational structure

The organisational structure of agencies dealing with passive and active labour market policies, and with job creation programmes intended to help unemployment in the city, is exceedingly complex and fragmented. The two main agencies dealing with the unemployed are the Employment Service and the Training and Enterprise Council (TEC). Both of these are funded by the national Department of Employment (DE) but whereas the Employment Service is under the direct control of the DE, the TECs, set up in 1988, are funded by central government, but are autonomous at a local level and are private independent non-profit making organisations, with a contract with the Secretary of State for Employment. The members of the decision making board of a TEC are made up of private sector employers and managers of local businesses, representatives of local industry and commerce, plus members from the voluntary sector, the public sector and training experts, but are dominated by employer representatives.

The Employment Service runs Job Centres where vacancies are registered; gives help in job search and finding an appropriate training course to the unemployed, particularly those out of work for longer than six months, or those living in inner cities; gives special help to the disabled; and has the job of verifying entitlement to unemployment benefit and fighting against fraud in the system. The Training and Enterprise Councils exist to provide opportunities for increasing skill levels, via a variety of training schemes adapted to the needs of the individual and the local economy; to improve the quality of training to help productivity in local businesses; and to encourage the unemployed to start up their own enterprises. In addition the central government Department of the Environment (DoE) regional office has responsibility for Urban Development Corporations – in the case of Manchester these are the Central Manchester Development Corporation and outside the city the Trafford Park Development Corporation. These latter bodies are private organisations funded by central government with one of their major aims, in redevelopment of an area, to provide maximum employment opportunities and training grants to local residents.

The DoE also has control of the Urban Programme funds for the area, including City Challenge, an initiative which operates in the inner area of Hulme/Moss Side in Manchester, with the highest unemployment level, and one of the aims of which is to improve employment prospects of the local population. City Action Team which comprises the regional directors of several national ministries, the Department of the Environment, the Department of Trade and Industry (DTI) and the Employment Service amongst others, aims to accelerate regeneration of the inner city by increasing and safeguarding jobs; increasing the employability of residents; generating economic activity and improving the quality of life. Economic development is also aided by government through the DTI, with Regional Selective Assistance within the most depressed areas of the city, co-ordinating with the local authority in providing support for job creation in industry. Yet another department of central government, the Home Office, gives grants to address the 'additional needs' of ethnic minorities to promote equality of opportunity in the labour market, where mainstream provision is not sufficient. The organisational structure of different levels of government and agencies dealing with policy towards the unemployed in the city is exceedingly complex and cumbersome and lacks coordination.[10] The following analysis will first of all look at benefits and income maintenance for the unemployed, and then at the active labour market policies that are in operation in Manchester.

Unemployment Benefit and Income Maintenance for the unemployed

Unemployment Benefit

Unemployment Benefit is available to those workers who have contributed within the previous two years for at least fifty times the lower weekly earning limit. It is paid out from progressive contributions from both employers and employees to the National Insurance Fund. The waiting period after which payment is made following job loss is three days if the unemployment was involuntary, and up to six months if the worker became voluntarily unemployed or became unemployed through misconduct. It was paid out to all qualifying beneficiaries at a flat rate of £43.10 per week for a single person in 1992. The duration of Unemployment Benefit up to the end of 1993 was one year. It was then reduced to six months. Once benefit has been exhausted the unemployed worker may then, under certain circumstances, claim Income Support.

Income Support

Income Support is a means-tested benefit and can be claimed by those who do not qualify for Unemployment Benefit, as well as those who have exhausted benefit. The means-testing takes into account the income of a spouse, so many unemployed may not be eligible to claim income support if the spouse is in employment. Several other means-tested benefits are also available, including housing benefit, to those eligible for Income Support. The benefit itself, in 1992, was £42.45 per week for single people over 25, with additions for dependents for other groups. The unemployed age group 16 to 18 have not been eligible to claim Income Support since 1987 without being registered on an official training scheme; also they cannot claim if they fail to complete training. This is particularly hard amongst the young in Manchester as training places are not available for all this age group.

Minimum wage for those in employment

There is no official minimum wage in the United Kingdom. Wages councils in certain low-paid industries such as catering and hotels prior to 1992 set a minimum payment for certain grades of work within these industries. Wages councils were abolished in 1992.

Active labour market policies

The measures cited have applied since the beginning of 1991. Not every scheme in the city will be examined, but all major policies will be described.

General policies affecting those who are not young, long-term unemployed, or groups with disadvantages in the labour market are as follows:

Thirteen Week Reviews

This measure is to help those unemployed for thirteen weeks to find employment quickly. It includes a meeting with the counselling service and has a Job Referral Service which tries to match candidates to jobs available. It is run by the Employment Service. The following two schemes are linked to the reviews and also run by the ES.

Job Search Seminars

This scheme is aimed to help search technique and enlarge area of search for employment. Photocopiers, a telephone, stamps and stationery are provided for participants. Nationally £2.4 million was available. No figures for participants or expenditure were available from the ES in Manchester.

Job Review Workshops

The scheme is directed at helping unemployed professionals and managers. Groups of twelve work in workshops lasting two days. Each participant prepares a detailed course of action. National expenditure in 1991–92 was £1.2 million. No figures on participants or expenditure were available from the ES in Manchester.

Business Start-up (formerly Enterprise Allowance Scheme)

Since 1991 this scheme has been reserved for those unemployed, although formerly it was open to others. It is aimed to help the unemployed to set up new businesses. Grants of between £20 and £90 per week for periods from 26–66 weeks are available. Participants are encouraged also to benefit from other enterprise creation programmes, for example business advice services offered. The scheme is organised by local TEC. In Manchester TEC in 1991–92 1,601 participants were funded. Ninety-five per cent of the businesses were still in operation after a year. There are many more applicants than funds available. Expenditure on the business enterprise programme in 1992 in Manchester was £3,066,000.

Career development loans

For those aged 18 and over, £300 to £5000 to finance professional training of their choice is available, lasting from a week to a year, full-time, part-time or by correspondence. This is administered on behalf of the Department of Employment by three commercial banks, and is intended to encourage workers to take more responsibility for their own training and career prospects.

Measures to help the young unemployed

The overall aim in the UK is that by 1997 at least 80 per cent of all young people should attain level two of National Vocational Qualification (NVQ).

By 2000 the aim is for 50 per cent to have reached level three or its academic equivalent. Training credits that make up NVQs are under the control of TECs. The main programme is called Youth Training.

Youth Training

This is principally for the young aged 16 and 17 years old but can apply to those up to the age of 25. In the year 1992–93 national government support was £881 million. The aim is that there should be greater flexibility in training with a balanced proportion of practical and theoretical content, and that the training is adapted to local labour market needs.

Young people who are disabled, who are not fully healthy, have been in prison or have linguistic difficulties can benefit from schemes between the ages of 18 to 25. In Manchester in 1991–92 £17,565,000 was spent on Youth Training by the Manchester TEC.[11] Outcomes of this scheme are shown in Table 5.11.

Table 5.11 Performance indicators Manchester TEC, 1991–92

Young people participating	Number/%
Participants in YT	6892
School leavers entering YT	60%
YT leavers gaining NVQ	36%
YT leavers gaining employment	60%

Source: Annual Report, Manchester TEC (1991–1992)

Training is undertaken with firms in the area and the amount paid by the TEC to employers will vary according to the type of training. If there is a shortage of skills, firms are willing to accept less than where there is a great demand for apprenticeships, as in motor engineering. The average amount paid to employers was around £30 per week. Trainees on the scheme over 17 years of age received £35 per week from the employer. New school leavers are given priority on the YT scheme. The take up rate among ethnic minorities is low. They constitute 9 per cent of the eligible population of the age group but take up only 6 per cent of places.

Compacts and Education Business Partnerships

This scheme is integrated into Action for Cities and involves employers actively in schools. They offer advice on study programmes. The aim is to increase knowledge in schools of business and participation in further education and training after the age of 16. The EBP and compact schemes were established by the TEC in Manchester.

Measures to help the long-term unemployed

Employment Training

This was initiated in 1988 to help the long-term unemployed and others with special needs to acquire the necessary skills to find employment, and respond to the needs of the local economy by ensuring relevant training. The aim is to provide recipients, as far as possible, with a training for professional qualifications or credits towards them. All trainees follow an individual programme. The training is a mixture of on-job and formal training in a centre. This scheme is run by Manchester TEC.

In 1992, £8,616,000 was spent on Employment Training by Manchester TEC, slightly more than on Youth Training. Fourteen per cent gained an NVQ and 24 per cent gained a positive outcome from ET training i.e. were reintegrated into the labour market, became self-employed or went on to further full-time training or study. This compares with 37 per cent nationally.

Employment Action

This was started in 1991 to help the long-term unemployed to contribute work of value to their neighbourhood in order to maintain skills and benefit future job search. Some 400 people within the Manchester TEC area benefited in 1991–92. The scheme was organised by the TEC.

Restart interviews

To help the long-term unemployed become more active in their search for employment and to furnish them with the ability to be more competitive in the labour market, this scheme operates for those unemployed for over six months. The adviser gives information on training, schemes for setting up enterprises, Job Interview Guarantee and Job Clubs. Since 1990 those registered unemployed for longer than two years who refused to take part in a placement programme were obliged to follow a Restart programme. If not, a proportion of benefit can be lost. The scheme is organised by the Employment Service. No information on numbers benefiting was available from the Manchester Employment Service.

Job Interview Guarantee

This scheme was started in 1989. Employers guarantee an interview for their vacancy to a suitable long-term unemployed worker in return for services given by the Employment Service. Nationally there were 96,000 participants in 1991, 27,500 of whom found a job. No information on figures for Manchester was available from the Employment Service.

Job Clubs

This scheme was initiated in 1984 to help the long-term unemployed find work more quickly. It aims to give members the skills necessary for efficient employment search. Eight half days every six weeks are spent at the Job Club, where motivation and interview advice is given. Members have access to facilities to aid application for jobs. After initial training members must report for four half days a week and follow ten leads a day until work is found. Participants receive income support plus expenses.

Measures to help other disadvantaged groups in the labour market

The disabled

Assistance with fares to work

Financial aid is available to help the disabled who are unable to use public transport to take the least expensive alternative means of reaching work. The scheme is operated by the ES.

Special aids to employment

Special equipment needed for work can be provided by the Employment Service. Further grants are available for adaptation to premises and equipment for employers to adapt the workplace to the needs of the disabled. They generally cover half the cost.

Job Instruction Scheme

This is to encourage employers to take on a disabled worker on a trial basis. It provides a grant of £45 per fortnight to subsidise the wages of the disabled worker for the six weeks trial period.

Placing Assessment and Counselling Teams (PACT)

Set up in 1992, it aims to furnish advice, evaluate and help the disabled to find work. It also aims to promote recruitment of the disabled amongst employers. It is run by the ES.

YT and ET schemes

These schemes are open to handicapped trainees who are able to follow normal training.

Law on employment of disabled workers

There has been a quota system in operation for disabled workers in the UK since 1944. Employers of more than twenty workers must take on 3 per cent of their workforce from the registered disabled. At present there are not enough disabled people to permit all employers to attain this quota.

Ethnic minorities

All schemes are, of course, open to ethnic minorities, but grants are also available to supplement needs of Commonwealth migrants in the labour market. Since 1992 there have been funds available to help non-Commonwealth immigrants overcome linguistic and cultural problems. These totalled £4 million nationally in 1992. Under this scheme Manchester TEC had ten schemes approved for Home Office Ethnic Minority Grants in 1992–93. Actual expenditure in Manchester is not available but is unlikely to be a large sum as total national expenditure is small compared to levels of expenditure on other labour market measures.

Women in the labour market

ET/YT and child care

The national government recognises the difficulties of women in the labour market and both ET and YT schemes help women returners and single parents by furnishing grants to TECs to fund child care after school hours for women on these schemes.

Career development loans

Career development loans for women are adapted to take into account the fact that they may wish to undertake part-time training and may need child care expenses.

All disadvantaged groups

One of the six priorities for TECs set out by the Secretary of State for Employment concerns disadvantaged groups including lone parents, ethnic minorities, refugees, older workers and ex-prisoners. TECs must be flexible in providing training for these groups and give priority to their needs within the categories of training.

The Manchester Scheme

This scheme was set up in 1987 and is part of the YT scheme. The local city council pays an extra subsidy to the training allowance, and the rate of trainers to trainees is higher than on other YT programmes. It operates positive action to help young women into non-traditional areas of work; to help ethnic minorities; and to help the physically disabled. Part of the training is in the Manchester College of Arts and Technology and part on placement. In 1992 it had 600 participants from the city and the city spent around £1 million on this project.

Urban regeneration and the creation of new employment

Urban policy of the central government has aimed to promote economic development and environmental improvement in inner city areas in particular and other areas of deprivation in large cities. In Manchester there are various programmes initiated by central government that aim to increase employment in inner areas where unemployment is highest.

Urban Development Corporations

Urban Development Corporations (UDCs) are quasi-private organisations funded by the Department of the Environment, which has to approve local plans. Two operate in the Manchester area, the Central Manchester Development Corporation (CMDC) and Trafford Park Development Corporation (TPDC) just over the city boundary. Their task is to regenerate areas of dereliction and decay within the inner cities by environmental improvement and physical regeneration, with the secondary aim of providing more local employment. The CMDC was set up in 1988 and has rehabilitated housing, both private and social housing; encouraged tourism projects, offices and the hotel sector, transportation and car parking. Net job gains in the area by the end of 1991 were 1,100 with 350 in the new British Council headquarters established in the development area. Other permanent jobs were mainly in tourism, catering and other services. The TPDC set up in 1987, is a large area of derelict industrial land where the Corporation has encouraged relocation of twelve large companies and around one thousand small companies. Manufacturing is particularly encouraged, but many speculative office blocks have also been built. The official estimate for new jobs created in the area between 1987 and 1991 is three thousand five hundred, but this includes all employees brought with firms when they relocated. The CMDC arranged with the British Council to have job interview guarantees for inner city dwellers who may not have qualifications but have been on a relevant training scheme. The TPDC had two schemes to help the long-term unemployed, the Job Offer Training Scheme whereby the Corporation paid 75 per cent of the cost of training if the company took on someone unemployed for longer than six months; and an Extra Skills Training initiative subsidising 50 per cent of the cost of upgrading the skills of an existing worker if it releases a job for an unemployed worker. Under these projects one hundred and thirty people were helped up to 1992.

Action for Cities/City Action Teams (CAT)

Action for Cities, was initiated in 1988 to promote inner city regeneration by means of encouraging aid to new and existing firms, increasing employment prospects and training, and improving housing and the environment. Within this plan City Action Teams of which Manchester/Salford is one of eight in the UK, co-ordinate government action at local level and ensure all other different programmes operate efficiently with no overlap. The Manchester team works on a modest budget, £4.4 million, for example, in 1992–93.

Hulme City Challenge

The most economically depressed areas of the city are Hulme, with an overall unemployment rate of 38.8 per cent in the 1991 Census, and neighbouring Moss Side with unemployment at 28.1 per cent. A Task Force, another central government funded body, was set up to work in partnership with the TEC, CAT, CMDC and other government departments within these areas; its aim in 1991 was to provide 880 training places, 290 jobs, and aid 236 small businesses. This was superceded by Hulme City Challenge, its aim to regenerate the area physically and economically with a budget of £7.5 million for 1992–93. The scheme runs for five years and is under the management of the regional office of the DoE. No employment results are yet forthcoming.

EVALUATION OF MEASURES AFFECTING THE UNEMPLOYED IN MANCHESTER

Manchester has experienced structural change and a fall in population of over 20 per cent in the twenty years up to 1991. Overall job losses in the metropolitan areas were 15 per cent in the decade 1977–87, while growth of small firms occurred in Greater Manchester and Cheshire at the same time as a loss of small firms in the city. The greatest number of redundancies in the city were amongst males working in manufacturing industry, both skilled and unskilled. Growth in service sectors occurred in the 1980s particularly in property, finance, professional services and personal services. Women took up the majority of the new service sector jobs, resulting in twice as many men as women unemployed by 1991. A high percentage of females employed were in part-time and/or low-paid employment. Just over one third of all those unemployed in the city were under 25 years of age, with unemployment of young ethnic minorities averaging over 40 per cent. The long-term effects on the labour market of high unemployment of the young will have serious implications. Most of today's older workers did not experience unemployment when young. The rate of long-term unemployment increased from one third of the unemployed in 1991 to half the unemployed at the end of 1993, with highest rates for male, prime age and older workers. Unemployment rates varied across the city with inner area residents and one outer area with over a quarter of the active population jobless. Those with no qualifications, either professional or educational, accounted for nearly half of all those unemployed in the area.

Unemployment Benefit levels are very low compared to wage levels, as is Income Support for the long-term unemployed. It is possible that because of various other means-tested benefits for those on Income Support, they may have a fairly high reservation wage, but there is no evidence for this. It may affect employment of women in households where the husband is among the long-term unemployed if total benefits exceed income brought in by the wife, which may nevertheless bring the family above Income Support levels. In this case it would be financially beneficial for the woman to become unemployed.

In Manchester there are complex organisational structures with different public and state funded private organisations dealing with unemployment and job creation. Ten major organisations are described, but many smaller organisations also exist. Coherence of policy and problems of communication and overlap occur where this sort of situation exists.

If we examine the type of policy and scale of aid in Manchester one thing which becomes apparent is that little is done for those who are neither young nor long-term unemployed, although they constitute over a third of the unemployed at 11,113 people. If this group, neither young nor unemployed over a year, do not wish to set up their own business, there is no free training or retraining available, and only minor forms of advisory help from the Employment Service. This suggests that government policy is very much affected by the European Union subsidies available. This lack of more extensive training policies in a situation of changing skill needs, probably results in a greater number becoming long-term unemployed than would otherwise occur.

Turning to the young unemployed, the aims of Youth Training are modest considering the fact that European economies require increased skill levels. Only 60 per cent of young people in the city stay at school to gain qualifications which leaves 40 per cent with little or no qualification. To have an aim of level 2 NVQ for 80 per cent of young people compares unfavourably with the situation in Germany where 80 per cent of 19-year-olds are still in education or formal apprenticeship schemes. The outcomes from the Manchester TEC show that of those going on schemes, bearing in mind the shortfall of places available to 16–18-year-olds, only 36 per cent gain an NVQ. Sixty per cent of these gain employment, bearing out the findings of Main and Shelley (1991) that there is a positive effect of training on the probability of employment. One of the problems of training schemes which offer subsidy to employer trainers is that employers may substitute participants for other employees, the so-called 'displacement effect'. This displacement effect from youth training schemes could be anywhere between 17 per cent and 62 per cent of all jobs created through the programme (Dolton 1993). Youth Training is open to question as being a subsidy scheme for low-cost labour rather than a professional training for the longer term needs of the local economy. Employment Training for the long-term unemployed in Manchester showed low positive outcomes. Only 14 per cent gained a qualification and less than a quarter of participants went on to a job, self-employment or further training. In a situation of falling employment it is not very realistic to train for jobs that are not available locally. Jobs that are available – the shortage of professional and managerial workers, for example – could not be filled realistically by unemployed manufacturing workers after a short training programme. This brings into question the validity of short-term programmes of this kind in a depressed economy, and in an economy which is radically changing in structure.

Ethnic minorities have very little recognition of their greater difficulties in the labour market. Lower numbers of the young are attracted to YT schemes in the city. Schemes funded by government, aimed to help ethnic minorities in the city, have very small grants of around £30,000 compared to the millions of pounds spent on YT and ET.

For women in the city the problem of unemployment appears less acute but their unemployment rate is still high. As previously stated, a large proportion are in part-time or low-paid unskilled service jobs. Career prospects and improvement in income are very much reduced for this group, who have little prospect of further on-job training to increase their skill levels. For unemployed women, unless young or long-term unemployed, there are no child care facilities for mothers to allow them to make job searches or take up training (unless they borrow money). Only the Manchester Scheme trains women in non-traditional areas to provide greater long-term opportunities.

Urban regeneration policy and planning policy is providing positive results in raising the level of economic development in areas hardest hit by unemployment. The various schemes have resulted in around four and a half thousand new jobs in inner areas up to 1991. Compared to the number unemployed it is small but valuable. It is helping to bridge the gap caused by the loss of jobs which in roughly the same period was six thousand five hundred in the city as a whole. Policies to encourage relocation are more successful in times of general economic growth, and since the recession, after 1991, new jobs creation has been considerably slower.

Finally the cost and availability of transportation may have some bearing on the opportunities for the unemployed to find work outside their own area. There is no rapid transit system throughout the city as in most other cities of this size, and fares are high per mile.

While it is difficult to reduce the level of unemployment in situations of general falling demand by active labour market policies, the type and level of training, where most expenditure goes, is doing little to help the longer term opportunities of employment, especially for the young, when the local economy grows. Levels of education and formal professional qualifications must be raised to meet the changing needs of a potentially high-skill service economy.

6

ROTTERDAM

INTRODUCTION

Rotterdam, the largest port in Europe,[1] is situated on the estuary of the river Maas some twelve miles from the North Sea, and linked through a network of canals to the Rhine. The urbanisation of Rotterdam began around 1875 when the port expanded after the construction of a direct connection with the North Sea. The population increased fourfold between 1875 and 1925, but has seen an absolute decline of around a quarter since 1965, when residents moved to outer suburban rings. In 1991 the population stood at 582,000 people. It is the second largest city in the Netherlands after Amsterdam. The city was heavily bombed in the second world war and twenty-eight thousand houses were lost in addition to enormous damage to the port facilities. Reconstruction needs increased the demand for labour in the building and construction industries and for harbour workers. In the 1950s many Dutch people emigrated to Australia, New Zealand and Canada (Gemeente Rotterdam 1991), and immigrant labour was sought to meet the shortfall in labour supply. Workers came mainly, at that time, from Turkey and Morocco, and later from ex-Dutch colonies. The local economy flourished in the 1950s and 1960s, but came under heavy pressure after the two oil price crises, which hit Rotterdam particularly hard as the economic structure of the city concentrated on transport, trade and petrochemical industries. Like most European cities with a manufacturing and port base Rotterdam had to adapt from being an industrial to a service economy. Nevertheless, Rotterdam has maintained its position as Europe's most important seaport and distribution centre. The loss of jobs in industry is more marked in Rotterdam than in the surrounding region. In the years 1985 to 1990 the city lost 2 per cent of jobs in industry while the region gained 2 per cent. Employment in the transport and communications sector fell in the city and region in the same period, but by 10 per cent in Rotterdam and 2 per cent in the region (COS). Containerisation of most of the port activity contributed to losses of employment in the transport sector. The construction industry also suffered heavy decline. In the Rotterdam region[2] changes in employment patterns were as shown in Table 6.1.

100

Table 6.1 Percentage change in employment
by sector in Rynmond, 1977–87

Sector	Change (%)
Services	+18
Manufacturing	– 29
Transport	– 9
Construction	– 12
Commerce	– 18

Source: Rotterdam Werkt (1992)

Overall the city lost thirty-six thousand jobs in the period 1970–91, a loss of over 11 per cent of total employment. The structure of employment in 1990 demonstrates that the city has become a largely service economy (see Table 6.2).

Table 6.2 Percentage employment by sector
Rotterdam, 1990

Sector	Employment (%)
Manufacturing	15.2
Construction	6.4
Transport	17.2
Financial services	15.0
Commerce, hotels, catering	17.3
Other services	29.9
Total	100

Source: COS Rotterdam (1991)

The city has undergone enormous economic structural change since the late 1960s from a situation where most jobs were in port, construction and manufacturing sectors to one where over 60 per cent of employment was in various service sectors. There has also been a growing suburbanisation and exurbanisation of both residents and jobs to the areas around the city. Economic planning by city government is, as will be shown, seeking to reverse the process of work suburbanisation. Residential out-migration began in the 1950s as those parts of the population who could afford to left the older housing in central areas, for newer suburban dwellings and out-lying villages. Migrant workers moved in to join the increasingly elderly population in the inner areas. Unlike most Northern European cities the per-centage of owner-occupiers in cities in the Netherlands is very low. Only 11 per cent of residents in Rotterdam owned their own house in 1989, the vast majority rented from the private or social housing sector. No single sector of housing is dominated by low-income groups (Van Kempen et al. 1989). In terms of income per head Rotterdam has more than 58 per cent of population with incomes less than 23,600 guilders, compared to 50 per cent nationally, and fewer residents, therefore, in higher income groups (COS 1991). Out of a population of 582,242 the non-Dutch population totalled 114,373, approximately 20 per cent, in 1991, with over a third of those under 15 from various ethnic minorities.

Rotterdam has 62 per cent of the population of the wider city region, Rynmond, within its boundaries. Both region and city grew around 2 per cent in population in the period 1985–91. The workforce population grew by 2 per cent in the city and 12 per cent in the region in the same period. The greatest increase came from participation by women in the labour market. In the six year period women in work increased by 15 per cent in the city and 27 per cent in the region as a whole.

UNEMPLOYMENT IN ROTTERDAM

Compared to the Netherlands as a whole Rotterdam's unemployment rate is nearly four times as high and represents 13.9 per cent of all unemployment in the country.

Table 6.3 Percentage and number unemployed, Netherlands and Rotterdam, 1990[3]

	Netherlands			Rotterdam		
	Male	Female	Total	Male	Female	Total
Number unemployed	208,000	137,000	345,000	32,000	16,000	48,000
% unemployed	4.2	6.5	5.0	21.1	16.5	19.3

Sources: COS Rotterdam (1991), MISEP (1991)

The discrepancy between the national and city rate is higher in Rotterdam than for all the other cities under study. Rotterdam, with 62 per cent of the regional population, had 74 per cent of regional unemployment in 1991. Its position vis à vis the region has, however, improved since 1985 when Rotterdam's unemployed were 79 per cent of those unemployed in the wider area (COS Rotterdam, 1991). It is possible that both employment policy and urban planning policy in the city have reduced job losses compared to the region since that date. The national/city unemployment rate could be explained by the fact that the city has an adverse economic structure, determined by its relatively higher numbers of low-skill, low-education work seekers. Loss of employment has been overwhelmingly in the 'simple' (*eevondige arbeid*) sector in Rotterdam (GBOS 1991) – 70 per cent of total jobs lost in recent years, which represents low-skill work. While the working population of the Netherlands has 60 per cent of people with upper secondary, higher vocational and university levels of education, only just over a third of Rotterdam's workforce have attained these levels of qualifications. Over 80 per cent of the unemployed in Rotterdam in 1990 had low levels of educational attainment (GBOS 1991).

The average unemployment rate in Rotterdam in 1990 was 19.3 per cent, with 48,400 registered unemployed. A breakdown by age and sex is shown in Table 6.4.

Table 6.4 Unemployment rate by age and sex, Rotterdam, 1990

Age	Male		Female	
	No.	*%*	*No.*	*%*
15–24	6,800	24	6,000	24
25–44	18,300	21	8,100	15
45–64	7,300	19	1,900	11
Total	32,400	21	16,000	16

Source: COS Rotterdam (1991)

Activity rates were 76 per cent for men and 51 per cent for women. Numbers unemployed of men and women were similar for the youngest age groups, but higher for men than women aged over 25. Although it is not possible to disaggregate activity rate by age groups it seems likely that female activity rates were high for the young but low for prime-age workers. Men comprised 61 per cent of those in work, and women 39 per cent. Overall 130,000 men and 81,000 women were in employment in 1990.

Although it appears from Table 6.4 that female unemployment is less of a problem than male unemployment, it is apparent that in the younger age groups under 30 seeking work, a higher proportion of women are unemployed compared to men (see Table 6.5).

As women in younger age groups have higher activity rates, one would expect more women to be unemployed in younger age groups. It does, however, indicate that with greater numbers participating in the labour market, the numbers unemployed are similar to the number of male unemployed as indicated in the youngest age group in Table 6.4. Information on types of jobs undertaken by sex are not available but educational levels of the unemployed indicate that women with lower educational qualifications are slightly less likely to be unemployed at all ages than men with the same education.

Table 6.5 Percentage unemployed of total
unemployed in Rotterdam by sex, 1990

Age	Male	Female
15–19	4.8	11.6
20–29	34.5	47.1
30–39	26.9	21.8
40–49	20.4	13.2
50–59	13.0	6.1
60–64	0.5	0.5
Total	100.0	100.0

Source: GBOS Rotterdam (1991)

This may indicate that women are taking up lower level service jobs for which little qualification is needed, while men are more excluded or self excluded from this type of work, where employment opportunities are growing. Those with higher levels of education and training form a smaller proportion of the unemployed for both men and women, but women with higher education form a higher percentage of total unemployed than men. There is a high percentage of women compared to men who work part-time. More than half of working women work less than thirty-five hours a week, and around 30 per cent work for less than twenty hours a week (Gemeente Rotterdam 1991).

This suggests that less qualified women have less of a problem finding work, and are more heavily represented in lower level jobs. It is interesting to note that over a quarter of all prime age unemployed women had a high

Table 6.6 Unemployed by age and education level, Rotterdam, 1990

Age/education	Male %	Female %
15–24		
Basic, lower secondary	85.9	81.9
Higher, vocational/university	14.1	18.1
25–44		
Basic, lower secondary	81.7	72.6
Higher, vocational/university	18.3	27.4
45–64		
Basic, lower secondary	93.9	89.5
Higher, vocational/university	6.1	10.5
Total all ages		
Basic, lower secondary	85.3	78.1
Higher, vocational/university	14.7	21.9

Source: GBOS Rotterdam (1991)

level of education. This suggests that there may be problems in educated women returners to work finding employment at a suitable level.

Duration of unemployment

Rotterdam has over 60 per cent of the unemployed in the long-term unemployed category i.e. out of work for longer than one year. Table 6.7 analyses duration of unemployment by age and sex.

Table 6.7 Length of unemployment by age and sex in Rotterdam, 1988 and 1990

Age	1988		1990	
	Male %	Female %	Male %	Female %
15–24				
< 1 year	61.2	55.4	55.5	52.2
1–2 years	18.1	19.0	21.7	21.5
> 2 years	20.8	25.6	22.8	26.3
Total No.	8,054	6,656	6,796	6,000
25–44				
< 1 year	34.0	36.8	29.5	32.6
1–2 years	16.0	18.1	16.7	19.1
> 2 years	48.4	45.1	53.8	48.2
Total No.	18,274	7,245	18,326	8,116
45–64				
< 1 year	24.9	24.9	15.4	21.2
1–2 years	12.5	14.7	13.9	19.2
> 2 years	62.6	60.5	70.7	59.6
Total No.	7,282	1,621	7,296	1,893
All ages				
< 1 year	38.9	36.5	31.8	38.6
1–2 years	15.8	17.8	17.1	20.1
> 2 years	45.4	45.7	51.1	41.3
Total No.	33,610	34,700	32,418	16,009

Source: GBOS Rotterdam (1991)

Long-term unemployment in 1990 for younger workers is lower than for prime age workers, but over a fifth of young men and a quarter of young women had remained unemployed for longer than two years. The incidence of long-term unemployment rises with age with 70 per cent of prime age men and 85 per cent of older men unemployed for longer than a year. The same is true for women but with a slightly lower percentage in each age groups (67 per cent and 79 per cent respectively). Another feature to note is that for the over-45 age group the majority of long-term unemployed had been without a job for over two years. Taking all age groups together a higher percentage of women than men were unemployed for between one and two years, but a lower percentage of women than men came into the more serious category of unemployment, being without a job for longer than two years. This may reflect the fact that older women are more likely than men to withdraw from the labour market if they cannot find work. The total number of long-term unemployed in the city was nearing thirty-two thousand workers. There had been an increase in the number and proportion of long-term unemployed since 1988 for all groups of the unemployed, except for older women.

Unemployment and ethnic origin

Around 16 per cent of the total population in Rotterdam belongs to ethnic minority group but workers from these groups constitute around one third of the total unemployed (Gemeente Rotterdam 1987). In 1978 31 per cent of ethnic minority groups were unemployed and this rose slightly by 1987. The position in the 1980s did not worsen with respect to the indigenous Dutch. The high level of unemployment of ethnic minorities is attributed to their weak labour market position, the result of low educational levels coupled with a traditionally limited job orientation that has failed to adapt to changes in the labour market (Gemeente Rotterdam 1991).

Table 6.8 Unemployment by country of origin and age, Rotterdam, 1991 – percentage of total

Age	Dutch	Sur/Ant	Guest workers*	Others	Total
15–24	59.6	12.1	24.4	3.8	100
25–44	64.6	13.9	14.8	6.7	100
45–64	66.2	8.4	20.5	4.9	100
Total %	63.7	12.4	18.2	5.2	
Total No.	27,709	5,394	7,917	2,480	43,500

Source: COS Rotterdam (1991)

Note:* Turkish, Moroccan, Yugoslav, Italian, Portuguese, Spanish, Cape Verdian, Algerian and Tunisian

The majority of guest workers in the above category are of Turkish and Moroccan origin and are largely the families of the original influx of migrant workers in the 1950s and 1960s. While the proportion of Dutch people decreased from 1989–91 in each age group the number of unemployed workers from elsewhere increased, particularly in the youngest age group, and most for the guest worker category.

The highest incidence of unemployment is amongst workers from Surinam and Antilles where the rate increased from 30 per cent to 45 per cent in the 1980s. The number of indigenous Dutch unemployed increased only a little over the 1980s. During the decade guest workers from Mediterranean countries were made redundant on a massive scale, having previously, in the 1970s, only suffered from low levels of unemployment.

The chance of long-term unemployment for non-Dutch residents is also likely to be higher. As an example, 65 per cent of Dutch workers compared to 79 per cent of Turkish workers had been unemployed for longer than a year. The differences were most marked in the youngest age groups under 22 years of age, reflecting the difficulties of young people with low educational levels finding employment. There was no significant difference between levels of very long-term unemployment of over four years according to country of origin.

Disablement and unemployment in Rotterdam

Of those of working age there are 21,500 men and 10,400 women registered as disabled. Nearly 80 per cent of the total are incapable of work and of the rest their work capacity is between 15 per cent and 80 per cent. The proportion of people totally incapable of work due to physical or mental incapacity is decreasing. More and more new cases are partially capable of work (Gemeente Rotterdam 1991).

Location of unemployment

Rotterdam is administratively divided into ninety-nine boroughs ranging in population from a hundred to over two thousand. In the map (Figure 6.1) these have been grouped into sixteen larger areas. The variation in unemployment rates in 1990 is between 6.7 per and 33.3 per cent. Most of the areas of highest unemployment are in central areas around the river and to the north of the city centre. The areas of lowest unemployment are in the outer suburban rings to the north and east of the city towards the airport.

In districts with high unemployment the educational level is low and the number of residents from ethnic minorities is high. Dutch people living in these areas also suffer from the same high rates of unemployment, suggesting that it is low-skill, low-education, poverty, and urban localisation effects rather than racial discrimination which affect work opportunity. In the inner suburbs unemployment increased over the period 1981–87 particularly on the right bank of the Maas, where unemployment at the beginning of the period was around 8 per cent but increased to nearly 40 per cent of the labour force. The seventeen boroughs with the highest unemployment (shown in black) account for 45 per cent of all unemployed in the city, but represent only 26 per cent of the labour force. Unemployment in all areas is higher than the national average, and in all areas the majority of unemployed are of low educational background (Gemeente Rotterdam 1987). Districts

Percentage of active residents unemployed

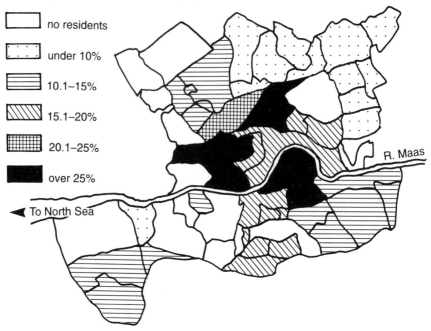

Figure 6.1 Unemployment rates in different areas of Rotterdam, 1990
Source: Gemeente Rotterdam, 1991

with high unemployment are unstable in the sense of frequent transfers in housing within the area or to nearby areas. Frequent moves can cause disruption to education, also estrangement from the local community making informal networking on job opportunities less accessible. Closures of industries and loss of port jobs, as has been mentioned, occurred in or near areas of higher unemployment, while growth of jobs, until recently, has been greater in outer suburban areas.

The major problems in Rotterdam result from changes in economic structure in the last forty years, and particularly the losses of manufacturing and harbour jobs in the late 1970s and early 1980s. These resulted not only in a new economy dependent on the service sector, but a fall in overall employment particularly within the city itself. The mismatch in skills resulting has not been rectified, and it is those with low educational levels and low skills who form the bulk of the unemployed. Lower level part-time jobs have been absorbed by an increase in women's participation in the labour force. The highest rates of unemployment were amongst the young but there was more short-term unemployed in this age group as is to be expected. The most worrying element is the very high proportion of long-term unemployed which has risen for all age groups in the past few years. This follows the pattern of labour queue theory, where those recently unemployed get jobs first, and the semi-skilled take up unskilled jobs. This has led to a 'consensus between civil servants and the long-term unemployed that they are unemployable'.[4] Accordingly city policy has recognised this in the policy on 'social renewal' discussed below. The group most at risk of unemployment are non-Dutch, especially workers from the Antilles, Surinam, Turkey and Morocco. They have twice the propensity to unemployment of Dutch workers; are more likely to be long-term unemployed (as the outflow of migrants from unemployment is lower than the inflow into it); have lower levels of educational attainments; and are more likely to live in areas of high unemployment. Unemployment is highly localised in inner city areas and to the south of the river reflecting the clustering of poorer residents and the location of employment losses. However, even in the suburbs, unemployment is higher than the national average.

In this context policies towards the unemployed in Rotterdam will be examined and evaluated.

Organisational structures and employment policy

At national level the Ministry of Social Affairs and Employment is responsible for health and safety of those at work, incomes policy and government, employment policy, also the development of social security policy. At the beginning of 1991 the structure within the ministry responsible for making Dutch employment policy underwent radical change. Central government was no longer the sole employment policy maker and a Central Employment Board (CBA) was set up with tripartite representation from central government, employers federations and employees organisations, all with equal responsibility. Policy implementation was decentralised to twenty-eight regional boards (RBAs) again dividing the responsibility in a tripartite system with government seats being taken up by local authority representatives. Once national policy has been established by the CBA, each RBA decides what is needed and how it will tackle labour market problems in its area. The national board assigns funds to regions on the basis of the level of unemployment and work opportunity figures in the region.

The general policies and targets set out are as follows:

1 to fill three quarters of vacancies of the Employment Service with unemployed persons, including women returners;
2 to reduce significantly the level of long-term unemployment;
3 to reduce significantly unemployment among ethnic minorities;
4 to provide equal opportunities for women;
5 to bring about a sharp reduction in youth unemployment;
6 to rehabilitate those partially incapable of work;
7 to have more preventative policing by promoting education more tailored to the needs of the labour market.

Private agencies and educational institutes can compete for training assignments with the Vocational Training Centre (CV) and Vocational Orientation and Preparation (CBB). Most policy is, however, implemented by local Employment Service offices and Vocational Training Centres. Total expenditure for the Employment Service in the Netherlands was 2.14 billion guilders of which central contribution provided 633 million, regional contribution was 1.28 billion, and the ESF 226 million.[5]

The city government of Rotterdam plays an important role. Rotterdam is an RBA, and the local authority has an important impact on decisions concerning what policies to implement and how to allocate expenditure on various programmes.

Unemployment Benefit and Income Support

Werkloosheidswet (WW) – Unemployment Benefit

Contributory Unemployment Benefit provides 70 per cent of the last earned daily wage (up to a maximum of 278.75 guilders). Those who have worked at least twenty-six weeks in the previous twelve months are entitled to benefits for six months. To claim benefit for a longer period workers must have been in employment for three out of the five previous years.

Those who have cared for children under 6 years of age have the period of care added to the employment record, plus half the years spent caring for children aged 6 to 12 years. The duration of benefit depends on calculated years of employment, for example a maximum of five years benefit can be claimed for forty or more working years. Those over 57½ can claim up to the age of 65. Income from partners is not taken into account when calculating benefit entitlement.

National Assistance (ABW) and State Group Regulation for Unemployed Workers (RWW)

For those who are not eligible, or are no longer eligible for WW, income maintenance can be claimed. Recipients must be registered as job seekers with the Employment Service. Any income of partners,[6] alimony and social security benefit are deducted, plus savings taken into account. ABW is 70 per cent of the statutory minimum wage (see Table 6.9). ABW can be claimed for an indefinite period, if the recipient is eligible. The rate paid depends also on age as the minimum wage depends on age (see next section).

Income Provision for Older or Partially Disabled Workers (IOAW)

This benefit is for persons aged between 50 and 57½ and the partially disabled who have run out of WW (Unemployment Benefit). The rate for a

Table 6.9 Example of the relationships of ABW to minimum wage, 1991

	Social security (guilders) per month	Minimum wage net + child benefit (guilders) per month
Single person	1,128	1,525
One parent + children	1,450	1,645
Couple	1,600	1,599
Couple with two children	1,600	1,625

Source: Rotterdam Werkt (1992)

couple, in 1991, was 2,463.72 guilders per month, and for single persons 1,829.42 guilders per month.

Disablement Insurance (WAO) and General Disablement Benefit (AAW)

Both of the above apply to the disabled. WAO is for those unfit for work after 52 weeks of disability. The amount depends on the degree of incapacity and the last earned wage of the claimant. Those not entitled to WAO can claim AAW. Claimants must be over 18 years of age and had an earned income for a year preceding incapacity to work. The amount depends on degree of incapacity, but a disabled worker can claim supplements if total family income is less than the social minimum.

Minimum wage and social minimum

Employers must pay at least the statutory minimum wage which varies according to age. In July 1991 this was 561 guilders per month for those aged 15–19; 1001 guilders per month for those aged 20–23; and 1,580 guilders per month for those over 23 years of age.

If income falls under a certain amount a supplement can be claimed to make up income to a social minimum. The social minimum per month for those over 23 was 1,471.47 guilders for a single person and 2,102.10 for a couple. If, therefore, one of a couple was earning the minimum wage but the other partner was not working and had no other source of income it would be made up to this social minimum. It is argued by Van Rintel (1986) that the legal minimum wage and social security system acts as a bottleneck and deterrent to young people entering the labour market. It is also reported by the municipality that it is a problem to get people to work and gain job experience in labour pools, as only minimum wage levels are paid, and for families the social service payment is equivalent to minimum wage (Gemeente Rotterdam 1987). Between 1975 and 1991 the number of unemployed receiving various forms of benefit in Rotterdam went from ten thousand to nearly thirty-seven thousand people.

Active labour market policies

General policies applying to groups who do not have special difficulties in the labour market, where special groups such as women, ethnic minorities and the long-term unemployed do not have priority are:

Vocational Training Centres (CV)

The aim of this scheme is to provide supplementary training to those who are unemployed or whose jobs are at risk. The centres provide both full-time and part-time day courses geared to present and future needs of the labour market. Unemployed workers retain their unemployment benefit while training. The schemes are organised by the Regional Employment Board. Nationally the drop out rate is 28 per cent, but this is often a result of finding employment. Eighty per cent of participants who complete training find employment at the end of the course. The cost per person trained was 7,342 guilders in 1990. Linked to training is the:

Framework Regulation for Training

This is to contribute to the expenses of those in CV schemes by making allowances to workers or employees in the form of wage costs, travel costs, child care costs and for development of training programmes by employers. Expenses for the unemployed are fully covered. Subsidies to employers are a maximum of 50 per cent of the cost. This is organised by Employment Offices. The average cost per applicant in 1989 was 3,600 guilders.

Training Scheme for Employees in the Private Sector (SSWB)

Subsidies are available to businesses, or joint training ventures of businesses and employees. They are given mainly to small and medium sized enterprises. The subsidies are allowed towards setting up a training infrastructure in the firm, compiling plans for training, developing and testing courses, and to provide information on training to entrepreneurs. Trade unions must be consulted on schemes. Subsidies cover between 50 and 70 per cent of the cost to a maximum of 150,000 guilders for regional projects. The scheme is organised by the Ministry of Economic Affairs.

Complementary Benefit Scheme for the Self-Employed (BZ)

The aim of this scheme is to give support to those unemployed who wish to start up a business. It is open to all the unemployed drawing benefit or income maintenance and those under threat of unemployment. It also applies to those on a low rate of disability allowance. People who are self-sufficient or whose partners have sufficient 'social income' cannot apply.

The new company set up must be viable and a positive report from an advisory body is required before support is given. The support available consists of income supplement plus the possibility of a loan, a maximum of 40,000 guilders in 1991. Income supplement is given for a six month period and can be extended in exceptional cases. One important point to note is that if growth in the economy stagnates and the prospects for small new businesses are poor, BZ is discontinued until the general economy picks up. BZ assistance is run by the City Social Services department.

Jobclubs (SOL)

The aim of Jobclubs is to help unemployed participants to find jobs as quickly as possible. The largest group are the unemployed who are expected to be able to find a job after job application training. The scheme involves four half days of training with two supervisors to every fifteen unemployed workers. The duration of Jobclub participation is between twelve and eighteen weeks. The approximate cost per place in 1990 was 2,500 guilders. The scheme is organised by the Employment Office.

Wage cost reduction at Minimum Wage Level (WLOM)

Minimum wage levels have been perceived as an obstacle to employment for some employers. The aim of this scheme is to improve the position of adult workers over 23 years of age whose jobs are threatened by minimum wage costs. Employers receive a subsidy of 3,200 guilders per annum for full-time workers, which is approximately 10 per cent of minimum wage costs, and a smaller subsidy for part-time workers. The subsidy is deducted from tax and social security payments made by employers each quarter. Finance is from AAW/AWBZ funds. The scheme was introduced in 1990 and intended to run for four years. It is organised by Employment Offices.

Many schemes are intended to help various groups of disadvantaged workers. These will be described first followed by programmes aimed specifically at the young, the long-term unemployed, ethnic minorities, women and the disabled.

Primary Job-related Adult Education (PBVE)

PBVE provides training for those over 18 years of age who have only a low level of formal education. Priority is given to members of ethnic minorities, women returners to the labour market, and the disabled who are unemployed or under threat of unemployment. The courses are designed to allow these groups to participate in higher level training schemes by giving preparatory courses. The cost per place is 3,200 guilders. Courses are organised by the Regional Education Office which then obtains training contracts from RBAs. The national drop out rate was high at 35 per cent in 1990 (MISEP 1991).

Labour Pools (BP)

The aim of Labour Pools is to place the difficult-to-place unemployed in supernumerary jobs in both the public and private sector. It is open to the unemployed whether they are eligible for benefits or not. Candidates are selected by Employment Officers after reorientation interviews. Jobs are temporary and are to give workers experience to make integration into the formal labour market less of a problem. Minimum wages and minimum holiday bonus are paid plus travel expenses. Finance comes from social security funds and the CBA. The approximate cost per place per annum was 36,100 guilders in 1991. The scheme ran from 1990 to 1994.

Youth unemployment programmes

Pre-Apprenticeship Training

The aim is to facilitate entry to apprenticeships for those under 21 years of age, who have incomplete and basic preliminary education, to enable them to undertake formal apprenticeships. The maximum subsidy is 8,500 guilders per person. If the unemployed young person does not transfer to an apprenticeship the subsidy is less – 5,000 guilders. Organisation is by RBA.

Youth Employment Guarantee Act (JWG)

The aim of JWG is to offer young workers, aged 16 to 21 years of age, and those unemployed for over six months aged 21 to 26, combined training and work experience to enable them to get a job. Work experience can be created in the public or voluntary sectors, or under the same conditions in the private sector. The work must satisfy the 'additionality requirement', i.e. it must be a supernumerary job causing no displacement effect. Participants are required to work a thirty-two hour week from 1992 onwards. The state reimburses local authorities for all wage costs based on hourly statutory minimum wage according to age. For every young person there is a subsidy of 150 guilders to cover implementation costs. The cost per place in 1992 was approximately 15,000 guilders per annum for each young beneficiary. The local authority is responsible for implementing JWG.

114

Apprenticeship Vocational Training Grants Scheme (BVL)

This scheme contributes towards training costs in apprenticeships. It is targeted at workers joining the first year of preliminary training courses and those admitted to advanced apprenticeship courses. There is an extra subsidy available for young women to train in traditionally male areas of employment, also extra subsidy for ethnic minority members and the disabled young.

In 1991 the level of subsidy was 3,500 guilders per apprentice, with an extra subsidy for special groups of 3,000 guilders per annum. At least 80 per cent of the subsidy goes to employers to offset costs, but not necessarily the same proportion of extra subsidy. Nationally in 1990 women comprised 29 per cent of participants and ethnic minorities 3 per cent.

Centres for Vocational Orientation and Preparation (CBB)

The aim of CBB is to improve the employment chances of young people who for socio-cultural reasons are disadvantaged and for whom existing training provisions are insufficient. Participants must be over 16 years of age. The national target is for 50 per cent of places to be filled by ethnic minorities. Courses are designed to eliminate deficiencies of knowledge and social skills and, for non-Dutch participants, to give a good command of Dutch language, society and labour relations. The approximate annual cost in 1990 was 13,000 guilders per place. The maximum length of the programme was twelve months. The scheme is run by the local authority (City of Rotterdam). Nationally the scheme had a 50 per cent drop out rate. Of those completing the course 45 per cent found a job, 25 per cent went on to further training and 25 per cent became unemployed.

Schemes for the long-term unemployed

Re-orientation Interview (HOG)

The aim of this programme is to promote labour market reintegration of those unemployed for longer than three years through individual counselling. Plans are drawn up with the unemployed person geared to training, work experience and placement. Ethnic minority participants are given a re-orientation interview after two years of unemployment. All potential beneficiaries are invited to a re-orientation interview by the Employment Office who run the scheme together with Municipal Social Services. The vast majority of those eligible attend an interview and nationally 54 per cent had an action plan agreed. For 23 per cent there was 'no plan possible' (MISEP 1991).

Integration into Working Life (KRA)

KRA aims to find the long-term unemployed (those without work for longer than two years, or one year if a member of an ethnic minority group) regular jobs or work experience. The scheme is also open to young people who have been on employment initiatives or JWG and are still without work after six months. The scheme has two parts. For the above target groups employers are offered a wage cost subsidy for supervision and training plus exemption from social security contributions for a maximum of four years, if they offer employment to one of the target groups. The subsidy was 4,000 guilders per year, or 6,000 per year if the worker had been out of work for longer than three years. Work experience under KRA is available to those unemployed for more than three years, or in the case of ethnic minorities more than two years. Jobs must be 'additional' and can be in either the public or private sector. Subsidy in 1990 was available at the rate of 22,000 guilders per worker in the public sector and 15,000 guilders per annum in the private sector.

Temporary Employment Refund Scheme (VU)

The aim of this scheme is to enable the long-term unemployed to acquire sufficient work experience through temporary employment that they are able to gain regular employment. The participants are those unemployed for over two years, or one year if the unemployed person belongs to an ethnic minority, and those who have already participated in training schemes for at least six months but are unemployed. After fifty days employment the worker is no longer considered to be in the above categories.

Social Renewal and employment in Rotterdam

Rotterdam believes in principle that people who receive benefits should be used productively (Gemeente Rotterdam 1991). They therefore took the initiative in giving paid jobs to people who would otherwise probably never have entered the formal labour market. In 1989 the city started by providing experimentally three hundred jobs in the community. This scheme was incorporated into what is known as the Social Renewal Programme set up in 1991. The philosophy behind the programme is to try and combine social and economic needs within particular areas of disadvantage and high unemployment in the city. Values of duties and responsibilities of both the state and individuals are incorporated in the plan. Renewal refers not only to investment in housing and environmental improvement, but also in the life chances and self esteem of individuals via employment in socially useful jobs. It is hoped that all those unemployed over three years who have low qualifications and poor prospects of work, which accounts for 5,000 people, can be offered permanent work in the community. All work is provided by the public sector and has to be agreed with trade unions as comprising additional work, not displacing existing jobs in any way. Participants are paid at minimum wage level and a contract is offered by local government covering the rest of working life. There is no compulsion to join the scheme and no loss of benefit for adults not taking part. In 1992 eight hundred long-term unemployed had joined the scheme. Highest unemployment levels (see Figure 6.1) are seen on both sides of the river in Charlois, Eiselmonde, Audenworden, Cool and Krossweg. The aim is to match jobs to people within their neighbourhood. Half of the participants were from ethnic minorities and 17 per cent were women. If people do not want to work in their own neighbourhood they are given the choice of working in other areas. The sort of work available is, for example, assistant caretakers in schools, car park safety officers, street cleaners, child care assistants.

One of the problems found was that many volunteers for the scheme were not physically healthy enough to undertake work, and that long-term unemployment and the stress it entails had taken a toll on health.

The scheme is organised by the city in cooperation with the social security system, the unions and employees, and is financed by the city and social security. Since a high degree of supervision is needed and for every five participants there may be one supervisor in charge who is paid a full salary, plus equipment costs per worker, on top of the minimum wage it is estimated that each job costs the city an additional 20,000 guilders per annum.[7] The total cost of community employment is, therefore, around 39,000 guilders per year, or 24,000 guilders more than income maintenance payments for the long-term unemployed.

Ethnic minority unemployed programmes

Apart from special classes in the Dutch language there is no special policy of identification for ethnic minorities. They are, however, a priority group in many of the above schemes. They are priority entrants for PBVE, CBB and KRA and employers are given additional subsidies in the BVL scheme for taking on workers from ethnic minorities. Ethnic minorities also constitute half the contracts given under the social renewal scheme in Rotterdam. There are three centres in Rotterdam providing job information and help with job applications with sections for ethnic minorities needing special help and for the disabled. Unlike in France it is not illegal to discriminate positively in favour of ethnic minorities 'positive discrimination is built into Dutch society'.[8]

Programmes for unemployed women

Women's Vocational Schools (VVS)

Women's Vocational Schools aim to train women with few qualifications, aged over 25, who have either never had a job or wish to return to employment.

They are trained in traditionally male dominated occupations such as computer science or business. Training must assist the women to find jobs or start up their own business. The scheme is organised by the RBA. Courses last around ten months on a three day a week basis, and the annual cost for a participant in 1991 was 14,000 guilders. Subsidy from the ESF is available for this scheme.

Women are also given extra subsidy on BVL apprenticeships and priority for training in the PBVE scheme.

Schemes to help the disabled unemployed

Temporary Employment Agency (START)

The aim of START is to provide temporary placement for difficult-to-place adults including the disabled. It was set up in 1977 and is closely linked to the Employment Office (Rotterdam Werkt). START is an independent legal body and works without subsidy.

Sheltered Employment (WSW)

WSW aims to create possibilities for disabled people who are able to work, enabling them to work in an adapted work situation designed for those where mental or physical disabilities rule out regular employment. It also aims to promote the capacity to work of the disabled. Local authorities have responsibility for sheltered employment and receive subsidies from the Ministry of Social Affairs and Employment. They are also awarded a financial incentive by being given an extra sum for every employee who transfers out of sheltered employment into the formal labour market. The approximate cost per place was 41,740 guilders in 1990 (MISEP 1991).

The Temporary Employment Refund Scheme (VU) described for the long-term unemployed also applies to the disabled.

The above schemes are financed in Rotterdam by a mixture of social employment provision by the city, contributions from the RBA and funding from the ESF (see Table 6.10). Expenditure per unemployed worker was, therefore, approximately 7,400 guilders. The total number on training and work experience courses during 1991 was 12,635.

Urban planning and regeneration policy and unemployment

Urban planning and development is the responsibility of the City Development Corporation, a part of local government in Rotterdam. There used to be many different agencies dealing with development but, from 1991, planning, economic development, administration and unemployment have been coordinated. The major role of the CDC is to deal with property

Table 6.10 Finance of employment schemes,
Rotterdam, 1992

Schemes	Guilders (million)
Social Employment provision	145
Job Pool	85
JWG	10
Other Local Authority schemes	7
Contribution RBA	108
ESF funding	15
Total	370

Source: Rotterdam Werkt (1992)

developers and sell land for 'necessary buildings'. City planners decide what is 'necessary' and try to attract relevant developers not by direct financial subsidy but by the flexible pricing of the land they own for sale. An example of this was to sell the land for a leisure and swimming pool complex 'Tropicana' in an inner area next to the waterfront to the developer for one guilder. The port is still the mainstay of the local economy but the CDC is helping to expand other activities, some of which, like banking and marine insurance, are linked to the port activities.

The main area due for development in the 1990s is the island areas to the south of central Rotterdam next to an area of very high unemployment. This site is to be developed for commercial use and headquarter offices, but, especially for the latter type of project, there are difficulties, as the city is in competition with Amsterdam. In the retailing sector shopping became more suburbanised in the 1980s, but city policy in the 1990s is only to give approval for large units such as motor or furniture sales in out of town areas. No integrated shopping malls are approved. The main plan is to extend shopping facilities in the central areas by building a large underground shopping complex for rent, with luxury shopping and department stores. This is aimed at increasing the quality of facilities in the city and giving an international atmosphere and status to the city. It will also provide more jobs centrally, initially in building and later in commercial and retailing sectors.

The CDC has tried to require new activities in the past to take on a percentage of unemployed workers for the new jobs created, but now assesses what the new activity will need in the way of skills, and trains the unemployed in the relevant skills before the project is completed. It has found using this new method of moral persuasion more effective in placing the unemployed.

Urban renewal projects for the poorest areas in the city have also taken into account employment factors. The areas of housing are rebuilt or improved, commercial and other business property is also renovated, with municipal subsidies amounting to 12–13 million guilders a year. If businesses are required to relocate for environmental reason they are provided premises on twenty industrial estates. Because renewal has not driven business out, half of the 18,000 businesses in the city are within urban renewal priority zones and employ 78,000 people.

Public transportation in the city consists of an extensive underground system, trams and railways. The latter serves both suburban ring areas and the wider travel-to-work area. The system is interlinked in its fare system, and a flat fare system operates on trams and the underground. The labour market area of Rotterdam stretches some sixty kilometres, partly because of easy and cheap access. It also means that 50 per cent of jobs within the city are taken up by people living outside the city.

EVALUATION OF MEASURES AFFECTING THE UNEMPLOYED IN ROTTERDAM

Changes in the economic structure of Rotterdam since the 1950s resulted firstly in an expansion of employment and encouragement of migration into the city, and subsequently a fall in employment in the sectors that had previously increased – transportation, construction and manufacturing. The process entailed fewer jobs overall for a growing working population and also a mismatch of skills needed for the growing service sectors of the economy. The 1980s saw a growth in female participation in the labour force, as was the case throughout Europe. Women took on many of the low-skilled service sector jobs with over half the female workforce working part-time and, therefore, having low take-home pay. Unemployment in the period under study was around one fifth of those registered unemployed but probably nearer 30 per cent if joblessness had been recorded. Although women's rate of unemployment was lower than that for men, for the youngest age groups where activity rates were similar, the rates were similar. A longer term problem can be seen for educated women returners, and in the fact that women could become isolated in low-skill service jobs with relatively low incomes. This factor is recognised by the special vocational training programme for women where high level and expensive training is available, also training in traditional male work areas.

Educational qualifications are crucial to the propensity to unemployment. Nearly 80 per cent of the registered unemployed are of low educational level and unskilled. The BVE scheme and Vocational Training Centres address this problem, and for the short-term unemployed they have high success rates in terms of participants finding employment at the end of training.

The young have only a slightly higher propensity to be unemployed than the active population as a whole. As in other European cities the emphasis is on training, but in Rotterdam one level of training is designed to lead to a higher level CBB, pre-apprenticeship training, BVL, and ideally to apprenticeships if participants are capable of this. The amount of subsidy to training the young can be as high as 13,000 guilders per place. Young people are also given work experience to help reintegration. No income benefits are paid out to those who refuse to participate in an employment scheme so participation rates are high for all sectors of the young.

Linked to education and skill levels is the very high incidence of long-term unemployed amongst those with low educational levels. Nearly two thirds of those out of work are long-term unemployed and nearly all of these have low educational attainments and low skill levels. The problem is most acute in older workers and those from ethnic minorities. Ethnic minorities have priority on various training programmes for the unemployed but the main emphasis is to provide help for reintegration into the labour market (KRA) through subsidies to employers for training and supervision on the job. Work experience can only be provided by 'additional' jobs, thus avoiding the displacement and substitution effects on the labour market that similar schemes can have elsewhere. It is in the field of 'social renewal' employment initiatives that Rotterdam is in the lead in the Netherlands and in Europe as a whole. It was the first city to offer lifetime contracts to the very long-term unemployed, recognising both the wastage of resources that unemployment represents and the contribution that community work can make to social welfare in an area, and to the individual concerned. It also represents official recognition of the fact that many of the long-term unemployed are unemployable on the formal labour market, and something should be done about it. The city estimates (Gemeente Rotterdam 1991) that there will probably be a need in the coming years for around ten thousand of these community based jobs in Rotterdam, and is planning on that basis. The scheme itself involves no displacement of existing workers or substitution for jobs that would be created in the public sector. In fact it acts as a creator of new employment in the formal public sector labour market by requiring organisers and supervisors of community workers. This form of employment policy is, however, expensive and entails spending the equivalent of more than £8,000 per year per job than if the unemployed person relied on income maintenance. The effects on local communities where unemployment is high and where the scheme was first implemented is very beneficial in raising the morale of the residents and in offering a high level of social welfare provision through useful employment.

Local planning and economic development policy takes into account locational factors in unemployment both in urban renewal policy and in the policy of reurbanisation of economic activity to try and make up for the loss of inner area jobs caused by market suburbanisation of activity in the 1970s and early 1980s. It is successful in doing this, but many more jobs need to be created in the city if the unemployed are to find work. Job creation has not kept pace with the demand for work.

Although unemployment is highly localised with nearly half the unemployed in a very small number of districts, the location of new employment is not a problem, nor is the cost of access to available work anywhere in the city, since the city has an excellent, cheap and extensive public transportation system.

One criticism which is often made in relation to unemployment in the Netherlands is that unemployment is the result of high levels of unemployment benefit. This would be difficult to assert for the Netherlands as a whole where unemployment was only 5 per cent in 1990, but could perhaps be applied to job search. Research has shown that in Rotterdam the level of job search in a very tight labour market becomes much more intensive when unemployment benefit entitlement runs out. Another passive labour market measure said to be related to long-term unemployment is the relatively high level of income support, or social assistance, in relation to the minimum wage. Income support is very generous by European standards and is roughly twice the amount in real terms of income support in Britain. As shown in Table 6.9, for a couple it is similar to minimum wage levels. The local authority has reported difficulties in trying to recruit the unemployed to work schemes that pay only minimum wage, so clearly income support does have some deterrent effect. The minimum wage may also be too high to support certain types of job. This is recognised by the WLOM policy where there is a wage cost subsidy for certain firms who cannot afford to keep on workers at the legal minimum remuneration. This to some extent recognises that while a minimum wage is socially desirable it may not always be economically feasible to pay it.

Overall the policies in operation for the unemployed in Rotterdam are of high quality, well directed towards the various groups at risk and take account of the fact that the unemployed are people and not just units of labour. It is difficult, however, in modern urban economies to provide suitable market employment for large numbers of low-education/low-skill workers. This problem can only be solved by starting within the education system itself to ensure that the cycle of unemployability does not recur in future generations of workers. It could be argued that the innovative policy of community work for the unemployable is 'giving up' on large sectors of the unemployed, but on the other hand it may be that Rotterdam is more realistic in expectations for large sectors of the unemployed than other cities are prepared to be.

7

BARCELONA

INTRODUCTION

Barcelona, Spain's second largest city and the capital of the region of Catalonia, is situated on the northern Mediterranean coast of Spain and has been a port since Roman times. It was an important trading centre in the Middle Ages. The city changed little until the second half of the nineteenth century when development of the Eixample, a new, grid-iron, planned development around the old medieval town took place, to accommodate the expansion of population and wealth resulting from new industrial and commercial enterprises. The major industry, as in Manchester, was textiles (there is in fact a district of the city called Manchester!) which continued to be the dominant manufacturing sector until the 1960s. Barcelona was the most developed industrial area of Spain, both before and after the Civil War, and was also the area with the highest growth of employment and incomes. From the 1950s, engineering and metal industries, chemicals and construction replaced textiles as the main employers. The need for a growing labour force within these industries boosted immigration, largely from the poorer agricultural regions of the south, particularly Andalusia. Over the twenty years from 1950 to 1970 the city grew from just over one million inhabitants to one and three quarter million. At the same time the outlying municipalities trebled in size. The Barcelona area grew in population at the rate of one hundred thousand people per year in this period. By 1970 half the population were immigrants from Castilian speaking Spain, working largely in unskilled and semi-skilled occupations in construction and transportation. Native Catalan workers were better educated and tended to work in the higher paid service and manufacturing sectors. Immigrant families initially concentrated in shanty towns to the west and south of the city, but in the 1960s tenement blocks were built in areas between the old nineteenth-century city and the new industrial estates, and those who could afford to buy them moved. Quality was low and density high. They formed many of the new poor areas of Barcelona.

The recession caused by the oil price rise of 1973 hit Barcelona very hard and had a negative effect on manufacturing industry, its prime activity. Income per head in Catalonia grew more slowly than for Spain as a whole, although Barcelona's income per head was still higher, but the region's and city's unemployment rate was above the national average for the remainder of the 1970s and early 1980s. Older industrial areas like Poble Nou declined with the closures of factories and workshops.

Three years after the death of Franco, democracy was introduced through the new Spanish constitution of 1978. Politics played an important part in the economic development of the city in the sense that Catalonia was the region most opposed to Franco in the Civil War, and continued in the 1970s to fight for workers' rights and greater democratisation of the system with mass protests and strikes (Balfour 1989). Apart from the fact that the area could expect no special favours because of this, governors and mayors were appointed by central government prior to 1979 and local councils had no autonomy and very little in the way of financial resources either to improve social conditions in the city or to promote the economy. Since 1979 Barcelona City Council has assumed an economic role, but it took nearly ten years to sort out a system of autonomous financing, resulting in difficulties in solving infrastructure problems, and congestion, poor social services and inadequate resources to aid economic development (Garcia 1991). Local government in the 1980s took various initiatives that affected employment. In 1984 a policy was adopted to try and attract investment from other European countries, the USA and Japan by various forms of subsidy. Barcelona's major coup was to attract the 1992 Olympic Games, and via the investment of seventy-five billion pesetas in infrastructure (telecommunications, transport and housing in particular) to upgrade business facilities in the city and raise its international profile. It was hoped that this would promote further investment in restructuring the local economy, and making the city a development pole in the wider region. The Olympic effect was dramatic in the labour market, reducing unemployment and causing some skill shortages. Positive effects were gained in the improvement of road links, public transportation, cultural and leisure facilities, all increasing the quality of life. Negative effects have been noted in the rise in land prices, building prices and house prices, and the unsuitability of Olympic housing for the needs, or ability to pay, of those needing homes. Future plans for the local economy and employment will be discussed later in the chapter.

Since the influx of immigrants in the 1950s and 1960s the population of the city has more or less stabilised (see Table 7.1).

There has been some outward migration of city population, largely to neighbouring townships in the metropolis. Unlike other cities under study, where the exodus has been of more prosperous employed sectors seeking benefits of suburbanisation amongst similar higher-income earners, leaving a poor inner core, in Barcelona incomes in the city are higher than in outer areas. In 1985 disposable income per head in metropolitan areas outside the

Table 7.1 Population: Barcelona and Barcelona
Metropolitan Area (AMB), 1981–90

	1981	*1986*	*1990*
Barcelona	1,752,627	1,701,812	1,707,286
AMB	3,071,680	3,083,353	3,031,672

Source: ABM (1991)

city was only 66 per cent of that of city dwellers.[1] Housing is generally more desirable within the city. It is young families who move, through lack of space, to areas of new housing.

The size of the active population changed only slightly between 1981 and 1991, increasing by 0.5 per cent during the decade, despite the increased employment opportunities offered by Olympic prospects in the latter half of the period.

The overall activity rate in 1991 was 60.6 per cent. The activity rate for women has increased from around 20 per cent in 1980 to around 40 per cent in 1991.[2] This reflects social and cultural change in Barcelona since the advent of democracy. Since the active population has only increased by a small amount this implies that the percentage of active working males has reduced. Barcelona has a large student population of around one hundred and fifty thousand over 16 years old, who are classified inactive. Of those in work 60.8 per cent worked in the service sector, 30 per cent in manufacturing and 6.8 per cent in construction. The numbers and change by sector of employment between 1985 and 1988 are shown in Table 7.2.

Apart from a reduction in employment in relatively unimportant sectors, manufacturing overall gained 9 per cent employment, and construction and retail, hotel and repair sectors increased jobs available by over a third. After the economic difficulties of the early 1980s Barcelona's economy recovered. The sectors with greater growth indicate that this was almost certainly the effect of forward investment for the Olympic Games. Manufacturing, which was still losing jobs elsewhere in Europe, and where there had been thousands of jobs lost in Barcelona in the early part of the decade, had recouped some of these losses as the local economy grew. Loss of manufacturing jobs in the late 1970s and early 1980s meant that greater Barcelona and Catalonia had unemployment rates higher than the rest of Spain in 1985,[3] but this had changed by 1991 (see Table 7.3).

The number of registered unemployed in the city nearly halved in the six years from 1986–91, from 126,000 in 1986 to 66,000 in 1991. Unemployment also fell in the Barcelona metropolitan area but to a lesser extent, the city itself benefiting most from the positive effects of the Olympics and economic actions of local government.

Table 7.2 Workers by occupational sector, Barcelona, 1988

	1988	%	% change 1985–88
Primary	593	0.09	−2.80
Energy and water	10.475	1.53	−12.90
Minerals, chemicals	42.348	6.20	8.0
Metal industries	83.626	12.24	1.7
Other manufactures	83.670	12.25	−0.7
Construction/public works	42.520	6.23	37.2
Retail, hotels, repairs	140.634	20.59	33.60
Transport and communications	49.052	7.18	9.4
Financial services	81.710	11.96	18.5
Other services	143.595	21.03	13.7
Not classified	4.749	0.70	19.1
Total	682.972	100.0	14.1

Source: ADES, Barcelona (unpublished)

Note: Statistics prepared for the author by ADES

Table 7.3 Comparative unemployment rates in Barcelona, Catalonia and Spain, December 1991

	Barcelona	Catalonia	Spain
Active population	680.330[4]	2563.400	15157.000
Registered unemployed	62.295	270.354	2329.258
Unemployment rate	9.74%	10.55%	15.37%

Source: Barcelona Activa (1992)

UNEMPLOYMENT IN BARCELONA

The unemployment rate at the end of 1991 was, as shown, 9.7 per cent. This refers to those registered at local unemployment offices which, according to local employment agencies, underestimates the amount of joblessness by several percentage points (ADES 1989). An analysis of unemployment by age and sex is shown in Table 7.4.

Age and unemployment

One fifth of those unemployed were under 25 years of age, 39 per cent were aged 25–40, and 36 per cent were over 40 years old. The largest number of the unemployed were prime age workers. It is not possible to ascertain what proportion of the active population in each age group was unemployed. It does not appear that the young were more at risk of unemployment than workers of other ages in Barcelona. The city had a lower proportion of this age group as a percentage of total unemployed than either the region or country, where the young constituted just under a third of the total number unemployed. In Spain as a whole 37 per cent of the unemployed were under 25 years old. This may be because of higher educational levels in Barcelona (see p. 129–30), or low registration rates, or the positive effects of policy.

Male/female unemployment

Women, constituted 62 per cent of the total number unemployed in the city, despite the fact that their participation rate in the labour market was much lower than that of men. In Spain as a whole 23.7 per cent of women were unemployed in 1990 compared to 11.8 per cent in the European Union as a whole. For Barcelona published statistics do not exist on the activity rate of women and men, so all that can be said is that female unemployment rates were considerably higher in all age groups than male unemployment rates. A greater number of women than men were unemployed in all age groups except for those over 55 years of age. Nearly half of unemployed women were between the ages of 25 and 39, while only a third of male unemployment was in this age group. Women returners to the labour market find it most difficult to find employment, which, it has been suggested, is the result of attitudes in Spain to women working, as a result of forty years of the Franco regime when women were considered to be predominantly mothers not participants in the labour market.[5] Women in Barcelona also worked mainly in the textile and clothing industries which suffered high job losses. New activities required higher educational levels, and women in Barcelona have low levels of education overall (Blanch 1990). Part-time work is not easy to obtain in Barcelona, because of the rigid structure of labour contracts, except in the civil service where working hours are from 9am to 3pm. As a result 80 per cent of civil servants in the city, mainly in lower levels of

Table 7.4 Unemployment by age and sex, Barcelona, 1991

| Age | Male | | Female | |
	No.	*% of total*	*No.*	*% of total*
16–19	1,157	4.17	2,025	5.25
20–24	4,152	14.98	6,387	16.56
25–29	4,120	14.86	7,731	20.04
30–39	5,163	18.63	10,395	26.95
40–54	7,936	28.63	9,506	24.65
55–64	5,193	18.73	2,530	6.56
Total	27,721	100.00	38,574	100.00

Source: INEM Barcelona Activa (1991)

the hierarchy, are women. The growth in employment since 1986 has benefited men more than women as shown Figure 7.1.

While more men were unemployed in 1986, the growth of employment in construction and manufacturing reduced male unemployment by over thirty thousand workers, at the same time as women's unemployment reduced by less than twenty thousand.

The distribution by age of female unemployment changed a great deal after 1986; young women under 25 comprised 47 per cent of female unemployment in 1986 but was 22 per cent in 1991. The greatest rise in the proportion of female unemployment was for the 30–39 age group, up from 17 per cent to 26 per cent and for those aged 40–54, up from 14 per cent to 25 per cent. Unemployment amongst young females became much less of a problem than that of women returners in mid-life. The percentage of the

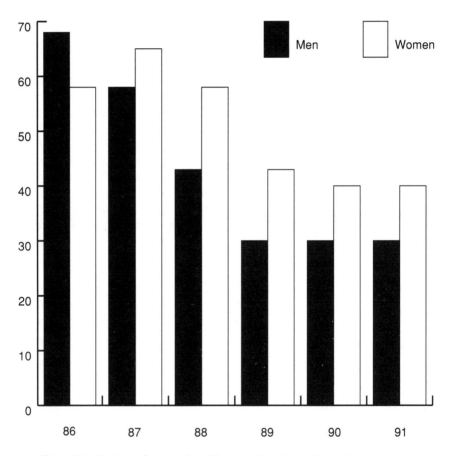

Figure 7.1 Registered unemployed by sex, Barcelona, December 1985–91
Source: Barcelona Activa

128

unemployed in Barcelona who are female, at 62 per cent is higher than the national rate of 51.6 per cent.

Unemployment and vacancies in the labour market
(National Statistical Institute, 1991)

Comparing the unemployed by previous sectors of employment with vacancies by sector gives some idea of changes in demand in the labour market and mismatch of skills in the local economy (see Table 7.5). Those unemployed from the manufacturing sector accounted for 28.9 per cent of those out of work, and those previously working in the service sector for 53.4 per cent of the unemployed. Vacancies in manufacturing were 13.9 per cent of the total and services 69.2 per cent. Vacancy levels in construction were higher than the proportion unemployed, reflecting the high demand for construction workers prior to the 1992 Olympics. The obvious mismatch between manufacturing local employment and services sector growth is a dominant feature of the Barcelona labour market. The likelihood for industrial workers to be reemployed in the same sector is much less than the likelihood of unemployed service sector workers finding employment. Redeployment of unskilled workers in industry to the services sector depends on training and initial level of education. Most service sector jobs require higher levels of education.

If we look at the registered unemployment in Barcelona by level of education, the greatest number have low levels of qualification (see Table 7.6).

Table 7.6 shows that those who have only completed primary education form 36.3 per cent of those unemployed and that together with the group who have left school at 15 they form nearly 60 per cent of the unemployed. The right-hand column shows the educational levels of the whole population of the city

Table 7.5 Registered unemployed and vacancies by sector, Barcelona, September 1991

Sector	Unemployed %	Vacancies %
Agriculture, Energy, Minerals	5.39	7.60
Metal Industries	9.51	5.87
Other Manufacturing	19.39	8.09
Construction	4.20	14.76
Retail, hotel, repairs	19.22	23.38
Transport and Communications	3.14	3.73
Financial Services	12.98	22.50
Other Services	18.20	19.57
Without previous employment	8.33	–
Total 5	100.00	100.00
Total number	66,285	26,074

Source: Barcelona Activa (1992)

Table 7.6 Registered unemployed in Barcelona by level of education, December 1991

Level of education	No.	% of total unemployed	Educational level of population (1986)
Illiterate	7	0.0	8.4
Primary, no certificate	205	0.3	27.2
Primary certificate	24,030	36.3	22.0
EGB	14,784	22.3	14.6
FP1/FP2	13,146	19.8	6.8
BUP	8,775	13.2	10.6
Titulacio Grau MIG	2,022	3.1	4.9
Titulacio Grau Superior	3,326	5.0	5.7
Total:	66,295	100.0	100.0

Source: AMB 1991, Barcelona Activa (1991)

Note: EGB is basic education to school leaving age; FP1 vocational training level 1 for ages 14–16; FP2 is second level vocational training for ages 16–18; BUP is academic secondary education equivalent to baccalaureate and Titulacio Grau MIG and Titulacio Grau Superior refer to those receiving higher education at lower and higher levels respectively.

in the 1986 survey of inhabitants. This is not a breakdown of the active population and would include people over retirement age, and so although it must be treated with great caution, it throws up some interesting points. Those with little or no education comprise over a third of the adult population but less than 1 per cent of the registered unemployed. Even allowing for the fact that these groups are less likely to register (ADES 1989), and so are under-represented in columns one and two, and that a higher proportion of elderly people belong to these groups, the likelihood of unemployment is probably still below that of those with higher levels of education. Those with primary certificates have an equal probability of unemployment to the size of their group, while those with some secondary education have a higher probability of unemployment than their group size would suggest. The people with higher education appear to have a propensity to unemployment in almost exact relation to their group size, i.e. you are no less likely to be unemployed if you have a degree.

Figure 7.2 shows that the growth in employment in Barcelona in the period 1986–91 reduced unemployment at all educational levels except EGB, had most effect for those with only primary education or FP1, and least effect on the groups with higher levels of education.

Long-term unemployment

There are no available statistics on duration of unemployment for Barcelona. In Spain as a whole in 1992 the long-term unemployed constituted 51 per cent of the total out of work.

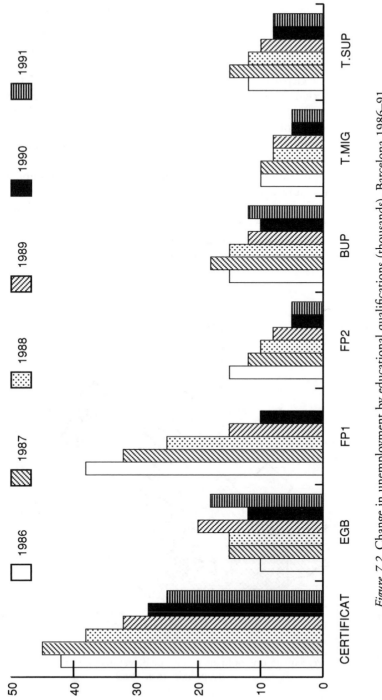

Figure 7.2 Change in unemployment by educational qualifications (thousands), Barcelona 1986–91

Source: Barcelona Activa (1991)

Urban factors in unemployment

Unlike Manchester and Rotterdam, the city of Barcelona overall has lower unemployment rates than many areas within the wider metropolitan region. This is illustrated in Figure 7.3.

Within the city itself unemployment varied by district from 5.6 per cent to 14.4 per cent of the active population in 1991. The districts shown in Figure 7.3 do not accord with administrative areas of the city but refer to local area offices of the Employment Office. They are fairly wide areas but within the Employment Services areas there are smaller districts where the unemployment rate was above 25 per cent. There are only thirteen offices serving a population of one and three quarter million. No complete information is available at ward level.

Figure 7.4 shows that central and northern areas of the city had lower unemployment rates than the old industrial areas of Poble Nou, Saint Andreu and Guineuta. Unemployment was also higher in the newer suburban areas built to house the immigrants of earlier decades mentioned before. While there is some

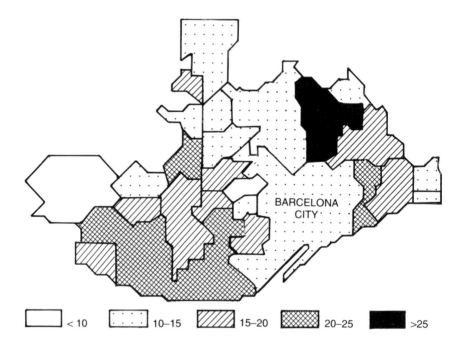

Figure 7.3 Percentage unemployment rate in Barcelona and other districts of the metropolitan area, 1989

Source: AMB (1991)

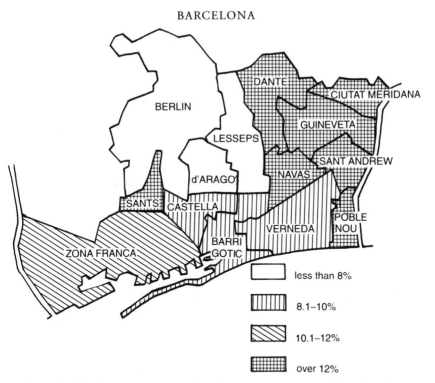

Figure 7.4 Registered unemployed by district employment offices, Barcelona, December 1991

Source: Ajuntament de Barcelona, Bulleti del Mercat Local de Treball, Barcelona (December 1991)

variation in unemployment rates between areas of the city they are not as wide as in Montpellier, Rotterdam and Manchester, as shown in Figure 7.4. This may be because smaller municipal districts previously used for comparison may show much greater variations. It may also be to do with the fact that in some areas, those without a job, particularly the illiterate and those of lower educational attainment, do not register as unemployed, according to officials. Neighbourhoods with higher proportions of those workers are found in Saint Andreu, Poble Nou and Zona Franca (ADES 1989). Most of the loss of manufacturing jobs has been in these areas of the city and growth of employment has been in tourism, financial and other services in more central areas of the city.

The change in types of employment may explain spatial differences in employment levels. Even allowing for the fact that differences in unemployment may have been greater between areas than official statistics suggest, rates did not vary a great deal, certainly not by the amounts experienced elsewhere. Two factors might account for this. One is that public transportation between areas of the city is extensive with a network of metro lines and integrated bus services. There is a cheap flat fare system in operation, journey times are fast and services frequent. The negative effects that lack of availability of access and high time and money costs of transportation can have on local labour markets, restricting job search to a very confined geographical area, do not appear to be present in Barcelona. Of those employed only 22.9 per cent live and work in the same Employment Office district, while 57.2 per cent work in other districts of the city, and 19.7 per cent outside the city area (Ajuntament de Barcelona 1990). The proportion of those employed working outside their own district does not differ significantly within different areas of the city.

The second reason may be to do with the fact that Barcelona has only a very tiny proportion of its population, less than 1 per cent, that is non-Spanish. There is, therefore, no ghettoisation of ethnic minorities, disadvantaged and discriminated against in labour markets, in certain sectors of the city. Older immigrant workers from the south, who speak only Castilian Spanish in a Catalan speaking city, have found difficulties in obtaining work, but they are spread over wide areas of the outer districts of the city. They currently form only a small part of the working population. Location of employment and cost and availability of transportation, together with ghettoisation of the poor and disadvantaged, which are urban factors in unemployment, do not appear to play such a large part in causing or perpetuating unemployment in Barcelona, as in other cities studied. Policy decisions have been taken, however, as will be shown, to concentrate resources in areas of the city with higher unemployment levels.

Barcelona has experienced a dramatic fall in unemployment levels since the mid 1980s with the great problem of youth unemployment falling from 30 per cent of all unemployment to 20 per cent in six years. This is not to say that youth unemployment is no longer a major problem, but that it has become less serious. More serious is the very high rate of female unemployment coupled with the rising participation rate of women in the labour market. Others most at risk are those made unemployed in the manufacturing sector, and those with only very basic educational qualifications, both groups out of line with the needs of the growing economy. One must remember that in 1991 the 'Olympic effect' was very strong in providing increased employment opportunities and, without this temporary demand, sustained planning of investment in the local economy will be needed to maintain the demand for labour within the city. Strategic plans of city government with this in mind will be discussed in a later section of this chapter. Firstly the policies towards the unemployment in Barcelona will be examined.

POLICIES TOWARDS THE UNEMPLOYED IN BARCELONA

Organisational structure

At national level in Spain the Ministry of Labour and Social Security (MTSS) has the responsibility for drafting, developing, evaluating and administering measures to promote employment and vocational training policy. It is also the central policy making body for social benefits. The body that administers employment policy is the National Employment Institute (INEM) which is autonomous but funded by the Ministry. Its function is to organise a nation-wide public employment service; assist workers in finding employment; promote workers' training; and administer and monitor unemployment benefit and subsidies for the promotion and protection of employment. INEM has offices at provincial, regional and local level. There are fourteen local offices in the city of Barcelona, and Vocational Training Centres (CFO) related to INEM to provide workers with locally needed vocational skills.

Also attached to the Ministry at national level is the General Vocational Training Council (CGFP). This is a tripartite body with equal representation from government, employers associations and trade unions. Its function is to propose to government a National Plan for Vocational Training (Plan FIP). A plan FIP was approved in 1985 and modified in 1990. The principles are:

• adaptation of the workplace to the new needs of the economy
• integration of vocational training with educational policy and employment policy
• co-ordination of activities of public and private sector
• participation by state, employers and workers.

Priority was to be given to those with greatest difficulty in finding employ-
ment. Schemes covering vocational training are financed by INEM out of contributions by employers (0.6 per cent of real wage) and employees (0.1 per cent of real wage) and contributions from the ESF.

At national level there is also the Economic and Social Council, a body issuing information and advice of a prescriptive nature on labour market policy to the Ministry. At city level the mayor's office set up a Department of Economic and Social Development (ADES) in 1984. Its aim was to generate the creation of employment, to encourage the unemployed to set up in business, and to respond to the training and professional needs of the city. Funding for the various projects came from the municipal budget, INEM, the Regional Government of Catalonia, the ESF and the ERDF.

Unemployment Benefit and Unemployment

Benefits for the unemployed in Spain take up over half the budget of the Ministry which spent nearly 1.6 billion pesetas in payments in 1992. There are two forms of benefit, unemployment insurance and unemployment assistance.

Unemployment Insurance

Beneficiaries must be contributors to the social security scheme and have paid contributions for a minimum of twelve months in the six years preceding unemployment. The amount received is linked to their previous wage and is 70 per cent for the first 180 days of entitlement and 60 per cent for days following. The duration of the benefit is dependent on the period of contributions in the previous six years. For example those having contributed for between a year and eighteen months will get 120 days' benefit, those who have contributed for the whole six years will get 720 days'. The monthly amount payable can under no circumstance be less than the level of national interprofessional wage (MISEP 1993) at the beginning of the period, nor more than 170 per cent of minimum wage except where the worker has dependents when it can be up to 220 per cent. The scheme is administered by INEM and financed by employers and employees contributions equal to 7.3 per cent of the wage (6.2 per cent of this paid by employers) plus a state contribution. The right to benefit starts on the first day of unemployment. Once Unemployment Insurance runs out the worker is then eligible for Unemployment Assistance.

Unemployment Assistance

Beneficiaries must be registered as job seekers and must not have refused suitable work. The unemployed who have exhausted contributory benefits are not automatically entitled to Assistance even if they are registered unemployed. In order to benefit they must have family responsibilities or, if without dependents, be over 45 years of age. Single persons younger than this cannot claim unless they are a returning emigrant worker; a released prisoner; have paid at least six months contributions previously and have been previously disabled; or workers over 52 years of age with at least six years unemployment contributions in their working life. Unemployment Assistance is 75 per cent of the minimum wage.

The duration of Unemployment Assistance is normally six months, renewable for a maximum of eighteen months, and depending on age and family responsibilities to thirty-six months. For workers over 52 years of age the benefit is paid until retirement. The scheme is administered by INEM.

Spain has no automatic social assistance for those who have no family dependents which means that young single workers receive no state benefits and must rely on the extended family to support them. Similarly the jobless who do not register for work at Employment Offices and are capable of work do not receive automatic assistance. Many of the unemployed live in great hardship. Of the 2,463,700 registered unemployed in Spain only 1,191,663 were receiving Unemployment Insurance or Unemployment Assistance in 1991. It would be difficult to argue that the generosity of benefit levels resulted in the high unemployment levels in this context.

Minimum wage

Legislation of January 1992 set a minimum wage at the following levels: full-time workers over 20 years of age receive 1,876 pesetas per day or 56,280 per month; full-time workers under 20 years of age receive 1,239 pesetas per day or 37,170 per month. Minimum rates of pay also apply for casual and temporary workers of 436 pesetas per hour for those over 18, and 288 pesetas per hour for those under 18.

Active labour market policies

The two main agencies dealing with policies for the unemployed and job creation in Barcelona are Barcelona Activa/ADES[6] and INEM. They concentrate most of their resources on districts within the city where unemployment is highest and job creation lowest, although programmes for the unemployed are available to people living in all areas of the city who qualify for particular programmes. Barcelona was seen as two cities (Ajuntament de Barcelona 1990), one with high levels of property ownership and high levels of professional and managerial workers (corresponding roughly to the lower areas of unemployment in Figure 7.4) and the other with predominantly unskilled workers of lower educational levels with higher unemployment. The aim is to increase economic activity, operate training schemes with a view to employment, promote initiatives to development and promote partnerships between the public and private sectors at district level, helping areas with the greatest socio-economic problems by integrated action.

Total expenditure in the city on programmes for the unemployed, job creation and economic development subsidies is shown in Table 7.7. Within the expenditure, programmes affecting different groups of the unemployed are described below, followed by policies to consume existing employment, and create jobs.

Table 7.7 Expenditure in Barcelona on employment creation and the unemployed, 1990

Source of funds	Amount (pesetas)	% of total expenditure
INEM of which:	1,343,967,971	28.9
FIP	183,929,492	
Other	1,160,038,479	
Municipality of Barcelona	2,601,520,782	56.0
European Social Fund	448,417,473	9.7
Catalonia Regional Gvt	67,482,187	1.5
Other external funds	180,701,107	3.9
Total[7]	4,642,089,521	100.00

Source: ADES. INEM (unpublished)

Note: Statistics prepared for the author by ADES

General policies

Workers over 25 years of age registered for less than a year

This part of the FIP national training plan allows for vocational training of adult short-term unemployed, and those in work whose jobs are threatened.

Workshop schools

Adult workers can attend workshop schools for building skills, both theory and practice, linked to the restoration of historic buildings and wider renewal projects and also the revival of building crafts. The length of the programme is between six and thirty months and participants receive 550 pesetas per day. This scheme is organised by INEM and operates nationally. The promoter of the projects are normally the municipal authorities who receive grants to finance teachers and premises. Grants are also available for transport, board and lodging costs of students and staff where necessary. The aim of the scheme is to stimulate entrepreneurial spirit in the trainees who are given advice and technical support to set up on their own, or as members of a co-op, once they have finished the course.

Measures to protect existing workers from unemployment

Support for maintaining jobs in cooperatives and workers' companies

Financial and technical support is available to decrease interest on loans for investment in these types of workplace and pay all the costs of technical assistance or training needed to keep the worker in employment.[8] The scheme is managed by INEM and financed by the national government. In addition to grants for setting up non-profit-making organisations and worker management schemes, Barcelona also has the PROGRESO programme for training managers of co-ops and supplying information to small businesses; and ENASIS, a programme to train experts to teach new technologies.

Temporary suspension and short-time working

The aim is to enable companies in difficulties as a result of economic or technical change to temporarily suspend the employment contracts of all or part of the workforce or to reduce normal working hours by up to one third. During temporary suspension the worker receives unemployment insurance. The scheme is administered by the Ministry of Labour and Social Security.

Vocational training for those in employment

Companies that are restructuring can apply to INEM for a grant to cover part of the wage costs while employees are being retrained for a new occupation or in new technologies or management techniques. The grant contributes to part of the wage cost and amounts to 50 per cent of the national minimum wage. It applies particularly to small companies and is not available to companies with over five hundred employees. It is a national scheme administered at a local level by INEM.

Practice work contracts

In order to foster the employment of skilled workers, contracts are organised by INEM to give these workers paid work and enable them to improve and apply their knowledge by work experience. The beneficiary must have a recognised academic or occupational diploma. The contracts are for not less than three months or more than three years. There are no financial incentives to employers.

Measures to help the young unemployed

There are 13,721 unemployed young people under 25 years of age, over 8,000 of them young women. Programmes are concerned with training and education, and work experience.

Aid for the young under 16

For young people who have left school with only very low educational levels the state provides supplementary general education or first level vocational training (FPI), paying the cost of teachers.

Vocational training of young people - training contract

This programme provides courses of vocational training with a certificate at the end of the course of Vocational Training in Practice. If the contract for training with a company is for at least six months the company receives a subsidy of 90 pesetas per hour of training. If the contract is in a training workshop the grant is 75 per cent of national minimum wage. Beneficiaries must be under 25 years of age. The training is adapted to the needs of the local labour market and is designed to help those whose qualifications are insufficient to enable them to enter the labour market. The scheme is run by INEM.

Vocational and work experience for FP2 level students, and university undergraduates

The aim of the national programme is to enable those young people without an employment contract to gain practical experience in a traineeship for a maximum of eighty days or four hundred hours. Bursaries are given to students of up to 800 pesetas per day, and to the companies up to 500 pesetas per day.

Youth Training Centres

Youth Training Centres are similar to workshop schools (see p. 138) but are for participants under 25 years of age. They provide training in trades and professions which improve the quality of urban life in infrastructure, the natural environment and social services. The training lasts between three and nine months and students receive 550 pesetas per day. On completion of the training the beneficiary receives a certificate to show the level of knowledge. The scheme is run jointly by INEM and the municipality.

Work orientation programmes for the young

Short orientation for work programmes are run by Barcelona Activa to provide general information on job search, knowledge of the employment market and job search skills.

Work experience contracts for the young

Work contracts are the most common form of help to the unemployed generally in Spain. Under these contracts, the worker must not replace a permanent worker, and the repeated renewal of short-term contracts in order to replace a permanent worker is not allowed. For the young 16- to 20-year old the contract is for a period between three months and three years. Training time must be not less than a quarter or more than half the contract time. The scheme is organised by INEM, but there are no financial incentives offered to employers.

Measures to help the long-term unemployed

Young long-term unemployed

For the long-term unemployed under 25, or up to 30 years of age, if the worker has not had a job for more than a total of three months, the contract is subsidised at the rate of 400,000 pesetas. This is jointly financed by the ministry and the ESF and this scheme was first implemented in 1992.

Contracts for long-term unemployed workers over 45

This scheme was introduced at national level in 1992 to promote the recruitment of workers over 45 years of age who had been out of work for more than a year. The scheme is organised by INEM and a grant of 500,000 pesetas is available for every worker given a contract. Reduction of 50 per cent of employers' social security contributions is also made. The scheme is financed by the Ministry and the ESF.

Measures to help unemployed women

As we have seen, women constitute the majority of the unemployed in Barcelona in nearly all age groups. In general programmes, women were 41.8 per cent of the total in occupational plans in 1988–89, but in district projects participation was low at 14 per cent (ADES 1990). Special projects for women are:

PILD (Incorporation of Women Programme)

This scheme is for women returners aged between 35 and 45, or long-term unemployed women with low educational qualifications. In practice most of the PILD beneficiaries have education only up to the statutory school leaving age. National policy promotes the full-time recruitment of these groups of women by giving grants of up to 500,000 pesetas to employers. It is financed by the Ministry and ESF.

ODAME (Women and Enterprise)

The aim of this scheme, run by the city, is to help women who wish to set up their own business. Hardly any participants have a low level of education and 23 per cent have higher education. The aim of the scheme is to help participants, but it is also hoped that they will provide further new employment when in business. A related measure is:

DIANE

This is a programme of research on the specific problems of women who wish to be self-employed. It gives training and advice to participants.

Measures to help disabled workers

Companies employing more than forty permanent full-time workers must employ not less than 2 per cent of their workplace from amongst the registered disabled.

Contracts for the disabled

To promote the integration of disabled workers into private enterprises and cooperatives, grants of 500,000 pesetas plus a 70–90 per cent reduction in employers' social security contributions are available, plus grants for adaptation of workplace. For each person per year a company increases its total of disabled workers it gets a reduction of 700,000 pesetas on taxable income. Finance comes from the Ministry and the ESF. The scheme is organised by INEM.

Employment initiatives for the disabled

Grants of up to two million pesetas are available to set up special employment centres for the disabled plus a wage cost subsidy. For self-employment a disabled worker can get a grant of up to 400,000 pesetas for fixed capital and a grant for interest on a loan.

Other employment creation measures

Capitalisation of Unemployment Benefits

This scheme exists in order to encourage the self-employment of unemployed workers, either in setting up their own business or as associate workers in a cooperative. Beneficiaries receive a lump sum of the amount of unemployment insurance benefit to which they are entitled, and a reduction in social security benefit. Older workers who have been in employment for most of their lives can receive a substantial lump sum, which acts as an incentive. The scheme is organised by INEM.

Outcomes of measures in Barcelona

Most of the participants of schemes in Barcelona are on work experience contracts, including some training either full-time or part-time with public or private employers. The next largest group are in training. Very few of those on contracts are over 45 years of age or disabled. The majority of work contracts are for less than twelve months, as is shown in Table 7.8. A high proportion, therefore, of the 66,300 unemployed are on these various work/training contracts. Participants of schemes co-funded by the ESF and the municipality in 1991 were as shown in Table 7.9.

The co-funded schemes work out at roughly 625,000 pesetas per participant. Within the ESF funded Objective 3 projects, 210 participants of the 280 were women; within Objective 4, for the young, the majority received only basic training. It was decided by the city that 'some programmes, co-financed by the ESF are to be discontinued due to the characteristics of

Table 7.8 Registered work contracts, Barcelona,
October 1991

Type of contract	No. of participants
Full-time work	11,168
of which less than 12 months duration	10,454
Part-time work	7,754
Workshops, etc.	2,081
Training	2,419
Over 45 years old	61
Disabled	32
Other	379
Total	23,894

Source: Ajuntament de Barcelona (1991)

Table 7.9 Barcelona city schemes funded by the ESF

Scheme	Participants	ESF (million pesetas)	Municipality (million pesetas)
Objective 2	307	70.2	85.8
Objective 3 (LTU)	280	79.8	97.6
Objective 4 (young)	502	137.4	167.9
Article 1.2	16	2.6	3.1
Innovatory	60	24.3	29.7
NOW (Women)	20	6.9	8.3
Other transnational	52	26.9	32.8
Total	1,237	348.0	425.2

Source: ADES Barcelona (unpublished)

financing that do not always identify with work insertion as an objective and which are not relevant' (ADES 1990). Participants on ESF schemes were forecast to fall from 1,237 in 1991 to 733 by 1993.

The city authorities evaluated the PILD programme for women returners and long-term unemployed women and also programmes for the young unemployed on schemes in 1991. The first stage of PILD covering December 1990 to February 1991, produced an outcome in terms of jobs higher than expected. Forty-five per cent of the 213 women selected for training found work. All the courses were between 150 and 700 hours long and were held in the evening. The courses covered telemarketing, family workers, administrative work, general assistants, hotel management, shop and restaurant work. Of those gaining work, 17.6 per cent were in administrative/clerical work, 16.2 per cent in personal services, 6 per cent in hotels and catering and the remainder in a variety of occupations. Many more women were offered jobs but were unable to accept them because of family or work conditions. Of the young people on council programmes (under 30 years old) most had only a low educational level (47 per cent), but 7 per cent were graduates. Those with some work experience formed 61 per cent of participants and they had mainly worked in domestic work, education and health services and restaurants. Those from industry came largely from metal manufacturers. One year after finishing training 92 per cent of participants had either found work or (in the case of 48 per cent of these) had gone on to further study. When questioned two months after the finish of the programme only 59 per cent were employed or studying. The highest job outcomes were for those with higher level vocational training or university studies. Permanent contracts of employment were few in comparison to short-term contracts of work.[9]

Of the projects concentrated in districts, information for the year 1988–89 shows that 179 people were trained locally. Of those nearly half were under 25, 26 per cent between 40 and 54 years of age, and 6 per cent over 55. The participants were nearly all male and half were trained in building skills, 25 per cent in other construction work and 25 per cent as gardeners. Participants were trained and employed by the municipality.

The policy of allowing workers to capitalise on unemployment benefits mainly in order to set up in business, attracted quite a lot of response. In the second quarter of 1991, two thousand five hundred and ten unemployed workers capitalised on their benefits and of those half set up in self-employment or co-ops (INEM Barcelona).

The future of employment in Barcelona - Barcelona 2000 Economic and Social Strategic Plan

Having achieved the siting of the 1992 Olympics in Barcelona, and the investment and employment opportunities accompanying this, Barcelona city government set forward a strategic plan up to the year 2000 (Ajuntament de Barcelona 1990). Barcelona sees its advantages as having strong manufacturing and commercial traditions with a diverse labour market; a strong centre of university education, cultural diversity and creativity; and an enhancement of the profile of the city since the Olympics. Its weak points are the pockets of poverty in some parts of the old centre and outlying areas; shortage of land; noise, congestion and poor functioning and coverage of public and social welfare services. It foresees also an ageing population and is expecting an increase in immigration from Eastern Europe and Africa. Barcelona's strategic plan is threefold. Firstly to make itself the centre of a macro-region, the so-called Golden Arc, coordinating with the cities of Saragossa, Valencia and Palma de Mallorca in Spain and with Toulouse and Montpellier in France. To this end the city intends to expand airport, port and high speed rail links; complete a network of major roads in Catalonia and build at least 120 kilometres of metro with complementary

bus routes; improve electronic communications; and provide land for industrial estates. Secondly, the city aims to promote industry and advanced business services. This will be done by the creation of business centres; a second
site for trade fares; a new conference hall; a centre providing information on
markets abroad; centres to promote diffusion of new technology to small
firms; attempts to attract headquarters of national and international companies; and encouraging development as a commercial and urban tourist
centre. All these measures should create permanent new employment. The
third strategy is to improve the quality of life. Measures to encourage reduction of pollution include regulating sources of pollution; encouraging use of
urban public transport and improving water and sewage plants. Within this
strategy a main policy area is training and education. The city envisages
creating centres of advanced technology linked to schools and INEM; link-
ing science parks to the universities; having postgraduate programmes related
to the needs of the labour market, and creating an institute of vocational
training. Alongside these measures there are aims to improve social welfare
via education, housing and welfare for the elderly in the most depressed
and needy districts. The city also aims 'to take account of the problem of
unemployment especially among the young and women' (Barcelona 2000).

EVALUATION OF MEASURES AFFECTING
THE UNEMPLOYED IN BARCELONA

Barcelona experienced a rapid growth of population into the city between 1950
and 1970 based on growth of manufacturing industry and construction. After
the oil price shock of 1973, the national economy suffered a steep rise in labour
costs and slow growth of output. Structural change in Barcelona was held up
as priority was given to restoring and developing democracy in the early 1980s.
Unemployment grew at a rapid rate with less manufacturing jobs and
Barcelona's unemployment was higher than that of Spain as a whole in 1985.
The Olympic effect and economic growth in Spain caused unemployment to
halve by 1991. The official unemployment rate underestimates actual unemployment by several percentage points. The informal cash economy grew as
well in the late 1980s, in domestic work, streetselling and catering, thus under-
estimating the number of workers with low skills who had no job on the formal
labour market. This cash economy was encouraged by the strict conditions of
unemployment assistance and the existence of a minimum wage on the formal
labour market. By 1991 there was still a mismatch between the number of
people unemployed from the manufacturing sector and the proportion of
vacancies in manufacturing. Clearly there was also a mismatch generally
between the educational levels of the unemployed, most of whom had only low
qualifications, and vacancies, where 40 per cent of jobs offered required knowledge of a foreign language. At the other end of the educational scale a relatively
high percentage, compared to other cities under study, are graduates.

Those most affected by unemployment are women, and those with low educational levels. The needs in policy terms are for training and retraining to match the needs of the labour market, and greater flexibility of working methods and reduction of discrimination to help the female unemployed. In Barcelona the municipal authorities have the power to implement policies for the unemployed as well as making plans for the future of the economy. They spend over half the funds allocated to unemployment policy in the city. National policy is administered by INEM which takes into account local needs and area problems. Policy is, therefore, designed to adapt to local economic and social conditions and the particular problems of groups of the unemployed in the city. INEM has the role of matching vacancies to the unemployed and 50 per cent of the unemployed use INEM to try to find a job, 43 per cent use press adverts and 31 per cent personal contacts. The most efficient method of job search has been found to be not INEM, but personal contact. Three quarters of the unemployed on programmes find a job in this way, and 38 per cent of the unemployed also do not take part in programmes (ADES 1991). This obviously makes it more difficult to find employment in areas of the city where there is high local unemployment. The majority of the unemployed helped by INEM are on temporary work experience contracts which give no financial incentives to employers. INEM appears to be very successful in arranging thousands of such contacts in the city. The benefits to employers are in the flexibility it gives in short-term contracts rather than employing permanent workers. Although a contract cannot displace an existing worker, the growth in jobs can be filled with those on short-term contracts. The unemployed could thus be re-cycled in this way, and the growth in stable permanent jobs reduced. Half of the participants on subsidised training schemes are young unemployed, many of whom are long-term unemployed as well. This applies to INEM/FIP, ESF subsidised and district schemes. The success rate of training for the young is very high with 92 per cent finding a job or going on to further training or study.

Women on PILD schemes have a relatively high rate of job gain (45 per cent) considering the discrimination by firms found by ADES. Women on special schemes, however, are only a very small proportion of the female unemployed, and those on schemes would be likely to have a more positive outcome as they are a selected and self-selected group. In general schemes, open to both men and women, women are less likely to find employment than men, despite the fact that there are many service jobs available, work that in other areas of Europe is often more likely to be filled with female workers. The measures in place have not reduced the high level of female unemployment. More effective programmes are needed to reduce discrimination, narrow the skills gap, and introduce flexibility within the labour market towards those who need to work part-time, for instance.

The urban factors affecting unemployment are on the whole positive in

Barcelona. Public transportation is fast and cheap and links potential workers with areas of job growth in the city. Plans for future development in the city concentrate on the important role of training and education of the labour force, and the social infrastructure needs of lower-income, higher-unemployment districts.

The policies promoted for Europe as a whole by the ESF were not considered the most appropriate for local employment problems by the city government. Subsidies from the ESF in 1991 constituted less than 10 per cent of total spending on employment creation and the unemployed, and the city has chosen to reduce its own matching expenditure on ESF funded schemes up to 1993. Available aid from the European Union is, therefore, largely rejected, and the influence of the commission on the structure of unemployment measures is small.

Overall the planned growth of the local economy has reduced general unemployment levels very successfully for the young and for unemployed men, but has been less successful in relation to the most serious problem of female unemployment. In the longer term it seems more of the unemployed will need high level training to adjust to the rapidly changing needs of the labour market for well-qualified workers in new technologies. Higher education must be directed more towards employment opportunities and greater emphasis must be placed on knowledge of foreign languages. The strategic plan of Barcelona may deliver this, but a great deal of investment in human capital will be needed to make the plan a reality.

8

FRANKFURT AM MAIN

INTRODUCTION

Frankfurt am Main, a city with a population of 641,261 in 1990 is the largest city in the land[1] of Hesse, and the seventh largest city in the Western part of Germany. It is situated on the river Main, a tributary of the Rhine, and has a central location within what was the Federal Republic of Germany. The old border with the German Democratic Republic lies one hundred and eighty kilometres to the east. It is the financial centre of Germany and home to the Bundesbank, and has recently been chosen as the site for the proposed new central Bank of Europe. It is also the hub of national and international travel with the largest airport in continental Europe and a railway station handling nearly fifteen hundred trains a day. In the 1960s, as in Rotterdam, expanding manufacturing industry needed a growth in workforce greater than the local economy could supply. This was filled with 'guestworkers' from countries in Southern Europe – Turkey, Greece, Yugoslavia, Spain and Italy. The highest level of recorded population in the city was in 1965, when there were approximately fifty thousand more people than in 1990, largely as a result of influx of workers to the manufacturing and construction industries. The city lost sixty-six thousand inhabitants between 1972 and 1984, some returning guestworkers, others suburbanising to the greater Frankfurt area. Between 1984 and 1990 the population rose again by twenty-nine thousand as the local economy improved. Manufacturing industry, as elsewhere in Europe, had lost workers through technological and market changes, but Frankfurt and its region rapidly adapted to a growing services economy. Frankfurt and the surrounding metropolitan area is the city in Europe with the lowest 'problem score' according to Cheshire and Hay (1989) with highest income per head and lowest unemployment rate of all Western Europe's large cities. West Germany had the lowest unemployment and highest income per head of the five countries under study so to some extent this is not surprising, but Hesse, in the 1980s, had a growth in income of 2.8 per cent per annum, a growth of employment of 0.7 per cent per annum while the average annual increases for West Germany were 2.2 per

148

cent and 0.5 per cent respectively. Since 1974 the GNP per inhabitant of these has been the highest of the German regions (Hessen Report 1992).

Although in the early 1980s, up to 1984, the Frankfurt area lost employment, between 1984 and 1990 the number in employment grew by 15.4 per cent.[2] Frankfurt's position as a transport centre and its strengths in trade and finance have allowed it to benefit from the growth in demand for services in the German economy. This demand has been generated as a result of high growth in income in the past decade, and the fact that there is a high income elasticity of demand for services; also the growing demand from the manufacturing sector for research and development, marketing and financial services.

The reunification of Germany has had consequences on the population of the city. Even before reunification people came to the city from the East, as Frankfurt was relatively near the border. Post 1989 saw a phase of job searchers flowing into the city with neither employment nor housing. In common with other large cities in Germany, to avoid an increase in social problems, the social services refused social benefit and provided return tickets to Eastern Germany. It is estimated, however, that in 1992 there were around twenty thousand workers commuting daily from the eastern länder to jobs in Frankfurt, despite daily journeys often in excess of four hours. Frankfurt's central airport function has also meant that the city has received a very high proportion of refugees, as it is the first port of call in Germany.[3] In addition German nationals from Russia and other East European countries, allowed national status after 1989, also came in large numbers to the city. The city accommodates the highest percentage of foreigners of all German cities with nearly a quarter of the population born outside West Germany. This has consequences on unemployment and on unemployment policy within the city, as will be shown later in this chapter.

STRUCTURE OF EMPLOYMENT

The Frankfurt labour market area,[4] shown in Figure 8.1, experienced a growth in employment in the period 1984–90 of 15.4 per cent, with 90,245 extra jobs, over half the growth in the period 1989–90. This was greater than the percentage increase in jobs in Munich, West Berlin, Hamburg or Cologne (ABF Aktuel 1991). If one looks at the relative growth in employment in relation to population for the city and the surrounding area, it is apparent that the surrounding municipality had gained a greater share of new jobs than the city itself, and had benefited more from the fast growth in the local economy in the late 1980s (see Table 8.1).

The number of jobs in Frankfurt and in the surrounding area exceeded the number of residents in both areas who were employed. While some residents of the city commuted outside the city to work, it appears that nearly half the workers in the city came from outside.[5]

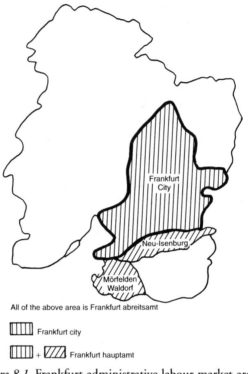

All of the above area is Frankfurt abreitsamt

⬚ Frankfurt city

⬚ + ▨ Frankfurt hauptamt

Figure 8.1 Frankfurt administrative labour market areas

Table 8.1 Employment and population, Frankfurt and area, 1990

	Frankfurt city	*Rest of Frankfurt ABM area*
Population	641,261	491.400
Growth in employment as % of population 1988–1990	3.9%	4.5%
No. of employed in area	481,961	194,745
No. residents in employment	235,803	138,477
Net commuting	+183,158	–43,732

Source: ABF Aktuel: Lands arbeitsamt Hessen (1991)

Because of the administrative areas included within the Frankfurt area by the Employment Office (AMB) (see Figure 8.1) the figures used, unless stated, will be for Frankfurt Hauptamt, a slightly larger area than the city itself.[6]

Employment by sector of activity in Frankfurt for 1991 and for eleven years previously is shown in Table 8.2. The table shows that while the small primary sector remained constant, manufacturing and construction lost 5.6 per cent of employment and the major growth in employment was in financial and other services (6 per cent). The economy of the city is heavily dependent on the services sector with 76.5 per cent of those employed in the local economy in various private and public sector service industries. This is in line with structural change in other cities in Europe. The city is unique, however, in having many more jobs available than the total active population in work or seeking work, having growth of employment higher than other major cities in Germany.

Table 8.2 Employment by sector, Frankfurt, 1980 and 1991

Sector	1980 %	1991 %	% change 1980–91
Primary sector	1.3	1.3	—
Manufacturing	22.4	17.6	−3.8
Construction	6.4	4.6	−1.8
Catering and hotel	3.1	3.8	+0.7
Financial services	10.8	13.8	+3.0
Transport and communications	12.5	14.3	+1.8
Trade/commerce	17.1	15.0	−1.9
Other services	17.6	20.6	+3.0
Public and non-profit sector services	8.8	9.0	+0.2
Total	100.0	100.0	

Source: AMB Frankfurt (ATOS 1992)

Note: The above statistics were provided by the Arbeitsmarkt und Berufsforshung Hesse, Frankfurt am Main from computer records (ATOS)

The growth of service sector employment has affected women in particular. They increased their share of jobs from 38.9 per cent in 1980 to 41.6 per cent by 1991 in the expanding jobs market. While men took more of the share of new jobs in manufacturing women had a greater share of the growth in the larger services sector (see Table 8.3).

As in other cities in Europe women are taking up a higher percentage of the growth in service sector jobs. Since the services sector throughout Europe is growing at a faster rate than other sectors, women's participation in the labour force is also likely to increase, as it has done in all cities under study. While the share of women in jobs is low at 41.6 per cent compared to Manchester at 45 per cent, women form a higher percentage of the population in work than in Rotterdam, Montpellier and Barcelona.

In this context it is surprising to find that the unemployment rate in the city is higher than that for other areas of the local labour market, the region and Germany as a whole (see Table 8.4).

Table 8.3 Change in employment in manufacturing and services, and male and female employment share, Frankfurt, 1980 and 1991

| | *Manufacturing employment* | | | *Services employment* | | |
	Total No.	*Men % share*	*Women % share*	*Total No.*	*Men % share*	*Women % share*
1980	99.586	72.4	27.6	331.606	57.3	42.7
1991	106.074	77.6	22.4	362.472	52.5	47.5
% change	+6.5	+5.2	−5.2	+10.9	−4.8	+4.8

Source: AMB Frankfurt (ATOS, 1992)

Note: The above statistics were provided by the Arbeitsmarkt und Berufsforshung Hesse, Frankfurt am Main from computer records (ATOS)

Table 8.4 Unemployment rates[7] in Frankfurt, surrounding area, Hesse and West Germany, 1990

Area	% unemployed 1990
Frankfurt	6.0
Other areas around Frankfurt[8]	3.8
Hesse	5.7
West Germany	4.3

Source: AMB Frankfurt Jahrebericht (1990); OECD Labour Force Statistics (1991)

In order to assess how these rates could be explained, an analysis of those unemployed in the city follows.

UNEMPLOYMENT IN FRANKFURT

For the whole of the Frankfurt labour market area the rate of unemployment varied between 4.4 per cent and 6.9 per cent over the period 1982–92. It rose from 4.1 per cent in 1982 to 6.9 per cent in 1987 and then declined to 4.1 per cent in 1991 rising slightly to 4.7 per cent the following year. Rates for the city moved in the same directions but were approximately 2 per cent higher than for the area as a whole. Unemployment rates by age and sex are shown in Table 8.5. Overall unemployment fell by over six thousand in the period 1985 to 1991 as a result of growth of employment in the city.

Age and unemployment

Over one thousand fewer young people under 25 were registered unemployed in 1991 than in 1985, and as a percentage of all those unemployed had shown

Table 8.5 Unemployment rates by age and sex, Frankfurt, 1985 and 1991

Age	1985			1991		
	Total M unemp. %	*Total F. unemp. %*	*Total unemp. %*	*Total M unemp. %*	*Total F unemp. %*	*Total unemp. %*
under 20	5.1	5.7	5.4	2.8	3.0	2.9
20–24	12.3	14.4	13.2	9.2	8.9	9.1
25–34	27.8	32.6	29.9	26.9	29.0	27.7
35–44	23.7	20.3	22.1	24.2	22.2	23.4
45–55	20.2	15.4	18.2	22.8	21.2	22.1
over 55	10.9	11.6	11.2	14.1	15.7	14.8
Total	100.0	100.0	100.0	100.0	100.0	100.0
Total No.	12,094	9,084	21,178	8,911	6,166	15,077
% of total						
No. unemployed	57.1	42.9	100.0	59.1	40.9	100.0

Source: AMB Frankfurt (ATOS, 1992)

Note: The above statistics were provided by the Arbeitsmarkt und Berufsforshung Hesse, Frankfurt am Main from computer records (ATOS)

a decrease from 18.6 per cent to 12.0 per cent. Over half those unemployed in both periods were prime age workers between 25 and 45 years of age. The share of total unemployment of those over 45 grew from 29.4 per cent to 36.9 per cent, and while the number of unemployed in the 45 to 50 age group fell by a quarter, the number unemployed over the age of 50 remained virtually static. Younger workers and prime age workers were both benefiting from a booming employment situation, whereas older workers, it appeared, were not. The difficulties faced by older unemployed workers is also demonstrated by the high proportion of long-term unemployed in this group (see p. 155). Eighty-two per cent of workers over 50 had been unemployed for longer than a year.

Due to the age structure of the population the number of active workers in the age group under 20 decreased in the late 1980s by 11 per cent and those over 59 increased by 4.1 per cent (AMB Frankfurt Jahresbericht 1990). Demographic factors may to some extent account for the changes in the numbers unemployed in the youngest and oldest age groups.

Male and female unemployment

Since the figures refer to registered unemployed and not to the jobless, the figures for female unemployment are likely to be underestimated, as previously discussed.

For West Germany as a whole the activity rate for men was 81.4 per cent and for women 57.7 per cent in 1991 (OECD 1992). There is no breakdown of activity rates by age for the city of Frankfurt, nor for number of residents working by age and sex in the city, so it is not possible to ascertain, for instance, whether men or women in a particular age group are more or less likely to be unemployed. As shown in Table 8.5 very similar proportions of men and women were unemployed in each age group as a proportion of total men and women unemployed, and the percentage of women in the total number of unemployed fell from 42.9 per cent in 1985 to 40.9 per cent in 1991. The proportion of women in the total number employed in Frankfurt (not necessarily resident in the city) was 41 per cent (ABF Aktuel 1992). This can be explained by the fact that women are employed in the services sector which is expanding more rapidly than manufacturing, where the vast majority of workers are men. If one takes this as a proxy figure for employment of those living in the city, this would mean that the unemployment rate for women as a whole was no higher than that for men. Again though, one must bear in mind that jobless women are likely to be underestimated in official figures.

Duration of unemployment

Of those unemployed in Frankfurt in 1991, only 23 per cent had been without work for longer than a year, 42.6 per cent had been out of work for less than three months and 61 per cent had been unemployed for less than six months. Long-term unemployment is lower in this city than in Montpellier, Rotterdam and Manchester. This is not unexpected in a local labour market with a high rate of employment growth compared to population growth and one of the most favoured economic structures of all European cities. For those three and a half thousand who have been without a job for a long period it is not unimportant. What are their characteristics?

Of all the long-term unemployed men comprise 57.6 per cent and women 42.4 per cent, a higher figure for women than for unemployment as a whole.

Table 8.6 Unemployed over one year by age and sex in
Frankfurt, 1991

	Male	Female	Total	% of LTU
under 20	1	–	1	0.0
20–24	25	17	42	1.2
25–34	225	191	416	11.9
35–44	459	276	735	21.1
45–54	673	444	1117	32.1
over 55	624	553	1177	33.7
Total	2007	1481	3488	100.0

Source: AMB Frankfurt (ATOS 1992)

Note: The above statistics were provided by the Arbeitsmarkt und Berufsforshung Hesse, Frankfurt am Main from computer records (ATOS)

Twenty-four per cent of unemployed women are long-term unemployed compared to 22.5 per cent of unemployed men. Only a very small number of young workers are long-term unemployed while 48.2 per cent of the long-term unemployed are over 50 years of age, and over a third are over 55. Around half of all the long-term unemployed have been out of work for longer than two years, with nearly 2,000 unemployed in the difficult-to-place category.

Nearly half the long-term unemployed have only basic education and are without training in any skill. Of those with training one third had technical, higher technical or university education. Klems and Schmid (1990) in their study of the long-term unemployed in the city noted that at the beginning of the 1980s the structure of long-term unemployment changed from a situation where nearly all the long-term unemployed had health handicaps or were unskilled to a situation in the late 1980s where a new group with training and education and without any obvious disadvantages remained unemployed for a long period, despite job availability. They reject the hypothesis of mismatch of skills and of low mobility of the long-term unemployed, maintaining that there is evidence to support the view that corporate selection procedures are more important as a cause of long-term unemployment. In other words, not only qualifications are important but sociability and work behaviour, the ability to 'fit in' are important criteria when choosing a worker. For older workers higher costs in terms of increased incidence of illness and lower job adaptability are perceived as important factors for employer rejection. Thirty-eight per cent of the longer term unemployed have some degree of disablement either physical or mental. Over a quarter of the long-term unemployed are non-German (see the next section on ethnic origin). The long-term unemployed are, therefore, more likely than other groups of the unemployed to be older workers with lower skill and educational levels, disabled, or a member of an ethnic minority group. It has already been noted that Frankfurt has a higher proportion of residents from outside Germany than either Hesse or the other areas of the wider labour market area. The incidence of unemployment by country of origin will now be examined.

Unemployment and ethnic origin

In Frankfurt the rate of unemployment differs according to country of origin as shown in Table 8.7. Non-German workers have a higher incidence of unemployment than German workers, with Yugoslav nationals having twice the unemployment rate, Turkish workers two and a half times the unemployment rate, and other foreign workers three and a half times the rate of Germans. This latter category includes refugees and asylum seekers, but they only form around 18 per cent of the total of this unemployed category. Comparing the above figures with the percentages of the employed population by ethnic origin of all those working in the city, 2.9 per cent were

Turkish, 2.8 per cent Yugoslav, 2.9 per cent other South Europeans, 4.2 per cent other foreign workers and 87.2 per cent were German nationals. It is clear, therefore, that the incidence of unemployment is higher and the work opportunities lower for those workers who are non-German. The groups most liable to unemployment are the Turks and 'other foreign workers', usually newly arrived, often with a low level of knowledge of the German language, and including those of German origin from Eastern Europe and the former Soviet Union.

Table 8.7 Registered unemployed as a percentage of working population[9] by ethnic origin in Frankfurt, 1991

Ethnic origin	%
Turkish	6.4
Yugoslav	4.8
Other South European	5.8
Other foreign[10]	9.7
German	2.4

Source: AMB Frankfurt (ATOS 1992)

Note: The above statistics were provided by the Arbeitsmarkt und Berufsforshung Hesse, Frankfurt am Main from computer records (ATOS)

Examining the changes in unemployment for each group over the years 1985 to 1991 in relation to total unemployment shows that Germans in this period of job growth had a falling share of total unemployment by 2.5 per cent, while the share of Turkish unemployed remained constant, Yugoslavs and South Europeans share decreased slightly but 'other foreigners' increased their share from 11 per cent to 15.4 per cent of the total (see Table 8.8).

Table 8.8 Percentage of unemployed by ethnic origin, Frankfurt, 1985–91

	Turkish	Yugoslav	South European	Others	German
1985	6.7	5.1	7.1	11.0	70.1
1986	6.7	4.4	6.9	12.0	71.0
1987	7.3	5.3	6.3	11.5	69.6
1988	6.9	4.8	6.8	12.7	68.8
1989	6.4	4.7	6.2	13.3	69.4
1990	6.0	4.5	5.9	14.4	69.2
1991	6.5	4.4	6.1	15.4	67.6

Source: AMB Frankfurt (ATOS 1992)

Note: The above statistics were provided by the Arbeitsmarkt und Berufsforshung Hesse, Frankfurt am Main from computer records (ATOS)

It is not altogether surprising to find that the unemployment probabilities of the migrant worker groups of the 1960s from Turkey, Yugoslavia, Spain, Italy, Greece and Portugal and their descendants are higher than for the national population. This is the case in Rotterdam, where there were similar groups of migrant workers with higher levels of unemployment than native Dutch. In Rotterdam it was the case that these groups had lower skill levels, and educational levels than the rest of the population. Information is not available on this for Frankfurt but information on unemployment by sector and educational level in general will now be analysed.

Unemployment, education and training

Over twenty thousand new jobs were created in the city in the year 1989–90. These were very largely in the tertiary sector. Of those unemployed in 1991 most (53.9 per cent) had no previous employment at all, and of the rest 35.6 per cent had had a job in the services sector and 9.7 per cent in the manufacturing sector. The total number of new jobs in the city exceeded the total number of unemployed residents. The education and training of those in work gives an idea of the needs of the local labour market in terms of qualifications. This is shown in Table 8.9.

Table 8.9 Employees in Frankfurt by education/training, 1991

Education/training	%
Primary/secondary school	22.9
Primary/secondary school and professional training	56.1
Abitur	2.1
Abitur and training	3.0
Technical higher level	3.5
Higher education	4.7
Unknown	7.7
Total	100

Source: AMB Frankfurt (ATOS 1992)

Note: The above statistics were provided by the Arbeitsmarkt und Berufsforshung Hesse, Frankfurt am Main from computer records (ATOS)

The demand for labour is predominantly for those who have secondary education plus a professional training, followed by those who have secondary education but no formal professional training. Higher education both technical and academic is required for 12.4 per cent of workers.

The unemployed, who are not analysed in exactly the same categories, are predominantly untrained in any profession, or only partly trained (see Table 8.10).

Table 8.10 Unemployed in Frankfurt by
education/training, 1991

Category	%
Without skill training	56.6 of which:
Illiterate/primary school	15.8
Secondary school	40.8
With training	43.4 of which:
On job training	26.2
Professional training in school	3.0
Technical School	2.4
Higher Technical School	3.1
University	8.7

Source: AMB Frankfurt (ATOS 1992)

Note: The above statistics were provided by the
Arbeitsmarkt und Berufsforshung Hesse, Frankfurt
am Main from computer records (ATOS)

While only 22.9 per cent of the employed population have no training or
higher levels of education 56.6 per cent of the unemployed are in this situation. One of the most striking features of the above table is the relatively
high percentage of those with higher technical training and university education who together comprise 11.8 per cent of the unemployed and match
their educational category in the employed sector. If one looks in more detail
at this highly educated group the incidence of unemployment is higher for
women than for men at 14.8 per cent and 10.9 per cent respectively. The
same picture emerges for the long-term unemployed as shown in Table 8.11.

The reasons for relatively high unemployment of those with higher education may be to do with an over-supply of graduates and their inappropriate
skills for the local labour market, as in Barcelona. It is more puzzling why
they form an even higher percentage of the long-term unemployed, as they
do not appear, as Klems and Schmid (1990) pointed out, to have other disadvantages. A reason for the percentage of long-term female unemployed

Table 8.11 Long-term unemployed by education/training, Frankfurt, 1991

Category	% of total	% of men	% of women
With no skill training and basic education	48.9	44.9	54.4
With on-job training	33.2	39.1	25.3
Professional training in school	0.9	0.9	0.0
Technical school training	2.9	3.4	2.7
Technical high school/university	14.0	12.7	15.7

Source: AMB Frankfurt (ATOS)

being higher than for males could well be to do with the problem of highly qualified women returners with little previous work experience having difficulty finding work appropriate to their skills, and the fact that there is competition from men who are more flexible in the location and timing of work. In general the availability of part-time work of a high level is low in Frankfurt compared to cities like Manchester, and this may limit female choice. Lower level part-time jobs are available in jobs such as office cleaning and auxiliary help in social services, and unskilled women have less difficulty in finding work than unskilled men in these sectors.

Urban factors in unemployment

As has already been noted unemployment rates in the city are nearly twice as high as those in surrounding areas of the labour market. This reflects the fact that the poor and disadvantaged and ethnic minorities are more likely to reside in the city than in neighbouring suburban municipalities. A breakdown of unemployment by area within the city is not available and would probably not show significant differences as the unemployment rate overall is so low. The one area that social services[11] noted as having higher unemployment than other areas was around the Central Station, an area of old low-rent housing, inhabited predominantly by ethnic minorities. Growth of manufacturing jobs has been largely in outer areas of the labour market. This should not present a problem of access for city dwellers as transportation by metro, tram and train is very comprehensive throughout the area. It is also fast, and with a flat fare structure that allows for transfers from one mode of public transport to another. It is probably also the reason why Frankfurt is relatively uncongested by motor traffic compared to cities of a similar size, and may not suffer from external diseconomies to location because of this. Growth of jobs both inside and outside the city, together with ease of access to employment, has meant that Frankfurt does not appear, as a city, to suffer from urban locational and planning problems that would affect employment opportunity for the unemployed. While it is clearly the growth in jobs that has resulted in low levels of unemployment, those that are unemployed are not hampered by urban factors which might in other circumstances – wholesale suburbanisation of jobs and lack of public transportation – have resulted in higher levels of unemployment than exist within the city.

Overall Frankfurt is one of the most fortunate cities in Germany, and in Europe as a whole, as far as unemployment is concerned. The rate of long-term unemployment is less than half that of Germany. Out of a population of six hundred thousand only three and a half thousand people have been unemployed for over a year, and most of the unemployed find work within six months, reflecting a booming demand for labour. Growth of employment in the wider Frankfurt area, and in the city itself has outstripped growth of the centre population, resulting in an influx of non-resident workers from other areas of the region and the country to fill the gap. The city, has, however, attempted to keep out potential residents from the eastern Laender by refusing access to social benefits and housing. Since twenty thousand people from the east are employed in the city, it seems reasonable to suppose that permanent migrants to the city would have been quite substantial. For those who did arrive without a home, tent cities were constructed – they accommodated around five thousand homeless in 1991 – largely as a deterrent to long-term residence. This form of 'urban policy', restricting the growth of migrants, has been effective in the sense that it has kept social problems, including unemployment, very much under control.

In the labour market women's share of total employment has risen, but more educated women find problems gaining employment. How much this is to do with suitability of work, flexibility of work organisation, or discrimination by employees is difficult to tell. Youth unemployment, lower in Germany than in other countries, is insignificant in Frankfurt, and the young unemployed do not enter into long-term unemployment. This is largely to do with training, as will be shown on p. 164. The main features of those who were long-term unemployed were that they were unskilled, or disabled, disproportionately from ethnic minorities, or a combination of these factors. A new group of long-term unemployed are graduates, particularly female graduates. In this context policies towards the unemployed will be examined. Not all policies of national government are relevant in the context of unemployment in Frankfurt, but they will be described together with the major measures in existence in the city.[12]

Organisational structure

At national level the Ministry of Economic Affairs is responsible for trying to achieve a higher level of employment and reduce unemployment through policies for investment and growth in the economy. The Ministry of Labour and Social Affairs is responsible for labour market policy, employment promotion and unemployment insurance. The federal government lays down rules for the promotion of training on the advice of the Federal Institute of Vocational Training, a tripartite body made up of representatives of workers, employers and government. The Länder, a regional level of government, each have responsibility for schools and vocational training in their area, as well as parts of the university system. The most important organisation as far as the unemployed are concerned is the Bundesanstalt fur Arbeit (BA), a Federal Employment Service responsible for placement, vocational counselling, placement of apprentices, promotion of vocational training, and the administration of unemployment insurance and unemployment assistance. The BA is a self-governing body, overseen by representatives of employees, employers and public bodies. The central level of the BA determines the budget and issues regulations on benefit and services. There is a regional body, in this case Hesse AMB and local offices which deal directly with the public – the Frankfurt AMB. The BA gets 90 per cent of its revenue from joint contributions of employees and employers amounting to 3.15 per cent of the wage. It appears that the more people are employed the greater the income of the BA and the fewer its responsibilities! The BA also pays out benefits on behalf of the Federal government. Function and lines of responsibility are clearly defined in this system. At city level, local government has the responsibility for social assistance which includes helping some groups of the particularly difficult-to-place unemployed. In Frankfurt this role is undertaken by Hilverbund Frankfurter Verein fur Soziale Heimstatten and Werkstatt Frankfurt.

Unemployment Benefit and Unemployment Assistance

Income for the unemployed who are insured workers and who have an employment record comes in two forms, Unemployment Benefit (Arbeitlosengeld) and Unemployment Assistance (Arbeitlosenhilfe).

Unemployment Benefit

To qualify for benefit an unemployed worker must have worked and made contributions for 360 days in the previous three years, or for seasonal workers 180 days in the previous three years. There is no waiting period and payment is made by cheque every two weeks. The amount received is 63 per cent of the last net wage, or in the case where the worker has at least one child 68 per cent of the last wage. The duration of benefit depends on previous contributions. If, for instance, the claimant has paid the minimum of 360 days in three years payment will be made for 156 working days (excluding Sunday); if for 720 days in the previous seven years payment will be made for 312 working days. Both the above apply to workers under 42 years of age. For older workers with 1,920 days contribution in the past seven years a maximum of 832 weekdays can be allowed for payment. An unemployed worker receiving Unemployment Benefit can also work part-time but 50 per cent of the supplementary income is deducted from benefit. In the case where total income is more than 80 per cent of last net wage, all earned income is deducted from benefit. A worker who left work voluntarily, or was dismissed through negligence, has to wait for eight to twelve weeks before benefit can be claimed. Similarly, someone who refuses to take up an offer of suitable employment can be disqualified for benefit for this period. In cases of hardship disqualification can be reduced from four to six weeks.

Unemployment Assistance

While Unemployment Benefit is paid out from contributions to the social insurance scheme, Unemployment Assistance is paid for by the Federal

Government. To be eligible an unemployed person must be available for work, registered at an employment office, have no entitlement to Unemployment Benefit, or be no longer entitled to it, or have been in contributory employment for one hundred and fifty days. Previous employment is not required for those who have been on social assistance for two hundred and forty days in the previous year. Unemployment Assistance is paid at the rate of 56 per cent of the last previous wage, or 58 per cent if there is a dependent child. The duration of benefit is in theory unlimited but must be reapplied for each year.

Social Assistance

If an unemployed worker has had no previous work then Social Assistance can be applied for. It is, however, means-tested and will depend on the income and assets of a spouse, or in the case of minors a parent or parents. There is no benefit available for those under 18 unless the young person is on a training scheme or comes from a very poor family living on subsistence level.

Active measures to aid the unemployed

First of all two measures aimed to prevent loss of employment will be specified.

Short-term working allowance

The aim of this measure is to maintain in employment workers, particularly experienced workers, who would otherwise be dismissed for economic reasons. If the worker can be kept by reducing working hours and at least one third of employees in a firm are affected, then the worker will get the rest of income equal to Unemployment Benefit for hours lost. This grant to the worker is paid for six months, which can, in special circumstances, be extended to two years. The Frankfurt employment area[13] helped 405 workers on short-time in 1990 with a total expenditure of 2.0 million DM, (approximately 4,938 DM per worker).

Promotion of worker productivity and weather allowances for the building trade

These measures aim to make it possible to continue working on buildings in bad weather, or to compensate employees who are unable to work because of weather conditions. Grants are available for the former to acquire facilities necessary to carry on construction in winter, such as shelters and heaters. For building workers unable to work employers apply for a subsidy equivalent to the Unemployment Benefit the workers would get. This must be applied for in advance. Workers must be paid their usual wage and maintained on the contract. Frankfurt area expenditure on this measure in 1990 was 3.9 million DM. No information is available on the number of workers affected.

The following measures apply to all unemployed.

Placement and Counselling Service

The local office of the BA informs employees and employers about trends in occupations; needs and opportunities for vocational training; and about all the incentives (listed below) for taking up a job.

Incentives to enter employment

The aim of these various incentives is to remove any financial obstacles that the unemployed might have in searching for or taking up a job. Expenses include:

(a) costs of applying for job; grant of up to 400 DM in six months;
(b) travelling expenses to attend employment counselling; travelling to an out of town job; travel to non-local vocational training; expenses for commuting to work outside the area for one year;
(c) removal costs for worker and family to new place of work;
(d) allowance for working clothes, 300 DM, and tools 500 DM;
(e) cost of travelling home once a month for workers separated from family;
(f) tideover allowance until first wage received, usually as a loan but can be a subsidy;
(g) grant towards acquisition of private means of transport.

Tideover allowance for self employed

For unemployed workers who enter into self-employment, Unemployment Benefit or Assistance is granted for six months to ensure a subsistence income during the difficult start-up period of a new business.

Support for vocational further training or retraining

The aim of this scheme is to improve occupational flexibility, to encourage career advancement of individuals and to prevent skill shortages in local economies. Participants are largely the unemployed. Participants on full-time courses are paid an allowance of 75 per cent of net wage if they have dependants, or 65 per cent if not. Part-time trainees can be made an allowance if they are looking after children. Training must be 'necessary' as defined by the ABM. The BA pays all or part of the expenses of training, not only course

163

fees but also cost of material, books, fares, working clothes and sickness insurance. A grant is also given for lodging expenses if training is away from home. Child care costs are paid up to 60 DM per month, a very small amount. In Frankfurt 1,126 people were trained under this scheme. Together with vocational preparation courses for the young (see p. 165), expenditure in Frankfurt in 1990 was 113.9 million DM.

Measures to help the young unemployed

Before looking at special aid to the young unemployed it would first of all be useful to examine the training available to all young people and undertaken by the vast majority of the young. It will help to explain why youth unemployment is relatively so low in Germany.

Vocational training in the dual system

The system of dual training in vocational schools and firms is open to all young people having had some secondary education. The training is for particular professional skills. There are three hundred and seventy-five recognised occupations for which training is required. The training is extensive and generally lasts for three years. The young person entering into a contract under this system has the status of employee and receives a training allowance which varies according to the industry concerned.[14] Training given in vocational schools and firms is often supplemented by courses in a joint training establishment, for example, in new technologies. This scheme of youth training has existed in Germany for many years, and as previously mentioned is based on assessment of economic needs in the long-term by the Tripartite Federal Institute of Vocational Training. It is seen as being advantageous to industry as well as young workers, and is incorporated into long-term economic strategies. Since most young people in Frankfurt, who are not in higher levels of academic or technical education, take part in this training scheme as a matter of course, the unemployment rate for the under 20s is very low.

Training allowances may be as low as 260 DM per month, and in order to allow trainees who do not or cannot live in the parental home there is the following subsidy:

Support for vocational training of individuals

Since 1989 trainees on the dual training schemes or trainees in companies (e.g. apprentices) can apply for an allowance if not living in the home, which takes into account the living and training expenses and income of the trainee. The scheme is financed and organised by the BA.

Vocational preparation course

This scheme facilitates the integration of difficult-to-place young people who for various reasons are unable to take up conventional training. The measures in operation include helping the young person to obtain a lower secondary school leaving certificate; to improve general educational skills; to give basic training to those who do not have access to vocational training; to provide information and motivation courses for the young; to provide sheltered workshops and prepare the disabled young for vocational training and employment. The courses last up to a year, or in the case of the disabled, up to two years. The scheme is financed by the BA and operated by the local ABM in Frankfurt.

Support for vocational training for foreign trainees and for socially disadvantaged German trainees or those with learning difficulties

Those who have participated in a vocational preparation course and cannot be placed in mainstream training without further help are aided within this scheme. From 1990–93 it included unplaced school leavers and trainees who had lost their place through company closure. The measures are of two kinds. One is to give support to on-job vocational training, by giving remedial tuition to reduce educational and language difficulties and to teach technical skills to ensure a successful outcome in mainstream training. The other is to give training in a training centre when it is not possible to provide normal dual training, even with support. After one year efforts are made to integrate these young people in training within a firm. Grants are given to the training and support bodies by the BA. Nationally the cost was 6,600 DM per person.

Integrated programme to help young unemployed

For young people who are very difficult to place in training or a work scheme, Frankfurt runs a special programme that is part-funded by the BA but is largely funded by the city. Under the Social Act a particular form of social policy is to help those with multiple social problems to integrate into working life. They have problems such as homelessness, drug and alcohol addiction or they may be abused women. Support is given by three departments to help with accommodation, employment and general social support. For the young, one quarter of the time is spent in a special vocational school and three quarters in a placement in public or private sector. There is no shortage of places available. If the participant has previously worked then Frankfurt Werkstatt (which runs the scheme) would try to find a placement in the same occupation. Social workers liaise with the work supervisors. The period of help is usually eighteen months but can be extended for a further eighteen months. For the young the outcome in terms of finding work is between 40–50 per cent. The most difficult to place are young foreign workers. The organisation reports that there is discrimination against blacks, Moroccans, refugees and Turkish workers, particularly young Turkish males. Between 60 and 70 per cent of those on this scheme are foreigners. Frankfurt Werkstatt also finds placements for another young group with particular difficulties, single parent mothers with pre-school children. Part-time placements are normally available with child-care provided. The ESF is a large contributor to this scheme. In 1990–91 some seven hundred people were aided at a cost of 30 million DM, approximately 42,880 DM per participant. These numbers include also the very long-term unemployed who are difficult to place (see next section).

Measures to aid the long-term unemployed

Employment assistance subsidy for LTU

The aim of this measure is to reintegrate the long-term unemployed into permanent work in the formal labour market by offering a wage subsidy to an employer who offers a permanent employment contract of at least eighteen hours a week. The subsidy is payable for twelve months and is available on the following scales:

- 1–2 years unemployed – 60 per cent for six months plus 40 per cent for six months
- 2–3 years unemployed – 70 per cent for six months plus 50 per cent for six months
- over three years unemployed – 80 per cent for six months plus 60 per cent for six months.

Employers apply to the Employment Office before entering into a contract. In the Frankfurt area in 1991 415 workers were placed in employment under the scheme, 207 unemployed between one and two years, 109 between two and three years unemployed, and 99 unemployed for over three years. It was most effective for those unemployed for a shorter period. Sixty-four per cent of those finding work were aged between 30 and 50 years old. In 1991 in the Frankfurt area, 620 workers were helped at a cost of 2 million DM (expenditure per participant 3225 DM).

Job creation for the LTU

Job creation schemes are aimed particularly at helping the long-term unemployed and those over 50 years of age. Priority is given to projects which are likely to result in employment in a permanent job, or improving social infrastructure and the environment. The job creation projects must provide 'additional' jobs (not substitute for existing jobs) and should benefit the community. A subsidy is given to the body creating the job (usually the public sector or a voluntary agency) of normally between 50 and 75 per cent of wages. Occasionally this can be up to full wage cost. Aid is usually given for a year, but can be given for two years for social reasons and over two years if a permanent job is created. In West Germany as a whole in 1991, 45 per cent of those who had been on this scheme found non-subsidised jobs.

Job creation for older workers

Under the above scheme workers over 50 who have been unemployed for longer than a year can be employed in 'additional' jobs for five years in the private sector or three in the public sector. The wage subsidy is 70 per cent for the private sector and 60 per cent for public bodies for the first year, reducing by 10 per cent per annum. If the older worker has been unemployed over eighteen months, the scheme allows for 70 per cent of wage costs for up to eight years – effectively the rest of working life. The scheme is financed, as is the previous one, by the BA, which also organises it. Higher levels of grant can be given under both schemes if the Land (Hesse) is willing to provide matching funds. Under both of the above job creation schemes 485 unemployed were helped at a cost of 13.7 million DM, of which the city paid 2 million DM and Hesse 1.9 million DM (expenditure per participant 28,247 DM).

Measures to help the disabled unemployed

Disabled workers in Frankfurt form a significant proportion of the long-term unemployed. The severely disabled have a special service provided within the general job placement service. Other measures specifically designed to help the disadvantaged group are of two types, subsidies as an incentive to employers and vocational rehabilitation schemes.

Incentives for the recruitment and employment of disabled workers

This scheme is designed to help difficult-to-place severely disabled workers registered at the Employment Office, who have neither work nor a training place. Subsidies are available to employers to cover 100 per cent of training costs or up to 80 per cent of the worker's wage for a maximum of three years.

Vocational rehabilitation

This scheme is designed to help physically, mentally or psychologically handicapped people to become integrated into a job or occupation. Grants are available to assist in maintaining, improving, establishing or restoring the earning capacity of workers in relation to their capabilities. Financial support from the BA ensures that there are a sufficient number of centres for vocational rehabilitation, including training centres, centres for medical occupational rehabilitation, sheltered workshops and the training of staff. All costs incurred by participants are covered, including subsistence allowance for disabled persons and their families. The duration of the scheme is effectively limitless, as it lasts until the disabled person is permanently integrated into working life. In Frankfurt the Hilferbund Frankfurt Verein and Werkstatt Frankfurt are responsible for those most difficult to place, and who are unlikely to be integrated into the formal labour market. They run two sheltered workshops, one for those who are psychologically disturbed or have chronic mental health problems. Here workers, under supervision of specifically trained staff, produce goods for sale on the private market. Grants are available to those projects for investment and the training of welfare staff. In the Frankfurt area in 1991 97.2 million DM were spent on vocational rehabilitation projects.

Measures to aid unemployed ethnic minority workers

As has been shown ethnic minorities suffer disproportionately high unemployment rates, form a high proportion of the long-term unemployed and are in the majority of the difficult-to-place young worker category. Frankfurt also has a large number of 'German' resettlers from Eastern Europe and Russia.

The national policies to aid foreigners are of two kinds, either encouragement to resettle in their country of origin or integration assistance.

Resettlement aid to foreign workers

These measures apply especially to migrants from former recruitment countries who arrived largely in the 1960s in Germany. In 1983 special repatriation allowances were given of 10,500 DM per worker plus 1,500 DM per child to allow unemployed foreign workers to return home. This no longer applies, but certain incentives are in operation. Counselling in opportunities in vocational reintegration, or setting up in business in the home country are supplied at main employment offices. Foreign workers can cash in savings and are given indemnity for pension rights accrued in Germany. Since 1986 there has been assistance with housing whereby building society savings made in Germany can be used to acquire a dwelling in the home country and can, up to 60,000 DM, be transferred tax free. On behalf of the Ministry for Economic Cooperation, the German Compensation Bank gives help on business start-ups to those with well formulated investment and financial plans. A subsidy of 5 per cent of total investment can be given up to a maximum of 9,000 DM. Overall in Germany a quarter of a million foreign workers and their families have returned voluntarily, of whom thirteen and a half thousand were unemployed. No figures are available on how many went from Frankfurt.

Integration assistance to foreign workers

These measures apply largely to young people. Help is given on language courses for new arrivals, with child care facilities provided. Assistance is also given for second and third generation young workers for employment preparation. Some bilateral training schemes are available to prepare young workers for employment in the home country with theoretical training in Germany and practical training in the home country. Such schemes exist in cooperation with Greece and Spain.

Measures to aid resettlers, refugees and asylum seekers

Language courses are provided for all 'German' resettlers to provide proficiency in written and spoken German, if they had been employed in the country of origin for at least one hundred and fifty days. In 1991 the BA covered the cost of these courses, plus the cost of travelling expenses, health and accident insurance and in certain cases a very small child care allowance of 60 DM per month. Those attending courses received 610 DM per week. Young resettlers, refugees and asylum seekers have the cost of the course, books, materials and travel expenses reimbursed. In the Frankfurt area in 1991, 33.5 million DM were spent on language courses.

Measures to aid women in the labour market

All of the above schemes are open to women as well as men. Retraining, as noted, can be done part-time for women and there may be child care facilities provided. Women participating in training can choose the type of training they wish to undertake. Frankfurt ABM noted that in the last three years there has been a trebling of willingness to participate in training in non-traditional areas, particularly amongst young women.[15] This is supported financially by the ESF. The city also, recognising discrimination against women in the local labour market, has arranged new schemes of positive discrimination in government administration and some private firms, e.g. IBM.

EVALUATION OF MEASURES AFFECTING THE UNEMPLOYED IN FRANKFURT

As noted, the unemployment problem in Frankfurt is not serious. It is an area of labour shortage, and fast growth of employment. Projections of growth and employment for Hesse show expected growth rates of 3.3 per cent per annum for 1990 to 2000 and 2.8 per cent per annum for 2000 to 2012. The number employed will also grow at similar rates since the employment content of service sector growth is high (Hessen Report 1992). The number of employed persons is predicted to grow faster in this region than the German average. This was even before news that the proposed Central Bank of Europe will be located in Frankfurt when it is established, which should lend an even greater boost to the economy of Frankfurt than predicted. The problems, such as they are, lie in the long-term unemployed sector of around five thousand unemployed workers. It is the characteristics of this group who are largely, but not exclusively, made up of those who are unskilled or have low educational qualifications, the severely disabled and those with multiple social disadvantages, including the discriminatory effect on ethnic minorities. Past labour needs of the city and the high number of refugees and resettlers have added to this group in recent years, although the number of long-term unemployed started to decline as the local economy boomed in the late 1980s. Compared to Montpellier, another city with fast growth of employment in growth sectors of the economy, the unemployment experience was not similar. Frankfurt is within a wealthy, low unemployment region, unlike Montpellier which attracted many migrants from its region. It has also slowed the potential growth of migrants, especially from the Eastern *Laender* by effectively barring residence.

The measures to deal with unemployment in this wealthy city are comprehensive, well directed and well run. Expenditure on the long-term unemployed is very high for those taking part in the variety of employment schemes. Although total expenditure on all active labour market measures is not known, the total expenditure on schemes shown in Table 8.12 will give a good approximation. It also indicates the generous level of expenditure on each participant.

In addition the city of Frankfurt spent 30 million DM in 1991 on those most difficult to place in employment at a cost of 42,880 DM per person, the most expensive scheme which involves multi dimensional help with the problems of this group.

The short-term unemployed do not figure greatly in expenditure, which in a situation where most are able to find work rapidly, via Employment

Table 8.12 Frankfurt AMB area expenditure on employment measures, 1990

Type of measure	Total expenditure (million DM)	Amount per participant (DM)
Vocational preparation/support	113.9	24,083
Vocational rehabilitation for disabled	97.2	39,789
Language courses	33.5	
LTU wage subsidy	2.0	3,225
LTU job creation	1.9	28,274

Service and other vacancy sources, is reasonable. The lack of young unemployed is splendid testimony to the BA's comprehensive system of professional training for young people, most of whom are automatically entered for a three year training on leaving school. What would appear to be a heavy cost on national resources is in fact the reverse, as skill shortages do not build up and neither does unemployment. The scenario of large numbers of young unskilled workers on the market, with firms disinclined to offer training in recessionary times is not a feature of the German labour market.

In Frankfurt the localisation of heavy unemployment in certain areas within the city is not apparent, except to a very small degree. Unlike other cities employment in central areas has not fallen as work has suburbanised. It has grown, albeit at a slower rate than in outer areas of the labour market. Access within the city to available work is also not impeded by the lack of availability or cost of public transportation.

The problems which appear to be least well solved are those of ethnic minorities, women and long-term unemployed with high levels of qualification.

Although ethnic minorities do not constitute as large a proportion of total long-term unemployed as Germans, they are often in the very difficult-to-place category. The main negative characteristic is that, on the whole, they have low educational attainments but this is compounded by the reported discrimination of employers, especially against male foreign workers. Ethnic minorities form a large proportion on schemes for vocational preparation and most difficult-to-place workers. The German Federal Government notes a marked improvement in educational standards as a result of these policies over the last few years (MISEP 1992b). It is apparent, however, that despite the fact that ethnic migrant workers on the labour market are second or third generation German-born, they are not considered as German. This is reflected in policies to encourage return to a 'home' country. It is also reflected in the policy of welcoming 'Germans', mostly non-German speaking but of German ancestry, back from past communist bloc countries. This strong sense of a 'national' identity is already causing not just discrimination in the labour market, but also violence in areas where unemployment is high in the eastern Laender. Germany's attitude is in marked contrast to the treatment of past migrant workers and their descendants in Rotterdam, where they are considered to be equal Dutch citizens, and have positive discrimination practised in their favour in employment measures. While recognising that racial discrimination is practised by employers, the Rotterdam attitude is to undertake very specific measures to overcome it. It will be interesting to see if German resettlers with language and cultural differences also face the same discrimination.

Women's problems in the labour market in Frankfurt are that there appears to be an underemployment of skills, and a number of well-educated women who are long-term unemployed. The local ABM report that although they try to provide child care in most training schemes, child care facilities in the city are not generally available for women with children wishing to work. This is borne out across Germany by Hujer and Schnabel (1992) who stated that married women with children suffer from a high rate of unemployment. This has longer term implications, since, when women are free to return to work when their children need less care, they have many years without work experience and are less likely to be employable. In Frankfurt, however, because of labour shortages, it has become a new trend for employers to provide child care facilities, but this system is not yet well developed.[16]

Women are found to be more difficult to place after training. There is a high demand from them for part-time work but employers are on the whole opposed to it. The final category that appears to be a problem that is not addressed is that of university and other graduates of higher education who are long-term unemployed. Overcoming the problem of corporate selection in terms of perceived personality or social requirements is somewhat difficult, however, for a training programme to address.

The unemployed in Frankfurt are fortunate that there is both the will and the resources to solve most of their problems.

9

UNEMPLOYMENT IN
EUROPEAN CITIES: CAUSES
AND POLICIES

The cities that have been examined are very different in economic structure, face different types of unemployment problems and have different policies in operation to reduce the level of unemployment. Cities rely largely on national interpretations of the causes of unemployment for their solutions, since it is national governments that set the policy agenda and levels of expenditure on active labour market policies. Action at local level is mainly through the agencies of central government, although in some cases city governments do have the power and the ability to initiate policy at an urban level.

In Chapter 1 the generally perceived causes of unemployment in the European Community (now the European Union) as a whole were discussed. These included demand factors and the role of restrictive macro-economic policy; distortions to the price of labour arising from minimum wage legislation and high levels of unemployment compensation; hysteresis effects of trade union action and discrimination; structural change and mismatch of skills; and the low labour content of economic growth in Europe. In Chapter 2 local factors affecting unemployment were discussed. As a rule it was considered that creation of new employment would reduce unemployment and loss of employment would increase it. In other words, those cities with a favourable structure for growth would be unlikely to suffer high levels of unemployment. Local factors affecting unemployment were the location of the unemployed; availability and cost of public transportation; and employer discrimination against certain groups either because of their residential location in the city or their ethnic origin.

Large European cities as a whole, as has been shown, have higher unemployment rates than the national averages. Can one use the findings on unemployment in cities as a microcosm of a wider pattern? Is there such a thing as 'European' unemployment that is fundamentally different from the problems experienced elsewhere in the industrialised world? Before attempting to address these questions, one must first ask whether or not it is valid to compare information on levels of unemployment and the numbers of unemployed and their characteristics, when the available statistics at city level do not exactly correspond, and precise information on different aspects of policy is not in all cases available? Clearly one cannot make a true comparison say, of female unemployment rates, as different bases have been used for calculating this figure in different cities. Similarly, in some cities youth unemployment is underestimated where those on unemployment schemes are excluded, compared to cities where they are included in the total of youth unemployment. Nevertheless it is possible to gain a fairly clear picture of both levels of unemployment and also of which groups within the cities are most seriously affected by unemployment.

To return to the causes of unemployment, first of all let us examine the cities in relationship to demand factors and the creation of loss of employment. European Union Member States suffered a loss or only slow growth of employment in the late 1980s and an overall loss of employment since 1992. The distribution of job losses and gains within Member States reflected the favourable or unfavourable aspects of local economies. It is not necessarily the case that cities in regions with low growth economies and loss of employment will also display the same features. Cities like Montpellier in a depressed agricultural region may experience fast growth of employment and be attractive to fast growth sectors of the economy. The studies have shown that unemployment rates in the cities are not necessarily related to employment growth or loss. The relationship is more clear between employment growth/loss and population growth/loss, but even here there is an exception. The changes in employment and population are shown below.

Montpellier 1982–90
Growth in employment   11.3 per cent
Growth in population   21.0 per cent
Unemployment increasing

Manchester 1981–91
Loss in employment   18 per cent (in Greater Manchester)
Loss in population   9.5 per cent
Unemployment increasing

Rotterdam
Loss in employment 1970–91   11 per cent
Loss in population 1965–91   24 per cent
Unemployment increasing

Barcelona
Growth in employment 1985–90   14 per cent
Loss in population 1981–90   2.7 per cent
Unemployment decreasing

Frankfurt
Growth in employment 1984–90   15.4 per cent
Growth in population 1984–90   1.1 per cent
Unemployment decreasing

Demand for labour increased in Montpellier, Barcelona and Frankfurt. In Montpellier growth in population through immigration was greater than employment growth, resulting in increased unemployment loads. In Barcelona employment growth coincided with loss of population, resulting in a dramatic decrease in unemployment. In Frankfurt growth in employment was accompanied by growth in population but the latter was much smaller than the former, again resulting in a decrease in unemployment.

The two cities with a fall in employment, Manchester and Rotterdam, both experienced a fall in population. The fall in employment in Manchester was greater than the fall in population and, as would be expected, unemployment increased. In Rotterdam however the fall in employment was only around half the loss in population but unemployment increased.

Growth or loss of employment reflecting changes in local demand do not, therefore, on their own, result in a decrease or increase in unemployment. Change in population (and by implication active population) must also be taken into account, as at a national level. One would expect to find that if population growth outstripped employment growth there would be an increase in unemployment, as in Montpellier; that if employment growth was higher than population growth there would be a fall in unemployment as in Barcelona and Frankfurt; and that if job loss was greater than population less unemployment would arise as in Manchester. What is not expected is that a loss in population greater than a loss in employment would result in increased unemployment, as in Rotterdam. Conditions of local labour market demand and population change do not appear to give a satisfactory explanation of changes in unemployment levels. Policies which assume that employment creation or job retention policies on their own will solve the problem of unemployment in cities are only relevant in some situations. While Montpellier experienced a fast growth of jobs in growth sectors, unemployment grew more serious since the prospect of work encouraged immigration from the surrounding region of very high unemployment.

In order to understand Rotterdam's problem one must examine the characteristics of the urban unemployed in relation to jobs available. In relation to this it would be useful to examine the concept of mismatch of skills in relation to local economies. The basic idea that structural change, for example from a manufacturing economy to one dominated by the service sector, will result in initial unemployment of workers from one sector in the short-term, is a simplistic one. Sectoral shift as such implies that in the medium term, with a modicum of training for adaptation to new skills, the problem should disappear, and that mismatch is only a temporary problem. If one looks at the cities studied, Montpellier has experienced little sectoral change in its economy. It has always been a predominantly high-skill service economy. Growth in employment continues to be in sectors requiring a very high level of professional skills and much of the demand for labour is supplied from the national market, not just the regional market. The local supply of labour is predominantly unskilled and of low educational attainments, migrants from the surrounding region and from North Africa. As has been pointed out, it is very unlikely that these residents could fill the vacancies, even with very extensive training. In Manchester there has been a shift from manufacturing to services in the past twenty years. The service jobs created have gone largely to women, many to part-timers, so while female unemployment has declined male unemployment has risen, and males are more likely to be unemployed in all age groups. Again though, the growth in demand for labour is for those with a high level of education and training in managerial skills, while over half the unemployed and a higher proportion of those long-term unemployed hold no formal educational qualifications. In the Rotterdam area manufacturing, construction and commerce all declined, while services grew to be the major employer during the 1980s. One third of all those unemployed come from ethnic minorities who had manual jobs in industry, the docks and construction, where most jobs were lost. This group has very low educational attainments on the whole, and this is the case also for the youngest age group of ethnic minorities, who account for 40 per cent of the young unemployed. There is a clear mismatch between the growth in white-collar work and the skill levels of the unemployed Dutch and non-Dutch citizens, and an increasing number of jobs being taken up by commuters from outside the city.

Barcelona, after a fall in employment in manufacturing in the 1970s and early 1980s, saw some increase in jobs in this sector during the 'Olympic boom'. The local economy was, however, as throughout Europe, concentrated in services with the largest increase in demand in hotels, catering and retail sectors. Of all vacancies, at the time of study, 40 per cent required knowledge of a foreign language. Prior to the late 1980s, however, those with lower levels of education and training constituted most of the jobless. Construction work and low-paid service jobs increased dramatically with investment for the Olympic Games and absorbed the majority of unqualified male workers. Women, who represented the majority of unemployed in the city, had low levels of education on the whole. In Frankfurt the demand for labour was predominantly for those workers with secondary education and a professional training, while over half the unemployed were without skills and had no previous employment, and a further quarter had only on-job training. The gap between demand and potential local supply was again great in terms of skill level, not something bridgeable by a short course.

The conclusion must be that in all the European cities examined in this study there is an enormous gap between the qualifications and education of the majority of the unemployed, available work, and areas of employment growth in the cities. Both male and female manual workers with low educational levels are most at risk of long-term unemployment, and unskilled jobs are becoming a smaller and smaller proportion of total employment. The depressing longer-term pattern is that the percentage of the young with qualifications is growing only very slowly, so the overall character of the labour force in the cities will not change significantly until educational standards of the most deprived groups are raised. Eighty per cent of the European workforce in the year 2000 are already part of the workforce now. The problem of mismatch and unemployment of the least qualified is unlikely to reduce much within the formal labour market.

Turning now to how far minimum wage levels and unemployment compensation schemes affect unemployment in the cities, the answer appears to be very little. The three countries with standardised national minimum wages are France, the Netherlands and Spain, with respective minimum monthly wages in sterling (1991) of approximately £658, £585 and £284.[1] Germany has different minimum wages in each industry, but they are the equivalent of French minimum wage, and in most cases considerably more. The UK has no minimum wage. Germany and the Netherlands with higher levels of minimum wage have lower unemployment rates than Spain, with lower minimum wage costs, and the UK, which abolished even minimum wages for low-paid workers previously set by the Wages Council for workers in, for example, catering and agricultural work. There appears to be little relationship in the city studies between the existence of minimum wage and the number of low-pay jobs on offer, nor the prevailing unemployment rate. Local Chambers of Commerce did not report high levels of basic minimum wages as a reason that inhibited job growth. In France the government attempted in March 1994 to introduce a lower pay rate for young people in work experience/employment, on an upwards scale from 30–65 per cent of SMIC (according to age) up to the age of 21, an effective cut of 20 per cent in remuneration. Vast and often violent demonstrations by the young in Paris and other large cities forced withdrawal of the scheme. A removal of minimum rates, once existing, does not seem to be a socially or politically acceptable option judging from this, even if it might, in the case of the young, result in more employment opportunities.

In 'Employment in Europe' (CEC 1992) rates of replacement ratio of unemployment compensation to previous wage were calculated as shown in Figure 9.1.[2] The Netherlands, Spain and France have the longest periods of wage-related unemployment compensation, and the Netherlands and Germany the highest replacement ratios. The UK had the lowest replacement ratio, and was the system least linked to the insurance principle, as it bore no relationship to an individual's previous wage.

While in all five countries fewer unemployed women than men received unemployment compensation in 1990, unemployment rates, except in Manchester, were higher for women than men. In Spain only 18 per cent of women received unemployment compensation, so that the existence and level of benefits is irrelevant to the vast majority of unemployed women in Barcelona. If one looks at the share of the unemployed in total receiving unemployment compensation, 63 per cent in West Germany received benefit but

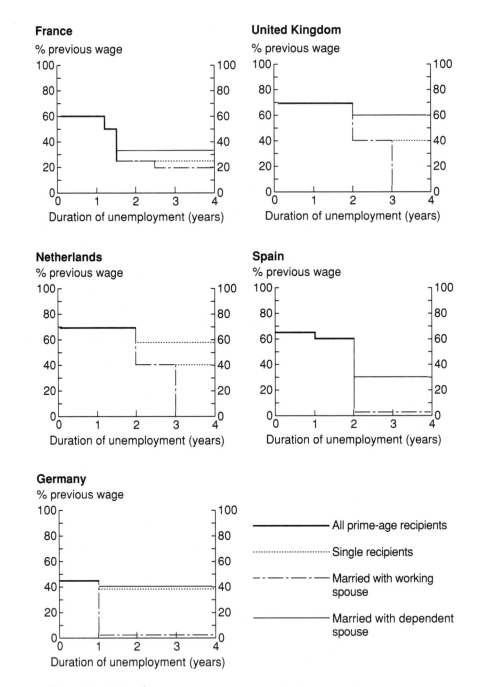

Figure 9.1 Unemployment compensation in relation to previous wage rate, France, UK, Netherlands, Spain and Germany, 1990

Source: Directorate General for Employment, Industrial Relations and Social Affairs, European Commission

only 25 per cent in Spain, yet Germany had a low and Spain a very high rate of unemployment.[3] The CEC report concluded that the relationship between unemployment compensation levels and their duration and the likelihood of individuals moving from unemployment to reemployment was very weak. Both Hujer and Schneider (1989), and Van den Berg (1990) found no or very weak effects of replacement rates on jobs taken up in Europe. Wadsworth (1991) found that benefits in the UK may have a positive effect on increasing good match between firms and workers, but that benefit claimants search more intensively for a job than other unemployed without benefit. The only indication in the studies of such a relationship, was that the 16–18-year-old age group in Manchester entered further education and training in greater numbers after the removal of social assistance for this group of unemployed, if no training place was accepted. The young, therefore, might be induced to be more active on their own behalf, if not by finding jobs at least by improving their skills and prospects, if benefit is reduced or curtailed. On the other hand evidence from Barcelona, where only a quarter of those under 30 who are unemployed can claim any form of social assistance, and where youth unemployment is very high, does not support this argument.

Local factors affecting unemployment can to some extent be gauged by the disparities in unemployment rates in different areas of the city. Very high levels of concentration were found in Montpellier and Manchester, with a fairly high degree in Rotterdam, low concentration in Barcelona, and very little evidence of concentration in Frankfurt. In Montpellier and Manchester low-income households were trapped in large social housing estates, with poor transportation links to areas of job growth around the city. In Rotterdam transportation was comprehensive and cheap, but growth of employment had largely taken place in outer suburban areas. Barcelona had had a sudden growth of employment in the city and together with a comprehensive flat fare rapid transit system appeared not to suffer from a high degree of localisation. Frankfurt, with such low overall unemployment, growth of jobs in the central area and good public transportation did not suffer at all from localisation problems. While it is not possible to state categorically that the location and planning of new employment location, and the cost and availability of transportation have an effect which reinforces unemployment in certain areas of a city, there does seem to be a strong possibility of a link. Certainly Rotterdam city government was working on this assumption in trying to relocate employment into the city, as were the Urban Development Corporations in Manchester. Further detailed research on the unemployed in areas of high concentration of joblessness is needed.

In looking at the causes of unemployment in the cities, clearly the most important factor in achieving low unemployment levels is the rate of job creation over and above population growth. The type of jobs created in relation to the skills of the unemployed was important in all five cities, where education and training levels were a strong determinant of the propensity to

179

be employed or unemployed. This was a factor also stressed by Wadsworth (1991), who found education had a significantly positive effect on the transition from unemployment to employment, and also on the duration of unemployment in Europe.

The unemployed, especially younger workers, will tend to migrate to large cities in the hope of finding work within a larger labour market. This is happening between regions and cities, from poorer countries in Europe to richer cities in Europe, and more recently from Eastern Europe to Western European cities. In accommodating these flows of migrants, large cities, and particularly those with any growth in employment, are likely to be affected in a free and open market for labour by increasing unemployment. Most of the migrants have low educational and skill levels and the growth in employment is predominantly in high-skill service sectors of the economy. Some cities, like Manchester and Rotterdam, are also suffering disproportionately because of a change in the demand for labour following manufacturing decline and technological change. Rotterdam also had the problem, together with Frankfurt, of migrant workers coming from poorer countries in the 1960s when there was a shortage of unskilled labour. In general their descendants have low skills and often language problems that make finding a job difficult, together with the problem of discrimination against ethnic minorities.

In all cities, except Frankfurt, there is a major problem of youth unemployment. In all cities, except Manchester, women are more at risk of unemployment than men. In all cities the proportion of long-term unemployed was growing. It is in this context that unemployment policy in the cities must be assessed.

GENERAL POLICIES FOR THE UNEMPLOYED

For the short-term (less than one year) unemployed adults, all the cities offer a placement and advice service. Frankfurt, in addition, has extensive subsidies to aid job search, including advancing salary to those finding employment.

The major forms of aid are measures for training, enterprise creation, job creation and maintenance of employment. Montpellier offers training through schools and in firms; Barcelona trains in building skills and subsidises work experience training; Frankfurt has training and retraining schemes; Rotterdam offers not only training subsidies but aid to child care costs for the unemployed worker in training; Manchester has Career Development Loans available to individuals. All the cities give either grants to the unemployed setting up in business, or a living allowance in the start-up period or both. Montpellier is unique in having a tax benefit scheme aimed at increasing employment in family care work. The other main area, trying to maintain existing jobs, is aided via subsidies to short-time workers when firms are in difficulties in Frankfurt and Barcelona, and subsidies to firms having difficulty paying minimum wages in Rotterdam. Frankfurt and Rotterdam, therefore, have the widest spread of policies and Manchester the fewest measures to aid the short-term unemployed. It could be argued that if this group received more help there would be fewer long-term unemployed, as more people would find work in a shorter time, but in fact although Frankfurt has only a relatively small group of long-term unemployed, the proportion in Rotterdam and Manchester are similar.

Measures for the young unemployed

Measures to aid the young unemployed fall into two categories – training or work experience. Barcelona provides training either in special centres or in a workplace, including a centre for those with higher levels of education. Frankfurt, Rotterdam and Montpellier have a variety of schemes, according to the needs of the individual including preparatory schemes for those with low educational attainments, subsidies to pre-apprenticeship and formal apprenticeship schemes; in the case of Montpellier training for a formal qualification for those with poor educational qualifications; and in the case of Frankfurt an integrated programme of training and social care to help the most disadvantaged and difficult-to-place young people. Manchester does not have the same comprehensive training systems for the young. Youth training is for most people a combination of on-job training and work experience. Montpellier, Barcelona and Rotterdam all have work experience schemes for the young. In Montpellier they are 'additional' jobs in the public sector and the Youth Employment Guarantee scheme in Rotterdam arranges 'additional' jobs in normally the public, but sometimes the private sector. Barcelona arranges work experience contracts that are not subsidised and arguably are not in all cases 'additional'. The problem of youth unemployment in Frankfurt is negligible, as already stated, as a result of the existing training structure for the young in Germany. Nevertheless for those not covered provision of aid is tailored to the needs of different sectors of the young unemployed. Rotterdam and Montpellier have high levels of young unemployed and a variety of different schemes for different groups. Barcelona has less provision in the way of skill qualification, and a non-subsidised work experience scheme. Manchester has a subsidised work experience scheme and training at lower rather than higher skill levels. Apprenticeships, for instance, are not subsidised.

Measures to aid the long-term unemployed

One of the main forms of aid to the long-term unemployed in the cities were wage subsidies paid to firms as an incentive to take on these workers. These were offered in Frankfurt for up to one year, in Rotterdam for up to four years, and in Barcelona only for the long-term unemployed under 30 or over 45 years of age. A second type of measure was the creation of additional jobs in the public sector to aid the community. Frankfurt provided jobs for not only the long-term unemployed, but also those unemployed over 50 years of age, as it was considered unlikely that they would be employed in the formal labour market. Rotterdam and Montpellier offered assistance through Labour Pools and the Solidarity Employment Contract respectively, and Manchester had a relatively small number on Employment Action. Training was the major form of aid in Manchester through Employment Training, largely in formal training schools, to acquire credits towards recognised skills. Montpellier subsidised some on-job training in firms and reserved places in training centres for the very hard-to-place long-term unemployed. Other measures are aimed at 'discouraged' workers via Restart Interviews, Job Clubs and Job Interview Guarantees in Manchester, and Reorientation Interviews in Rotterdam. The one unique policy operated in Rotterdam is area based 'social renewal' aimed to tackle the housing, social and employment problems of the areas of highest unemployment and highest long-term unemployment in the city via creation of a community based 'additional' job for life. Rotterdam, in effect, recognised that there are certain groups of the unemployed who are unemployable on the formal labour market, especially where there is a situation of high general unemployment. In this situation the least qualified will always be last in line for a job offer. Manchester, although not offering wage subsidies, aims to retrain in skills relevant to the local labour market, uses some job creation and tackles the problem of lack of confidence and withdrawal from the labour market of the long-term unemployed.

Measures to help unemployed women

Considering the enormous problem of female unemployment in Europe there were few special schemes in the cities. All schemes are, of course, open to male and female participants and in Rotterdam priority was given to women on all schemes. This, however, does not recognise the special difficulties that women workers have in child care responsibilities and resulting difficulties in times available, and suitable work locations nearer home. Childless women, without these difficulties, experience discrimination in certain areas of work that are typically male. The European Union recognised this and provided subsidies to schemes for training and recruitment of women in non-traditional areas. This type of scheme operates in Barcelona in the PILD scheme, and wage subsidies to non-traditional jobs in SMES; in Rotterdam through Women's Vocational School and subsidies to female apprenticeship; in Montpellier in the Plan for Vocational Equality; and in the Manchester Scheme. Numbers of participants are relatively small in all these initiatives. The problem posed by child care is best addressed in

Montpellier where the double-value policy of Family Employees creates a job (usually for a woman) and subsidises a large proportion of child care (or elderly person care) through the tax system for women in work, thus allowing women to become more flexible in their working practices. Business grants and advice are given to women in Barcelona in the ODAME project, with the hope that further jobs for women will become available in the new businesses created. Grants towards child care are available to participants on Youth Training and Employment Training Schemes in Manchester. There were no comprehensive crèche or child care facilities provided by city governments, and no subsidies available for firms to provide facilities. Frankfurt has no special schemes for unemployed women, but does, as a concession, offer some training schemes on a part-time basis to those with children.

Fewer women are unemployed in Manchester partly because there are many more part-time and flexible-time jobs available. Part-time work was not generally available, except in very low level occupations such as office cleaning, and neither did national or local policy in the other four cities try to promote the idea with employers, despite opinions expressed that it would help reduce the problem of female unemployment considerably.

Overall in the three cities where female unemployment was most serious – Montpellier, Rotterdam and Barcelona – no really effective policy existed to combat the problem. This is a major failure of employment policy throughout continental Europe where the lack of flexibility in working practices effectively discriminates very heavily against female employment, and is more important than the ability to enter non-traditional occupations.

Measures to aid ethnic minorities

The problem of high levels of unemployment amongst ethnic minorities in cities is largely the result of low educational and skill levels, together with, in some cases, language problems, and locational disadvantage by ghettoisation, compounded by racial discrimination in the labour market. These problems are encountered in Montpellier, Rotterdam, Frankfurt and Manchester to a greater or lesser degree. Very little is done for ethnic minorities as a separate group from the rest of the population with similar individual disadvantages. Frankfurt does have integration assistance for young settlers and refugees, with language classes to promote proficiency in German. Frankfurt also offers return of unemployment benefit entitlement to returning guest workers, and advice on resettlement in the country of origin. Rotterdam gives priority to young ethnic minority participants in most schemes. Older workers also have priority in the 'social renewal' programme with a 50 per cent target for minority participation. Positive discrimination is, therefore, a feature of this city's employment initiatives.

There are no special policies in operation in Montpellier, where it is considered illegal to discriminate on grounds of race, but where some language classes are available.

Overall the problems of unemployment of migrants, past or present, are largely ignored, with the exception of the Netherlands.

Measures to aid the disabled unemployed

Measures to aid the disabled without work were generous and comprehensive in all the cities. In Barcelona this was done via subsidies and grants to employers; in Manchester by grants to adapt premises and subsidies to employers; in Frankfurt by vocational rehabilitation and training and provision of jobs in sheltered workshops; in Rotterdam by subsidising employment placement and again the provision of sheltered workshops. In Montpellier, all of the above measures operated plus grants for the disabled worker to travel to work. In expenditure terms per worker, the disabled unemployed had a much higher amount spent on them than any other group of the unemployed.

Urban policy and unemployment

Urban policy – the planning of areas of employment growth, the siting of new science parks, the regeneration of city areas and public transportation policy in the cities can have an impact, as discussed, on the unemployed.

Rotterdam has addressed the problem of unemployment, in its economic development plan, by a policy to re-site jobs to central areas and forbid expansion of certain types of activity in the suburban areas. The package of renewal proposals incorporated in 'social renewal' also considers employment alongside other physical and social problems in the most deprived areas of the city. Manchester, also, has used Urban Development Corporations, a renewal policy judged successful by government partly in terms of the number of jobs created in distressed areas of the city. The City Challenge project aimed at improving one of the most deprived areas of the city with very high unemployment is, however, largely concerned with providing a new physical environment and capital expenditure on hardware rather than investment in human resources. Barcelona created the Freeport on the edge of the city with easy access by public transportation. The siting of the Olympic Games in the city resulted in massive increases in infrastructure investment by the city government in central areas, increasing employment quite dramatically within the city, and having a very positive effect in reducing the level of unemployment in the city. Market forces have ensured the location of new jobs in city areas rather than the metropolitan area so problems of access for the urban unemployed are not so acute.

Montpellier's economic development policy is totally divorced from consideration of the unemployed in both the location of new employment in 'poles' and science/industry parks outside the city, and in the type of activity attracted. Frankfurt has few urban problems in the sense of depressed areas, it has growth of employment in the city and easy, cheap access by public transportation to available employment.

Returning to the question, asked earlier, as to whether cities are a microcosm of the wider problem of unemployment in Europe, the cities studied exhibit all the major causes of unemployment. Changes in demand, changes in population, technological and structural change, mismatch of skills, and lack of mobility of the workforce have all been identified as causes at an urban level. Also, the interrelationship between public infrastructure investment, and other forms of social and economic policy, including the siting of social housing, planning policy, transportation policy, education policy, and the effect of local public expenditure levels, are important. What the studies do demonstrate is that causes of unemployment are complex, and the level in any one location cannot be put down to a single cause. Assumptions that labour market rigidities, wage levels or demand factors can provide a one track explanation of the problem can be discounted. The idea also that the mismatch of skills, initially the result of change in economic structure, can be solved by a training course is simplistic, since the qualification and educational levels of the majority of long-term unemployed are far removed from the skill needs of growth economies. The studies point to the need for an increase in long-term investment levels in education and professional skill training. In the short term job creation schemes in the public sector can help to bridge this gap by giving the opportunity for useful and needed activities in the community to those who are not employable in modern urban economies. This strategy is expensive and entails greater public expenditure than the payment of non-productive unemployment compensation, but this must be set against the other costs to society entailed in long-term unemployment. The studies do point to the fact that even in Europe's most successful city, Frankfurt, where there are more jobs available than those seeking work, there is a hard core of around 3–4 per cent of the labour force who are not employable on the formal labour market. This proportion increases in cities with greater employment problems where unskilled jobs available are filled by skilled workers in line with the queuing theory.

In Chapter 3 the role of the European Union in active labour market policies was examined. In the context of the cities how far has EU policy been appropriate and successful?

THE ROLE OF THE EUROPEAN UNION IN MEASURES TO AID THE UNEMPLOYED

The European Union, under Objectives 3 and 4, subsidises measures to aid the long-term unemployed and the young unemployed. Approved schemes concentrated on training programmes and adaptation to new technologies.

Matching funds were required from national governments and, as discussed, this resulted in greater allocations to wealthier countries under these objectives, as they were in a better position to afford a higher expenditure on the unemployed. In the report to the Committee of the ESF on the assistance given in 1992, actual payments to Member States were higher in total than planned by 11 per cent, but the distribution varied between countries. The UK and Germany received 28 per cent more than originally planned and Spain 2 per cent less. Actual expenditure on Objectives 3 and 4 by the ESF is shown in Table 9.1.

Table 9.1 Financial aid by ESF under Objectives 3 and 4, 1990–92

Country	Forecast aid	Approved expenditure
	(million ECU)	
France	872	1,033
UK	1,025	1,313
Netherlands	231	236
Germany	573	732
Spain	563	553

Source: Directorate General V (1992)

Share of ESF funds for the long-term unemployed and young unemployed in 1993 was as follows: UK 24.8 per cent, France 21.1 per cent, Germany 13.9 per cent, Spain 13.6 per cent and the Netherlands 5.6 per cent.

The ESF did not spend 58.4 million ECU of provisional expenditure in 1991 on the special schemes for employment – HORIZON, NOW and EUROFORM. Applications did not meet targets. If one looks at the percentage of total expenditure on active labour market policies in the cities, where this information was available – Rotterdam, Barcelona and Manchester – there is great variance. In Rotterdam only 4 per cent of funding comes from the ESF, in Barcelona 9.7 per cent, in Manchester the overall estimate is 30 per cent. Since there is a large incentive to undertake schemes which can be co-funded by the ESF, it is surprising that only Manchester has adopted policies that match the criteria set out by the ESF, and that in the other two cities, schemes in operation are not of the type to benefit. Barcelona, as has been mentioned, found the policies promoted for Europe as a whole under Objectives 3 and 4 were not considered the most appropriate for reducing local employment problems in the city. In situations where a wage subsidy or job experience are most effective or most feasible, ESF funding is not available. Unfortunately no detailed information on funding sources of all schemes was available for Montpellier and Frankfurt, so it is not possible to draw any over-all conclusion on the role of the ESF in cities with different types and levels of unemployment.

In the brief concluding section the revised regulations for Community Structural Funds in the period 1994–99 will be examined together with pre-scriptions for future policy within the European Union.

10

PRESCRIPTIONS FOR
THE FUTURE

Unemployment in Europe has worsened since the case studies were under-taken. In the European Union as a whole over 12 per cent of the working population was officially unemployed in 1994 with the total of jobless higher than registered rates. In the cities official unemployment rose from 9.7 to 12.7 per cent (1991–94) in Barcelona; from 6.0 to 7.5 per cent (1991–94) in Frankfurt; from 15.7 to 18.3 per cent (1991–94) in Manchester; from 16.9 to 22.0 per cent (1990-94) in Montpellier; and from 19.3 to 26.5 per cent (1990–94) in Rotterdam. The increase in unemployment ranged from 17 per cent in Manchester to 25 per cent in Frankfurt and 30 per cent in Montpellier, Barcelona and Rotterdam. All the cities suffered from the Europe-wide recession to a greater or lesser extent.

There have been some changes made to European Union aid for the unemployed, partly as a result of the increased seriousness of the problem, and also as a result of evaluation of the first Community Structural Fund Programme. These changes will be noted, followed by prescriptive actions proposed in the Report on European Social Policy of December 1993, and analysis of the so-called 'Delors Report' on Growth Competitiveness and Employment (CEC 1993). Suggestions on unemployment policy in Europe by the OECD (1994) and other commentators will also be briefly examined.

EUROPEAN UNION POLICY 1994–99

Six revised regulations were adopted in July 1993 by the Commission regarding the Community Structural Funds for the period 1994–99. The major principles of concentration of effort, partnership, programming and additionality were maintained and strengthened. New areas were included as Objective 1 regions. They were the border territories of France and Belgium, Merseyside and the North West Highlands in the UK, Cantabria, Flevoland in the Netherlands, and East Berlin and five of the eastern *Laender* in Germany. Over one fifth of the Community population is now within the highest priority regions and cities. Funds are targeted to rise from 20 billion

ECU in 1994 to over 27 billion ECU by 1999 in real terms, 70 per cent of which will go to Objective 1 region.

Objective 3 combines the task of the old Objectives 3 and 4, and also aims to 'facilitate the integration of those threatened with exclusion from the labour market'. The new Objective 4 is to give effect to a part of the Maastricht Treaty by facilitating workers' adaptation to industrial changes and changes in production systems. Allocation under all objectives is to be in relation to national prosperity, regional prosperity, population of regions and severity of structural problems, including unemployment. The principle of additionality is more flexible. Member States must maintain comparable expenditure to that of the previous programme period. Contributions by the CSF, as a general rule, will still not be more than 50 per cent of the cost of a programme outside Objective 1 regions, where they may be up to a maximum of 85 per cent of the cost. Interpretation of 'a general rule' is important in making the additionality principle more flexible. These two measures go some way to addressing the problem of marketing grants, but probably not far enough to have a significant impact. This can, however, only be judged by future evaluations.

The funding for special employment projects (NOW, HORIZON, Euroform, Rechar, etc.) has been increased, and constitutes 9 per cent of the total Structural Fund in the period to 1999. Assistance on all projects is only to be allocated where medium term economic and social benefit 'commensurate with the resources deployed' can be shown.

As we have seen the EU regards employment as necessary for social cohesion and that it should not be considered solely in terms of economic efficiency. In 1989 the Charter of Fundamental Social Rights for Workers was adopted by eleven of the twelve Member States (not the UK). It set out principles covering aspects of working and living conditions. This was incorporated in the Social Chapter of the Treaty of European Union in Maastricht in 1992, which clearly establishes the tasks of the Community as promoting a high level of employment and a 'proper' level of social protection (Article 2). It also recommends increasing dialogue between management and labour, and the development of human resources to both increase employment and combat social exclusion. No actual measures are included in the treaty. All Member States, including the UK, are however still bound by the existing articles of the Treaty of Rome on social policy affecting workers, particularly that of non-discrimination. This includes all health and safety directives of the Commission designed to improve working conditions, and the Directive on European Workers Councils of 1990. The latter requires consultations on proposals likely to have serious consequences for employees' interests in any company of one thousand or more workers with an establishment of at least one hundred workers in another Member State.

The Report on European Social Policy (1993) also recommends the encouragement of greater flexibility in careers and working hours and greater provision of child care facilities to reduce discrimination against women in the workforce. The key objective of integration, in the report, is that working and living standards throughout the Community should converge, with standards being levelled up not levelled down. The Commission recognised that 'the issue of minimum international standards is complex and difficult' but aims to search for a fair balance between safeguards against unfair competition based on exploitative labour conditions, and legitimate comparative advantage. These aims are seen as measures which increase labour costs and lose competitiveness by free marketeers, represented by the British viewpoint, but a necessary part of social progress and welfare for the inhabitants of Europe by other Members States.

Before looking at the Delors report which tackles the conflict of economic versus social priorities from a different viewpoint, one further report of the Commission on Social Exclusion and Poverty (CEC 1993c) is particularly relevant to cities. It points out that 70 per cent of European citizens live in cities, and it is in cities that the problem of social exclusion is found in its worst forms. Action at local level by co-ordination of economic and social institution is, therefore, seen to be the best way of combating urban deprivation. Recommendations are made that employment creation and vocational training should be undertaken in relation to local needs, and that there should be an improvement in access to information and activities which support families and local communities, in order to make them less passively dependent. For this purpose the ESF has set aside 112 million ECUs for the period 1995–96.

More detailed proposals to aid the urban poor, including those effectively excluded from the mainstream urban labour market, are being prepared by the Commission.

The major proposals of the European Commission concerning employment were announced by Jacques Delors, the President, in December 1993 and are incorporated in the White Paper 'Growth, Competitiveness and Employment: The Challenges and Ways Forward into the 21st Century' (CEC 1993). Analysis of reasons for high unemployment in the European Union in this document have already been briefly referred to in Chapter 1. It is the recommendations we are concerned with here. The Commission recommends an objective of creating fifteen million new jobs, and halving unemployment rates by the year 2000. Employment on this scale is viewed as necessary to 'make a significant dent in the human waste represented by unemployment'. In order to keep employment stable five million jobs must be created. The immediate objective is to overcome the recession, when four million jobs were lost in 1992–93. The prerequisites for the desired creation of employment are a 3 per cent p.a. average growth rate, an increase in the level of investment from 19 per cent to 23–24 per cent of income, and increasing the job content of growth. To start off the growth process Delors recommends that the Community invest some twenty billion ECUs per annum in the period 1994–99 in infrastructure projects, mainly highways and environmental projects but also in joint private ventures in information and communications systems. Two fifths of the sums needed would be financed from the issuing of bonds in order to avoid strain on national budgets. The proposed financing met with some opposition from finance ministers. Although the proposals were agreed at the Corfu summit of June 1994, the finance question remained unresolved at that time.

Overcoming the recession was seen as requiring both macro and structural policies. Lower interest rates to increase competitiveness would entail, in the medium to long term, a reduction in budget deficits. In the meantime governments should switch expenditure to areas influencing growth, particularly education, research and development and infrastructure investment. These measures are aimed at restoring confidence in the economy.

As far as promoting longer-term competitiveness is concerned, the White Paper sees no gains to be made in trying to reduce unit labour cost, as the gap between Europe and, for example, China is too great. Lowering wages will only depress demand further in an already recessionary economy. The way forward is through high productivity and superior products with emphasis on innovatory areas – health, environment, biotechnology, multimedia and culture are suggested. On the supply side the Community should support SMEs and stimulate the development of clusters of competitive activities – the idea of mini 'growth poles'. It was also thought necessary to redistribute the tax burden away from labour costs on firms and towards the taxing of usage of natural depletable resources. Knowledge-based investment through training and research should also be encouraged. Countries with the highest levels of general education and training, like Germany, it was pointed out, are least affected by problems of lack of competitiveness and low skills. Although increased investment in education is not seen as the panacea for all problems, there is a strong recommendation that Member States increase the proportion of children completing secondary education, and receiving higher education. Universities must be given the resources they need to play their particular role in developing lifelong learning and retraining in appropriate high level skills. While the Commission is normally seen as a body increasing regulation in the labour market, Delors proposes reduction in non-wage labour costs and a cut in welfare contribution especially in unskilled jobs; pay restraint; and flexibility of minimum wages for young workers.

A further change suggested is that the volume of work could be more effectively distributed into extra jobs by changes in work practices and shorter working hours, with greater numbers working part-time. The Netherlands is given as an example, where the average working week is thirty three-hours, growth of job creation is high, and productivity is not impaired.

In contrast to the macroeconomic policy recommended in the Delors report, the OECD (1994) sees a stable macroeconomic framework, with control of inflation as its central aim, and a reduction in public sector deficits, again in order to establish low inflation, as the primary requisite in the European economy. Expansionary fiscal policy is viewed as unacceptable since it could increase inflation and damage the growth of confidence within the private sector. Wage flexibility is viewed as essential for competitive advantage, and minimum wages are considered to be a form of social policy which, in most circumstances, results in decreases in employment.

The OECD, like the Commission, recommends increased investment in human resource development, with education as the most important feature of any policy to overcome the problems of structural adjustment. More work-orientated academic education is also thought desirable.

The main difference between these two prescriptions is that Delors is trying to coordinate the aims of economic and social policy within one framework while the OECD is making more conventional economic assessments of the role of wages and inflation on the economy.

The point made by the OECD on minimum wages has, in practical terms, been recognised by Member States in their policy. Minimum wage legislation has not been abandoned, but one of the more effective policies towards the long-term unemployed in the cities has been to offer wage subsidies in order to facilitate the entry of unemployed workers into employment. Rotterdam, to maintain employment, had a top-up subsidy to employers who were unable to keep workers at minimum wage levels and survive in the market.

This difference of approach on Europe's problems is, however, more realistically dealt with in the Delors report. Regulations that exist are unlikely to be changed in any significant way and most of Europe will not become a free market in the sense of deregulation. The desire to maintain gains in social welfare through wage rates and working conditions, which have been made in Europe in the last fifty years, are not easily abandoned. Throughout most of Europe deregulation of the labour market is socially and politically unacceptable, as was seen in the attempts of the French government to effectively lower minimum payments to young workers in 1994. To ignore the strong commitment of most European countries to the protection of workers' rights and social equity within the labour market is unrealistic. This is where Europe is unique and cannot be readily compared with labour markets such as the United States. While it may be possible to tinker at the edges with social rights in the labour market there is very little support in Europe for the idea that problems could or should be solved by becoming more like America. For this reason the Delors approach and the prescriptions put forward by the ESF are likely to be implemented in Europe.

The prescriptions are primarily concerned with the medium- and long-term problem, and there is little for the short-term. Increased infrastructure investment will help in some areas of Europe in the short-term, but is not going to touch the majority of the seven million long-term unemployed.

Wage subsidy and the creation of 'additional' jobs within the public sector would be the most effective measures in the short-term. In the long-term heavy investment in human resources and significant upgrading of skills will result in a European economy competitive in the world market. There is little future for those without high skill levels in knowledge-based sectors of the economy. Europe will never compete with the developing economies in cheap unskilled labour. This is something that the newly industrialised economies of East Asia have already recognised, and expansion and upgrading of education has become a major feature of economic policy in Singapore, Korea, Malaysia and Taiwan. The European Union must invest heavily in education to retain its advantage and improve its economic position in the next two decades.

One of the potential future problems in Europe on the employment front, which was largely discounted by the Delors report, was the effect of introducing a single currency and Central Bank for Europe. It has been pointed out (Michie and Grieve Smith 1994) that if the new central bank is dedicated to the achievement of price stability via tight control of monetary policy in Europe, this could result in levels of demand too low to support a growing supply of labour, and seriously impede progress on the reduction of unemployment. This is something that should be borne in mind when constructing the details of monetary union, an otherwise beneficial measure for Europe.

What of the unemployment problems of cities in Europe, the primary concern of this study? It has become evident that at a local level a more co-ordinated policy concerned with both economic and social policy is needed to combat the longer-term hysteresis effects of generations of unemployed being created and locked into social exclusion. In the short-term the comprehensive type of 'social renewal' scheme found in Rotterdam provides useful indications of the principle of coordinated activity for those with the most serious unemployment problems concentrated within the city. In the medium- to long-term planning policy, economic development policy, education policy and employment policy should be adapted to the needs of local communities, particularly in areas of multiple deprivation, but co-ordination is also necessary for the economic welfare of the city as a whole. In doing this the role of the modern centres within regions must be taken into account. Greater flexibility is needed in national policies to allow variation of methods and expenditure in a co-ordinated approach to the problems of the long-term unemployed.

In general the special problems faced by women and ethnic minorities within cities is poorly dealt with. Either the problem is ignored by regarding all units of labour as homogenous and, therefore, open to the same solutions, or intervention is on a very minor scale. The problems of these two groups are not, however, on a minor scale. Europe is experiencing, partly because of unemployment, a breakdown in traditional family structure.

Women are increasingly becoming effectively the bread winners for the next generation. Unless realistic policies are introduced with greater flexibility of working practice and help with domestic responsibilities, the effects on the life-chances of the workers of the future could be negative.

A failure to adequately address the problems of ethnic minorities will lead to further social tensions already apparent in incidents of racial violence in parts of Germany and on a smaller scale in most large cities in Europe. The growth in popularity of right wing political parties with an overt or covert racialist agenda is a worrying feature on the European political scene. The social costs of inaction are potentially very high, especially in large cities.

The financial costs of unemployment in the European Union were estimated to be some 210,000 million ECU in 1993 (CEC 1993) which included unemployment compensation, lost tax revenue, increased social service costs, increased health costs and increased crime. This, of course, does not include longer term social and political costs discussed above. Bearing this in mind any expenditure on short-term panaceas and long-term investment plans that would reduce the level of unemployment in Europe, would be a price well worth paying. Inadequate responses to the problem would be a form of short-termism the consequences of which would have severe repercussions in the future, not only on the economy of Europe, but on the civilised values of European society.

NOTES

INTRODUCTION

1 The terms European Community and European Union will both be used. When policies were formulated and when the case studies were undertaken, the Union was still called the Community.

1 UNEMPLOYMENT IN THE EUROPEAN COMMUNITY

1 Corporatism can be measured by the Calmfors–Driffel index of the centralisation of wage bargaining where high levels of centralisation indicate a greater degree of corporatism and where wage rates in different industries and locations are closer to each other.

2 These Eurostat statistics are not based on persons registered at employment offices because eligibility for registration does not produce comparable figures across Europe. They derive from a Community labour force survey and will, therefore, differ from figures produced by national governments.

3 Defined as the total labour force divided by population of working age (15–64) at mid year.

4 The figure for France is $4,600, the Netherlands $3,500 and the UK $5,000.

2 URBAN UNEMPLOYMENT IN EUROPE

1 FURs are metropolitan areas with boundaries determined on the basis of economic relationships rather than history or political and administrative divisions. In the study they are defined as areas over 330,000 in population.

2 For in-migration of population the period 1971–81 was used.

3 The same study by Robson also found that where new housing in central areas was available, developers had no trouble selling it.

4 Not all commentators agree that the shift in population preceded shifts in employment, but, in general, it appears that the decentralisation of employment lagged behind outward movement of population while inducing further move-

ment of workers at a later date (Keeble et al. 1983).

5 Further information on the role of local planning in the location of employment will be given in later chapters.

6 Berthoud (1980) found managerial and professional groups were five times more likely to migrate for job reasons than manual workers who are held back by financial circumstances, an inadequate supply of private rented housing and constraints on cross-authority transfers in public housing.

3 THE ROLE OF THE EUROPEAN COMMUNITY IN HELPING THE UNEMPLOYED

1 Vasco Papandreou, Director General of ESF (CEC, *Social Europe*, 1991).
2 Official Journal of the European Communities, 24 February 1989.
3 CEC, *Social Europe* 1991.

4 MONTPELLIER

1 All figures given are for the administrative area (commune) of the city of Montpellier not the labour market area. This is to some extent unsatisfactory but is necessary as no breakdown of figures is available for the city region.

2 Metropolitan France is equivalent to 'mainland' France and excludes overseas departments as well as all other countries.

3 Source INSEE. From the census, for 8.5 per cent of the unemployed there was no precise information on duration of unemployment.

4 Interview with Jacques Rouzier, urban economist, University of Montpellier, CNRS, January 1992.

5 Montpellier has the third highest cost of living in France after Paris and Ajaccio (Donzel 1991).

6 Interview with M. Mascheotti, ANPE, January 1992.

7 The quartiers have a minimum population of 5,000 people.

8 Observatore Régional de l'Emploi Dynamique des Emplois et des Formations dans le Sectour Agricole en Languedoc-Roussillon, February 1991.

9 Observatoire Régional de l'Emploi 'Le Tertiaire en Languedoc-Roussillon', March 1992.

5 MANCHESTER

1 The unemployment rates for the UK, the North West and Greater Manchester are calculated on the narrow base denominator i.e. employees in employment plus the unemployed. The figure for Manchester is Manchester City Council's estimate based on Department of Employment claimants register of the unemployed.

2 The other 9 per cent were self-employed.

3 In March 1994 following a decision by the courts on Equal Opportunities for women, redundancy and unfair dismissal law now applies to part-time workers.

196

4 The figures for Manchester refer to October 1991, those for Greater Manchester to July 1991.

5 The 16–19 age group excludes all those in the age group 16–18 who are not eligible for benefit and so are not registered. The number is likely, therefore, to be higher.

6 The Department of Employment estimates that only one third of all job vacancies are registered at Job Centres.

7 The eight highest wards of youth unemployment, and seven of the ten highest wards of long-term unemployment in Greater Manchester were in the city of Manchester (Census 1991).

8 Wards are administrative districts varying in population from seven to fourteen thousand population, with the majority having around twelve thousand.

9 The powers of local government were largely devolved to individual boroughs within the metropolitan area, of which the city of Manchester was the largest borough in terms of population. There are nine other separate local authorities in the urban area.

10 Measures were announced in the Budget of November 1993 proposing a Single Regeneration Budget and integrated regional offices of the various ministries concerned.

11 Manchester TEC is responsible for not only the city of Manchester, but also the boroughs of Salford, Trafford and Tameside.

6 ROTTERDAM

1 Rotterdam handles the most tonnage of all ports in Europe.

2 Comprehensive statistics for the city of Rotterdam were not available before 1987.

3 Central Bureau of Statistics, Netherlands, states total figure for jobless (ILO definition) is 510,000 for the Netherlands as a whole, compared with registered unemployed of 345,000. Throughout the analysis figures are only available for registered unemployed, and thus will underrepresent unemployment compared to Montpellier and Manchester where census figures are largely used representing joblessness.

4 Interview with Dr van Wijk, Rotterdam Werkt, February 1992.

5 Current exchange rate 1994 was 2.8 guilders = £1.

6 Partners/couples can be spouses or persons of the same or different sex with whom the claimant lives.

7 Interview with Mr G de Kleyne, Town Hall, Rotterdam, February 1992.

8 Interview with Dr van Werf, Social Services, Rotterdam 1992.

7 BARCELONA

1 Barcelona city statistics.

2 Estimate of Professor J.M. Blanch, Barcelona Autonoma University. Interview,

13 March 1992. No official statistics were available on male/female activity rates.

3 Comparative unemployment rates in 1985 were AMB 22.0 per cent, Catalonia 20.6 per cent, Spain 20.0 per cent (Area Metropolitana de Barcelona Estadiques Basiques 1989).

4 Barcelona active population from survey of inhabitants, 1986.

5 Interview, Maria Belil, International Centre for Urban Studies, Barcelona, 11 March 1992.

6 The two bodies were joined to make one municipal organisation dealing with the promotion and development of economic activity in 1991.

7 This sum is roughly equivalent to £24 million, or £360 per registered unemployed person.

8 The encouragement and financial subsidy for workers to take over their firms, if there is a threat of closure, was a measure taken in Spain to encourage a new 'social economy' and increase workers' involvement in company direction, in addition to the aim of retaining/creating jobs. For historical and cultural reasons, Holstrom (1993) claims that it was particularly strong in Catalonia.

9 The fall in permanent work contracts may be related to the fact that there are restrictions on working time under labour law in Spain. There is a maximum working week of forty hours, with only eighty hours of overtime allowed per annum. Also paid leave must 'under no circumstances be less than thirty calendar days per year' (MISEP 1993).

8 FRANKFURT AM MAIN

1 Germany is divided into Federal States (Läender).

2 In the same period, employment in Munich grew by 11.9 per cent in West Berlin by 12.4 per cent and in by Hamburg 5.11 per cent (Hessen Report 1992).

3 Germany had the most liberal definitions of refugee status in the EC.

4 This is defined as the wider Frankfurt area covered by the Frankfurt ABM (Figure 8.1).

5 For example, 115,000 Damstadt residents work in the Frankfurt area, 16,000 from Giessen, 9,000 from Nordrhein–Westphalen (ABF Aktuel October 1991).

6 Frankfurt Hauptamt area includes the boroughs of Morfelden–Waldorf and Neu–Isenberg. The population of Frankfurt city in 1990 was 641,161 and working population 235,803. Including the two boroughs it was 705,994 and 262,712 respectively.

7 Unemployed persons are defined as those who are not in employment, or are working for only very few hours a week, who are registered as unemployed at the Employment Office. The rate is the ratio between registered unemployed and active resident population.

8 This is an average rate for surrounding municipalities such as Bad Hamburg, Bad Vilbel, Ffm Hoechst and Langen.

9 Working population refers to the number employed by ethnic origin plus the number unemployed within the Frankfurt Hauptamt area.

10 'Other foreign' category includes other European Union workers, workers from other countries, plus refugees and applicants for asylum.

11 Interview Herr Mayer, Frankfurt Verein fur Soziale Heimstatten e.V. 26 March 1992.

12 As this has been done for other cities in the study, it provides useful national comparisons.

13 Expenditure and outcomes of unemployment measures are for Frankfurt ABM unless specified, which covers the whole of the labour market area. Frankfurt Hauptampt has 65 per cent of all unemployed in the area.

14 In Germany an agreed minimum wage is negotiated between workers and employees in each industry. The training allowance is related to the minimum wage in the industry in which the trainee has a contract.

15 Interview ABM Frankfurt, March 1992.

16 ibid.

9 UNEMPLOYMENT IN EUROPEAN CITIES: CAUSES AND POLICIES

1 These are rough figures based on exchange rates, current in June 1994, translating national currencies into pounds sterling.

2 The figures shown on the diagram refer to prime age workers, who were either single or married but without children, who had been in work for the previous ten years. In France, the Netherlands, Germany and Spain unemployment compensation was initially linked to past wages (gross or net in the case of Germany). In the United Kingdom estimates were made, as there was no official replacement ratio.

3 Labour Force Survey Europe, 1990.

BIBLIOGRAPHY

ABF Aktuell (1992) 'Struktur Analyse No. 2', Frankfurt: AMB Landesarbeitsamt Hessen.

ABM (Arbeitamt) Frankfurt am Main (1990) 'Jahresbericht', Frankfurt: ABM.

Addison, J.T. and Siebert, W.S. (1992) *The EC Social Chapter: recent developments and the Maastricht Summit*, Birmingham: The Birmingham Business School, University of Birmingham.

ADES (1989) *Projecte PLA de formació occupational*, Barcelona: Ajuntament de Barcelona.

—— (1990) *Caracteristiques dels participants i resultats d'Inercio*, Barcelona: Ajuntament de Barcelona.

—— (1991) *Informatiu de L'Area de Desenvolupamont Economic i Social*, Barcelona: Ajuntament de Barcelona.

Ajuntament de Barcelona (1990) *Enquesta Metropolitana de Barcelona*, Paper 7, Barcelona.

—— (1990a) 'Barcelona 2000: Economic and Strategic Plan', Barcelona: Ajuntament de Barcelona.

—— (1991) Bulleti del Mercat Local de Treball. Barcelona.

Alogoskoufis, G. and Manning, A. (1988) 'On the persistence of unemployment', *Economic Policy* (7).

AMB (Area Metropolitana de Barcelona) (1991) *Estadisticas Municipales,* Barcelona: AMB.

Andrews, H.F. (1978) 'Journey to work considerations in the labour force participation of married women', *Regional Studies* 12: 12–20.

Armstrong, H. and Taylor, J. (1983) 'Unemployment stocks and flows in the travel-to-work areas of the North-West regions', *Urban Studies*, 20: 311–25.

Atkinson, A.B. (1986) 'Income maintenance and social insurance', in Auerbach A. and Feldstein, M. *Handbook of Public Economics* 2, Amsterdam: North Holland.

Atkinson, A.B. and Micklewright, J. (1991) 'Unemployment compensation and labour market transitions: a critical review', *Journal of Economic Literature*, xxix: December.

Atkinson, A.B., Gomulka J., Micklewright, J. and Rau, N. (1984) 'Unemployment benefit, duration and incentives in Britain', *Journal of Public Economics* 23.

Auer, P. (1984) *Reintegration of the long-term unemployed: an overview of public programmes in eight countries*, Berlin: International Institute of Management.

Auerbach, A. and Feldstein, M. (1986) *Handbook of Public Economics* 2, Amsterdam: North Holland.

Aydalot, P. (1986) 'The location of new firm creation. The French case', in Keeble W., Wever, D. *New firms and regional development in Europe*. London: Croom Helm.

Balfour, S. (1989) *Dictatorship, workers and the city. Labour in Greater Barcelona since 1939*, Oxford: Clarendon Press.

Banks, M. and Ullah, P. (1986) 'Unemployment and unqualified urban youth', *Employment Gazette* 94: 205–10.

Barcelona Activa (1991) Estaistiques del Mercat de Treball. Barcelona: Ajuntament de Barcelona.

Barron, J.M., Bishop, J. and Dunkelberg, W.C. (1985) 'Employer search: the interviewing and hiring of new employees', *Review of Economics and Statistics*, 67, pp 43–52.

Bean, C.R., Layard, P.R.G. and Nickell, S.J. (1986) 'The rise in unemployment: a multi-country study', *Economica* 53.

Begg, I.G. and Cameron, G.C. (1988) 'High technology location and urban areas of Great Britain', *Urban Studies* 361–79.

Begg, I., Moore, B. and Rhodes, J. (1987) 'Economic and social change in urban Britain and the inner cities', in Hausner, V. (ed.) *Critical issues in urban economic development*, 1, Oxford: Clarendon Press.

Bentolina, A. and Blanchard, O. (1990) 'Spanish unemployment', *Economic Policy*, April.

Berg, S.V and Dalton, T.R. (1977) 'United Kingdom labour force activity rates: unemployment and real wages', *Applied Economics* 9: 265–70.

Berger, A., Catanzano, J., Fornairon, J.D. and Rouzier, J. (1988) *La Revanche Du Sud*, Paris: L'Harmattan.

Bernard, A. (1991) 'Place et dynamique des observatoires regionaux et de l'emploi et des formations' *Revue de L'Economie Meridionale* 39(2).

Berthoud, R. (1980) 'Employment in a changing labour market', in A.W. Evans and D.E.C. Eversley *The Inner City: Employment and Industry*, London: Heinemann.

Beumer L., Harts M., and Ottens H. (1983) *Ontwikkelingen ruimtelijke struktuur en ruimtelijke funktierverschuivingen in der vier grote stadsgewesten*, Utrecht: Utrecht Geografisch Institut.

Birch, D.L. (1987) 'Job creation in America', Free Press, London: Macmillan.

Blanch, J.M. (1990) *Del Viejo Al Nuevo Paro*, Barcelona: PPU-INEM.

—— (1992) *Mujer y Trabajo*, Barcelona: Barcelona Autonoma University.

Blanchard, O.J. and Summers, L.H. (1986) 'Hysteresis and the European unemployment problem', in *National Bureau of Economic Research Macro Economics Annual*, Cambridge, Mass: MIT Press.

Blanchard, O.J. and Diamond, P. (1990) 'Unemployment and wages. What have we learned from the European experience?', London: Employment Institute.

Blau, D.M. and Robins, P.K. (1990) 'Job search outcomes for the employed and unemployed', *Journal of Political Economy* 98: 637–55.

Borchert, J.G., Bourne, L.S. and Sinclair, R. (1986) 'Urban systems in transition', *Netherlands Geographical Studies* 16.

Brown, C. and Gay, P. (1987) *Racial discrimination seventeen years after the act*, London: Policy Studies Institute.

Brunet, R., Grasland., L., Garnier, P., Ferras, R. and Volle, J.P. (1988) *Montpellier Europole*, Montpellier: Reclus.

Bruno, M. and Sachs, J. (1985) *The Economics of Worldwide Stagflation*, Cambridge, Mass: Harvard University Press.

Buck, N. (1988) 'Service industries and local labour markets: towards an anatomy of service job loss', *Urban Studies* 25: 319–32.

Buck, N. and Gordon, I. (1987) 'The beneficiaries of employment growth: an analysis of the experience of disadvantaged groups in expanded labour markets', in Hausner, V. (ed.) *Critical Issues in Urban Economic Development* 2: 77–115, Oxford: Clarendon Press.

Budd, A., Levine, P. and Smith, P. (1986) 'The problem of long-term unemployment', *Economic Outlook* 1985–89 10(5), London: London Business School, Centre for Economic Forecasting.

Bundesanstalt fur Arbeit (1981) *Employment policy in Germany – challenges and concepts for the 1980s*, Berlin.

Burtless, G. (1987) 'Jobless Pay and High European Unemployment' in Lawrence R.Z. and Schultz, C.L. (eds) *Barriers to European Growth: a Transatlantic View*, Washington D.C.: Brookings Institution.

Bushell, R. (1986) 'Evaluation of the young workers scheme', *Employment Gazette*, May.

Cameron, S.J., Dabinett., G.E., Gillard, A.A., Whisker, P.M., Williams, R.H. and Willis, K.G. (1982) 'Local authority aid to industry. An evaluation in Tyne and Wear', *Inner Cities Programme* 7, London: Department of the Environment.

Campbell M. and Duffy, K. (eds) (1992) *Local Labour Markets: Problems and Policies*, London: Longman.

CEC (1991) *Social Europe, the European Social Fund*, Luxembourg.

CEC (1992) *Commission of the European Communities, European Social Fund, Community Support Framework, 1990–92*. (1) Federal Republic of Germany, (2) The Netherlands (3) United Kingdom, (4) France, (5) Spain, Luxembourg.

CEC (1992a) *Second Annual Report on the Implementation of the Reform of the Structural Funds*, Luxembourg.

CEC (1993) 'Growth, competitiveness, employment, the challenges and ways forward into the 21st century', *Bulletin of the European Communities*, Supplement 6/93, Luxembourg.

CEC (1993a) 'Growth, competitiveness, employment, the challenges and ways forward into the 21st century', *White Paper Part C*, Luxembourg.

CEC (1993b) *Community structural funds 1994–1999, regulations and commentary*, Luxembourg.

CEC (1993c) 'Social exclusion and poverty' Background Report Note ISEC/B 34/93. Brussels: CEC.

Centre for Employment Research (1990) *Social and economic profile of the North West*, Manchester: CER.

Champion A.G., Green, A.E. and Owen, D.W. (1988) 'House prices and local labour market performance: an analysis of building society data for 1985', *Area* 20: 253–63.

Chandler, J.A. and Lawless, P. (1985) '*Local authorities and the creation of employment*', London: Gower.

Cheshire, P., Hay, D., Carbonara, G. and Bevan, N. (1988) *Urban problems and regional policy in the European Community*, Luxembourg: CEC.

Cheshire, P.C. and Hay, D.G. (1989) *Urban Problems in Western Europe*, London: Unwin Hyman.

Clark, G.L. and Whiteman, J. (1983) 'Why poor people don't move: job search behaviour and disequilibrium amongst local labour markets', *Environment and Planning* 85–104.

Coombes, M.G., Green, A.E. and Openshaw, S. (1985) 'Britain's local labour markets', *Employment Gazette* 93: 6–8.

Coombes, M.G., Green, A.E. and Owen, D.W. (1981) 'Substantive issues in the definition of localities: evidence from sub-group local labour market areas in the West Midlands', *Regional Studies* 22: 303–18.

Coombes, M.G., Storey, D.J., Watson, R. and Wynarczyk, P. (1991) 'The influence of location upon profitability and employment change in small companies', *Urban Studies*, 28(5).

Corry, B.A. and Roberts, J.A. (1974) 'Activity rates and unemployment, the UK experience', *Applied Economics* 6: 1–21.

COS (Centrum voor Onderzoek en Statistik) (1991) 'Kerncijfers van de Gemeente Rotterdam', Rotterdam.

Dasgupta, M. (1982) 'Mobility and access to employment opportunities: a comparison of inner and outer areas of Greater Manchester', *Ekistics* 297: 480–82.

Danson, M.W., Lever, W.F. and Malcolm, J.F. (1980) 'The inner city employment problem in Great Britain, 1952–76: a shift share approach', *Urban Studies* 17: 193–210.

Deakin, S. and Wilkinson, F. (1992) 'European integration. The implications for UK policies on labour supply and demand', in E. McLaughlin (ed.) *Understanding Unemployment*, London: Routledge.

Delegation à L'Emploi (1987) *Chomage de Longue Durée*, Paris.

Delors, J. (1988) *Our Europe*, London: Verso.

Demery, P. (1988) *Jobclubs. Report on a postal survey of individuals who joined Jobclubs in Autumn 1987*, The Employment Service, Research and Evaluation branch, Report 6, September, London.

Department of Employment (1988) 'Ethnic origins and the labour market', *Employment Gazette* 96: 164–77.

Dilnot, A. and Kell, M. (1987) 'Male unemployment and women's work', *Fiscal Studies* 8(2), 1–16.

Directorate General, Employment, Industrial Relations, Social Affairs (1992) *Employment in Europe*, Brussels: CEC.

Disney, R., Bellman, L., Carruth, A., Franz, W., Jackman, R., Layard, R., Lehmann, H. and Philpott, J. (1992) *Helping the unemployed, active labour market policies in Britain and Germany*, London: Anglo-German Foundation.

Dolton, P. (1993) *The econometric assessment of training schemes; a critical review*, Mimeo, University of Newcastle-upon-Tyne.

Donzel, A. (1991) 'Urbanisation et Fonction des Villes en Europe. Le cas de Montpellier', *Revue de L'Economie Meridionale* 153.

Drèze, J.H. and Bean, C.R. (eds) (1990) *Europe's unemployment problem*, Cambridge, Mass: MIT Press.

Dyson, K. (ed.) (1989) *Combating long-term unemployment local/EC relations*, London: Routledge.

Eurostat (1989) *Schemes with an impact on the labour market and their statistical treatment in the member states of the European Community*, Luxembourg: CEC.

—— (1991) Labour Force Survey, Brussels: European Commission.

—— (1992) Employment Statistics, Brussels: European Commission.

—— (1992) *Unemployment in the European Community*, Brussels: CEC.

Elias, P. and Keogh, G. (1982) 'Industrial decline and unemployment in the inner city areas of Great Britain: a review of the evidence', *Urban Studies* 19: 1–15.

Flanagan, R.J. (1987) 'Labor Market Behavior and European Economic Growth' in Lawrence, R.Z and Schultz, C.L. *Barriers to European Growth: a Transatlantic View*, Washington D.C.: Brookings Institution.

Fornairon, J.D. (1987) 'La Mutation des Activités et des emplois', *Revue de l'Economie Meridionale* 35.

Fothergill, S., Kitson, M. and Monk, S. (1985) 'Urban industrial change: the causes of the urban rural contrast', *Manufacturing Employment Trends*, London: HMSO.

Fothergill, S., Monk, S. and Perry, M. (1987) *Property and Industrial Development*, London: Hutchinson.

Franz, W. (1987) 'The end of expansion in employment in Germany. Beginnings of an attempt at evaluation of structural unemployment as a partial component of joblessness', in Pedersen, P.J. and Lund, R. (eds) *Unemployment: theory, policy and structure*, Berlin: Walter de Groyter.

Frost, M. and Spence, N. (1981) 'Employment and work travel in a selection of

English inner cities', *Geoforum* 12(2): 107–60.

Gabsi, Abdallah (1988) 'Les tunisiens en aquitaine midi-Pyrenées et Languedoc-Roussillon', *Bulletin de La Societe Languedocienne de Geographie* 3–4.

Garcia, Soledad (1991) 'Politique économiques urbaines et autonomie locale le cas de Barcelone', *Sociologie du Travail* 41–91.

Garfield Schwartz, G. (1981) *Advanced Industrialisation and the Inner Cities*, Lexington, Mass: Lexington Books.

GBOS (1991) *Werkloosheidscijfers van Rotterdam (1988/1989/1990)*, Rotterdam: Gemeentelijk Bureau, voor onderzoek en Statistiek.

Gemeente Rotterdam (1987) *Werkloosheid in de Rotterdamse Wijken 1987*, Rotterdam: Gemeente.

Gemeente Rotterdam (1991) *Social Innovation in Rotterdam*, Rotterdam City Council.

Gold, M. (ed.) (1993) *The social dimension: employment policy in the European Community*, Basingstoke: Macmillan.

Gordon, I.R. (1988) 'Evaluating the effects of employment changes on local unemployment', *Regional Studies* 22: 135–47.

Gordon, I.R. (1988) 'Housing and labour market constraints on migration across the North–South divide', Paper prepared for the NIESR conference on housing and the national economy, 14–15 December.

Gordon, I.R. (1989) 'Urban unemployment', in Herbert D. and Smith, D. (eds) *Social Problems and the City*, Oxford: Oxford University Press.

Gordon, I.R. and Molho, I. (1985) 'Women in the labour markets of the London region: a model of dependence and constraint', *Urban Studies* 22: 367–86.

Gould, A.E. (1988) 'Unemployment duration in the recession: the local labour market area scale', *Regional Studies* 19(2): 111–30.

GMRIPU (Greater Manchester Research, Information and Planning Unit) (1991) *Monthly Unemployment Bulletin July 1991*, Oldham: GMRIPU.

—— (1991a) *Employment Trends in Greater Manchester 1990*, Oldham: GMRIPU.

—— (1991b) *Labour Supply Monitor 1991*, Oldham: GMRIPU.

—— (1991c) *Quarterly Unemployment Bulletin 3/91*, Oldham: GMRIPU.

—— (1991d) *The Relative Performance of the Small Business Sector for Greater Manchester 1980–89*, Oldham: GMRIPU.

—— (1993) *Quarterly Unemployment Bulletin 3/93*, Oldham: GMRIPU.

Greenhalgh, C. (1977) 'A labour supply function for married women in Great Britain', *Economica* 44: 249–65.

—— (1989) *Employment and structural change in Britain. Trends and policy options*, London: Employment Institute.

—— (1990) 'Participation and hours of work for married women in Great Britain', *Oxford Economic Papers* 32: 296–318.

Gregg, P. (1990) 'The 1988 labour force survey', *National Institute Economic Review* 2, May.

Gudgin, G., Moore, B. and Rhodes, J. (1982) 'Employment problems in the cities and regions of the UK: prospects for the 1980s', *Cambridge Economic Policy Review* December 8(2).

Hall, P. and Hay, D. (1980) *Growth centres in the European urban system*, London: Heinemann.

Hartog, J. and Theeuwes, J. (1985) 'The emergence of the working wife in Holland', *Journal of Labor Economics* 3(1) Part 2.

Hasluck, C. (1987) *Urban unemployment: local labour market and employment initiatives*, London: Longman.

Haughton, G., Peck, J. and Steward, A. (1987) 'Local jobs and local houses for local workers: a critical analysis of spatial employment', *Local Economy* 2: 201–7.

Hausner, V. (ed.) (1987) *Critical issues in urban economic development*, Oxford: Clarendon Press.

—— (ed.) (1987) *Urban economic change: five city studies*, Oxford: Clarendon Press.

Hausner, V. and Robson, B. (1986) *Changing Cities*, London: ESRC.

Hedges, B. and Prescott-Clarke, D. (1983) 'Migration and the inner city', *Inner Cities Research Programme*, London: Department of the Environment.

Hessen Report (1992) *Prognose der Wirtschaftlichen Entwicklung in Hessen bis 2010 HLT*, Wiesbaden.

Hofbauer, H. (1981) 'Untersuchungen des IAB uber die Wirksamkeit der Beruflichen Wetterbilung', *Mitteilungen aus der Arbeitsmarkt und Berufsforschung*, 14(3).

Hofbauer, H. and Dadziow, W. (1984) 'Mittelfristige Wirkungen Beruflicher Weiterbildung. Die Berufliche Situation von Teilnehmern Zwei Jahre nach Beendigung der Massnahme', *Mitteilungen aus der Arbeitsmarkt und Berufsforschung* 20(2).

Holen, A. (1977) 'Effects of unemployment insurance entitlement on duration and job search outcome', *Industrial and Labour Relations Review*, 30(4).

Holmström, M. (1993) *Spain's new social economy: workers' self-management in Catalonia*, Oxford: Berg.

Hughes, J.T. (1991) 'Evaluation of local economic development: a challenge for policy research', *Urban Studies* 28(6).

Hujer, R. and Schnabel R. (1992) 'The impact of regional and sectoral labour market conditions on wages and labour supply: analysis for married women', *Working Paper*, Dept. of Econometrics, University of Frankfurt.

Hujer R. and Schneider H. (1990) 'Unemployment duration as a function of individual characteristics and economic trends' in Mayes I.U. and Tuma N.B. *Event History Analysis in Life Course Research*, London.

Ihlanfeldt, K.R. and Sjoquist, D.L. (1991) 'The effect of job access on black and white youth employment', *Urban Studies* 28(2).

Ileris, S. (1986) 'How to analyse the role of services in regional development' in Borchet J.G., Bourne L.S. and Sinclair R. *Urban Systems in Transition*, Netherlands Geographical Studies 16, Amsterdam.

INSEE (1990a) 'Communes, metropoles, regions: l'espace français', *Economie et Statistique* 230.

INSEE (1990) Recensement de la Population, Montpellier.

Jackman, R. (1992) 'An economy of unemployment', in E. McLaughlin (ed.) *Understanding unemployment*, London: Routledge.

Jackman, R. and Layard, R. (1991) 'Does long-term unemployment reduce a person's chance of a job?' *Economica* 58.

Jackman, R. and Roper, S. (1987) 'Structural unemployment', *Oxford Bulletin of Economics and Statistics* 49.

Jackman, R., Pissarides, C. and Savouri, S. (1990) 'Labour market policies and unemployment in the OECD', *Economic Policy* 11.

James, F.G. and Clarke, T.A. (1987) 'Minority business in urban economies', *Urban Studies* 24: 489–502.

Johnstone, D. (1986) '*Programme of research and actions on the development of the labour market: the role of local authorities in promoting local employment initiatives*' Luxembourg: CEC.

Johnstone, D. (1989) 'The European Community and long-term unemployment', in Dyson, K. (ed.) *Combating Long-Term Unemployment*, London: Routledge.

JURUE (1986) *Assessment of the employment effects of economic development projects funded under the urban programme*, London: Department of the Environment, HMSO.

Kaiser, M. (1989) 'Long-term unemployment and locally based initiatives. West German experience', in Dyson, K. op. cit.

Kaufman B.E. (1988) *How labour markets work: Reflections on theory and practice.* Lexington, Mass: Lexington Books.

Keeble, D. and Wever, E. (1986) *New firms and regional development in Europe*, London: Croom Helm.

Keeble, D., Owens, P.L. and Thompson, C. (1983) 'The urban-rural manufacturing shift in the European Community', *Urban Studies* 20: 405–18.

Khelfaoui (1992) 'Pour un renouvellement des methodes d'aroches de l'emploi et de la formation par la localité', *Revue de l'Economie Meridionale* 39(2).

Klaasen L. (1987) 'The future of the larger European towns', *Urban Studies* 24(4).

Klems W. and Schmid A. (1990) *Langzeitarbeitslosigkeit, Frankfurt am Main*, Berlin: Sigma Bohn.

Laget, M. (1987) 'Le Systeme economique du Languedoc-Roussillon', *Revue de l'Economie Meridionale* 35.

Lawless, P. (1988) 'British inner urban policy: a review', *Regional Studies* 22: 531–42.

Lawrence, R.Z. and Schultz, C.L. (eds) (1987) *Barriers to European growth. A transatlantic view*, Washington DC: Brookings Institution.

Layard, R., Barton, M. and Zabalza, A. (1980) 'Married women's participation and hours', *Economica* 47: 51–72.

Layard, R., Nickell, S. and Jackman, R. (1991) *Unemployment*, Oxford: OUP.

Lindbeck A. and Snower D.J. (1988) 'Cooperation, Harassment and Involuntary Unemployment: an Insider-Outsider Approach' *American Economic Review* 78.

McCormick, B. (1985) 'Employment opportunities, earnings and the journey to work of minority workers in Great Britain', *Economic Journal* 96: 375–97.

McGregor, A. (1978) 'Unemployment duration and re-employment probability', *Economic Journal* 88: 693–706.

—— (1988) *Unemployment in Glasgow: problems of peripheral housing estates*, Training and Employment Research Unit, University of Glasgow.

McLaughlin E. (ed.) (1992) *Understanding unemployment*, London: Routledge.

Madden, J.F. (1981) 'Why women work closer to home', *Urban Studies* 18: 181–94.

Madden, J.F. and Chiu, L.C. (1990) 'The wage effects of residential location and commuting constraints on employed married women', *Urban Studies* 27(3)

Main, B.G. and Shelley, M.A. (1988) 'School leavers and the search for employment', *Oxford Economic Papers* 40: 487–504.

Main, B.G. and Shelley, E.M. (1991) 'The effectiveness of the youth training scheme on manpower policy', *Economica*.

Manchester City Council (1992) *Economic Development Strategy*, Manchester.

Mason, C.M. (1980) 'Industrial decline in Greater Manchester 1966–75: a components of change approach', *Urban Studies* 13: 869–84.

Meadows, P., Cooper, H. and Bartholomew, R. (1988) *The London Labour Market*, London: HMSO.

Meager, N., and Metcalf, H. (1987) *Recruitment of the long-term unemployed*, London: Institute of Manpower Studies.

Michie, J. and Grieve Smith, J. (eds) (1994) *Unemployment in Europe*, London: Academic Press.

Minford P. (1985) *Unemployment Cause and Cure*, Oxford: Blackwell.

MISEP (Directorate General Unemployment, Industrial Relations and Social

Affairs)
—— (1991) Policies Netherlands
—— (1992a) Policies France
—— (1992b) Policies Germany
—— (1992c) Policies United Kingdom
—— (1993) Policies Spain
Luxembourg: CEC.
Molho, I. (1983) 'A regional analysis of the distribution of married women's labour force participation rates in the UK', *Regional Studies* 17: 125–34.
—— (1986) 'A time series study of household participation decisions through boom and slump', *Oxford Economic Papers* 38: 141–59.
—— (1991) 'Patterns and trends in local pay in Great Britain 1975–76 to 1987–88', *Urban Studies* 28(4).
Molho, I. and Elias P. (1984) 'A study of regional trends in the labour force participation of married women in the UK, 1968–1977', *Applied Economics*, 16(2): 163–5.
Moore, B. and Townroe, P. (1990) *Urban Labour Markets. Reviews of Urban Research*, London: DOE/HMSO.
Moore, B., Tyler, P. and Elliott, D. (1991) 'The influence of regional development incentives and infrastructure on the location of small and medium sized companies in Europe', *Urban Studies* 28(6).
Morris, J.L. (1988) 'Producer services and the regions: the case of large accountancy firms', *Environment and Planning* A20: 741–59.
Morris, L.D. (1987) 'Local social polarization: a case study of Hartlepool', *International Journal of Urban and Regional Research* 11: 331–50.
Nabarro, R. (1980) 'The impact on workers from the inner city of Liverpool's economic decline', in A.W. Evans and D.E.C. Eversley (eds) *The inner city: employment and industry*, London: Heinemann.
NEDO/TC (1988) *Young People and the labour market: a challenge for the 1990s*, London: NEDO.
Nickell, S. (1979) 'The effect of unemployment and related benefits on the duration of unemployment', *Economic Journal*, 87: March.
OECD (1988) *Measures to assist the long-term unemployed and recent experience in some OECD countries*, Paris: OECD.
—— (1990) *Implementing change: entrepreneurship and local initiative*, Paris: OECD.
—— (1990) *Labour market policies for the 1990s*, Paris: OECD.
—— (1991) *Labour Force Statistics,* Paris: OECD.
—— (1992) *Employment outlook, July 1992*, Paris: OECD.
—— (1994) *Job study: facts, analysis and strategies*, Paris: OECD.
OPCS (Office of Population Censuses and Surveys) (1991) Local Base and Small Area Statistics, Manchester City Council.
Owen, D.W., Gillespie, A.E. and Coombes, M.G. (1984) 'Job shortfalls in British local labour market areas: a classification of labour supply and demand trends, 1971–1981', *Regional Studies* 18: 469–88.
P.A. Cambridge Economic Consultants (1987) *An evaluation of the enterprise zone experiment*, London: Department of the Environment.
—— (1989) *The government's Handsworth task force – an evaluation report*, London: Department of Trade and Industry.
Peck, F. and Townsend, A. (1987) 'The impact of technological change upon the spatial pattern of UK employment change within British corporations', *Regional Studies* 21: 225–39.

Pederson, P. and Westergard-Nielsen N. (1993) 'Unemployment: a review of the evidence from panel data', *OECD Economic Studies* 20: Paris.

Pennings, F. (1990) *Benefits of doubt*, Deventer: Kluwer.

Philpott, J. (1990) *A solution to long-term unemployment: the job guarantee*, London: Employment Institute.

Pissarides, C. and Wadsworth, J. (1992) 'Unemployment risks', in E. McLaughlin (ed.) *Understanding unemployment*, London: Routledge.

Priester, T. and Klein, P. (1992) *Hilfe zur Arbeit*, Augsburg: Maroverlag.

Rajan, A. (1988) *Job subsidies: do they work?*, London: Institute of Manpower Studies.

RBA Rijnmond (1991) *Arbeidsmarkt Aanpak Wordt Maatwerk, Jaarplan, 1992*, Rotterdam: RBA.

Robinson, F., Goddard, J. and Wren, C. (1987) *Economic development policies: an evaluation study of the Newcastle Metropolitan Region*, Oxford: Clarendon Press.

Robinson, P. (1991) *Full employment in Britain in the 1990s*, Aldershot: Avebury/Gower.

Robson, B.T. (1987) 'Local employment: a success story?', *Business in the Community* 4: 16–18.

—— (1988) *Those inner cities*, Oxford: Oxford University Press.

Roseingrave, T. (1989) 'The role of local employment initiatives in combating long-term unemployment in the European Community', in Dyson, K. (op cit.).

Rotterdam Werkt (1992) 'Soziale Zaken en Werkgelegenheid', Mimeo Rotterdam Werkt.

Sachs, J. (1985) *High unemployment in Europe*, Mimeo, Harvard University.

Schmid, G. (1988) 'Labour market policy in transition, trends and effectiveness in the Federal Republic of Germany', *EFA Report* 17, Stockholm.

Simpson, W. (1982) 'Job search and the effect of urban structure on unemployment and married female participation rates', *Applied Economics* 14: 153–66.

—— (1987) 'Workplace location, residential location and urban commuting', Urban Studies 24, 119–28.

Spitznagel, E. (1985) 'Arbeitsmark Politische Massnahmen: Entlastungswirkung und Kostenvergleiche', *Mitteilungen aus der Arbeitsmarkt und Berufsforschung* 18(1).

—— (1989) 'Zielgruppenorientierung und Eingliederungserfolg bei Allgemeinen Massnahmen zur Arbeitsbeschaffung (ABB)', *Mitteilungen aus der Arbeitsmarkt und Berufsforschung* 22, (4).

Stern, J. (1988) 'Methods of analysis of public expenditure programmes with employment objectives', *Working Paper* 53, London: HM Treasury.

Storey, D.J. (1990) 'Evaluation of policies and measures to create local employment', *Urban Studies* 27(5).

Storey, D.J. and Johnson, S. (1987a) *Job generation and labour market change*, Basingstoke: Macmillan.

—— (1987b) 'Regional variations in entrepreneurship in the UK', *Scottish Journal of Political Economy* 34: 161–73.

Symes V. (1992) 'Migration, the urban environment and the success of European cities' in *Metamorphosis in Europe*, Greece: University of Thessalonika.

Theeuwes J., Kerkhofs M. and Lindebookm M. (1990) 'Transition intensity in the Dutch labour market 1980–85', *Applied Economics* 1043–61.

Thélot C. (1985) 'La croissance du chomage depuis vingt ans: interpretations macroeconomiques' *Economie et Statistique* 183.

Townroe, P.M. (1983) 'United Kingdom', in L.H. Klaasen and W.T.M. Molle (eds) *Industrial mobility and migration in the European Community*, Aldershot: Gower.

Townsend, A. (1992) 'Regional and local differentials in labour demand', in E.

McLaughlin (ed.) *Understanding employment*, London: Routledge.

Turner, P. (1985) 'After the Community programme – results of the first follow up survey', *Employment Gazette*, January.

Turok, I. and Wannop, U. (1990) *Targeting urban employment initiatives*, Inner Cities Research Directorate, London: DOE, HMSO.

Van den Berg, G. (1990) 'Search behaviour, transitions to non-participation and the duration of unemployment', *Economic Journal* 100(402) 842–65.

Van den Berg, L., Drewett, R., Klaassen, L.H. and Ross, A. (1982) *Urban Europe, a story of growth and decline*, Oxford: Pergamon.

Van Kempen, R., Teule, R. and Van Weesep, J. (1989) 'Low income households and their housing situations in large Dutch cities', *Netherlands Journal of Housing and Environmental Research* 4(2).

Van Rintel, P.J.L. (1986) *The fight against youth unemployment in the Netherlands*, Ondenemengen: Verbond van Nederlandse.

Van Winckel, E. (1991) 'Women's situation on the labour market in 1992', *Social Europe* 3/91, Brussels: CEC.

Vickerman, R.W. (1984) 'Urban and regional change, migration and commuting. The dynamics of workplace, residence and transport choice', *Urban Studies* 21: 15–30.

Wadsworth, J. (1991) 'Unemployment benefits and search effect in the UK labour market', *Economica* 58: 17–34.

Willis, K.G. (1985) 'Estimating the benefits of job creation from local investment subsidies', *Urban Studies* 22: 163–78.

Wiltshaw, D.G. (1985) 'Jobs and local authority subsidies', *Urban Studies* 22(5): 433–37.

Wren, C. (1987) 'The relative effects of local authority financial assistance policies', *Urban Studies* 24: 268–78.

INDEX

Action for Cities 96
active labour market policies 14–17, 28;
    Barcelona 137–42; Frankfurt 162–9;
    Manchester 89–96; Montpellier 64–71;
    Rotterdam 112–18
Addison, J.T. 33
age and unemployment: Barcelona 126–7;
    Frankfurt 152–3; Manchester 78;
    Montpellier 54–5; Rotterdam 103; *see
    also* long-term unemployment; youth
    unemployment
agencies 29–30; Barcelona 134–5; Frankfurt
    160–61; Manchester 87–8; Montpellier
    63; Rotterdam 109–10
aggregate demand 4–5
agricultural sector 7–8; rural-urban
    migration 12, 19
Alogoskoufis, G. 6
apprenticeships: Montpellier 67; Rotterdam
    114–15
Atkinson, A.B. 7
Aydalot, P. 52, 53

Balfour, S. 124
Barcelona 123-47; active labour market
    policies 137–42; age and unemployment
    126–7; Barcelona 2000 144–5; disabled
    141–2, 184; economic development
    planning 124, 144–5; educational
    qualifications 129–30; ethnic minorities
    134; female unemployment 127–9, 182;
    female unemployment programmes 141,
    146, 182; European Social Fund funding
    147, 186; income support 136;
    Incorporation of Women Programme
    (PILD) 141, 143, 146; industrial decline
    123–4; job creation 144–5; labour
    market vacancies 129–30; long-term

unemployment 130; long-term unem-
    ployment programmes 140–41; male
    unemployment 127–9; migrant workers
    123, 134; minimum wage 136–7;
    National Employment Institute (INEM)
    135–6, 146; Olympic Games 124, 125,
    134, 176, 184; organisational structure
    134–5; population changes 20–21,
    124–5, 174–5; skills mismatch 129–30,
    145, 176; strategic planning 144–5;
    suburbanisation 24; training 138, 139,
    180; transport 26, 133–4, 144–5;
    unemployment 126–34, 188; unemploy-
    ment benefits 135–6; unemployment
    policies 134–47; unemployment
    prevention 138–9; urban factors 132–4,
    146–7; youth unemployment 126–7,
    134, 139–40, 181
Bean, C.R. 4, 5
Bentolina, A. 7
Berger, A. 53
Blanch, J.M. 12, 127
Blanchard, O.J. 4, 5, 6, 7
Brown, C. 26
Bruno, M. 6
Budd, A. 9, 10
budget deficits 33
building workers 162–3
Burtless, G. 7
Business Start-up (Enterprise Allowance
    Scheme) 90

career development loans 90, 94, 180
Central Bank for Europe 33, 193
Central Manchester Development
    Corporation 88, 95–6
Charter of Fundamental Social Rights for
    Workers (1989) 189

210